Belding

W9-CVA-762

Experiencing
International
Management

The Kent Series in Management

Belding

Experiencing International Management

Betty Jane Punnett
University of Windsor

PWS-KENT Publishing Company
Boston

To Dad with thanks

And thou beside me singing in the wilderness
And wilderness is paradise enow

 PWS–KENT
Publishing Company

Acquisitions Editor: Rolf A. Janke
Production Editor/Text Designer: Susan L. Krikorian
Compositor: Carlisle Communications, Ltd.
Interior Illustrator: George Nichols
Cover Designer: Joanna Steinkeller
Manufacturing Coordinator: Marcia A. Locke
Cover Printer: John P. Pow Company
Text Printer/Binder: The Book Press, Inc.

Copyright © 1989 by PWS-KENT Publishing Company. All rights reserved. No part of this book may be reproduced, stored in a retrieval system, or transcribed in any form or by any means, electronic, mechanical, photocopying, recording, or otherwise, without the prior written permission of the publisher, PWS-KENT Publishing Company, 20 Park Plaza, Boston, Massachusetts 02116.

PWS-KENT Publishing Company is a division of Wadsworth, Inc.

Printed in the United States of America

1 2 3 4 5 6 7 8 9 — 93 92 91 90 89

Library of Congress Cataloging-in-Publication Data

Punnett, Betty Jane.
  Experiencing international management / Betty Jane Punnett.

  Includes index.
    1. International business enterprises—Management—Simulation methods. I. Title.
HD62.4.P86   1989   658.1′8—dc19   88-39859
ISBN 0-534-91699-6

Preface

It seems clear that the business world of today is no longer limited by national boundaries, and that organizations need to have a global perspective if they are to survive and prosper in this international environment. Many will succeed or fail on the basis of their ability to deal with this dynamic environment.

Managing virtually any business in the 1990s will mean some international contacts. This is just as true of the small manufacturer that buys foreign materials and employs immigrant workers, as it is of the global company, which views the world as both a market and a source of supply. The scope of these two examples is different, but both face an international environment, and neither can overlook its implications.

The international environment is complex because of the interactions and transactions that take place across national boundaries; this is the key difference between international companies and those that are essentially domestic. The increasing need to interact with the complex international environment means that international expertise is of growing importance to companies. In spite of this, it appears that there is a decreased availability of individuals with such expertise. In the past, most international managers acquired international expertise on-the-job through assignments abroad. But fewer Americans and Canadians have been stationed abroad in the 1980s than previously.

One solution to this problem is an increased emphasis on international management in business programs offered by universities. Many universities have responded to this challenge by internationalizing their curricula. The complexity of the international environment means, however, that it is often difficult for students to appreciate the practical implications of international management decisions in the classroom. The purpose of this book is to give students an opportunity to address international decisions in a simulated real-life setting. The exercises and projects included here encompass many of the major management processes in international management and include decisions that relate to the various business functions. They are intended to give the student an appreciation of decision making in the complex international environment. It is the author's hope that the experiential approach provided in this book will serve to increase students' readiness to work in the international environment of the 1990s and beyond.

Acknowledgements

It is impossible to thank individually all of the people who have contributed to this book. I could not have written it without the training and insights provided by my colleagues and teachers. I could not have written it without the support of all my family and friends. I would like to mention individually Allan Date and Jeanne Drouillard who put many hours into gathering data for the Country Profiles, Paula Gignac who put many hours into typing and retyping parts of the manuscript, and the reviewers of the manuscript who made very helpful comments. I owe special thanks to my husband, Don Wood, who untiringly read and reread the manuscript through all of its stages; without his patience and insight it would never have been completed. Finally, I would like to mention particularly my father and mother, Langley and Betty, without whom I would not have reached the stage of attempting to write such a book, and my children, Amanda and Justin, who have encouraged me in all my academic endeavors.

Betty Jane Punnett

Contents

Introduction and Overview   1

Part 1   Exercises   27

Introduction
and Overview

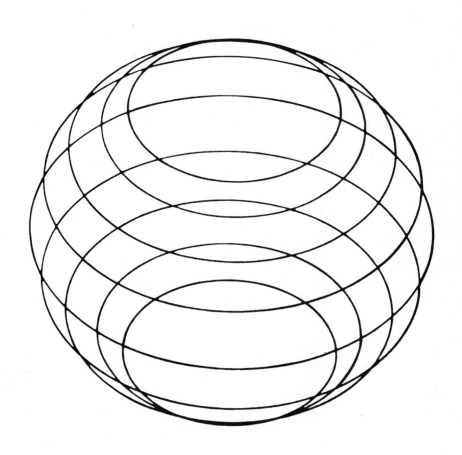

International aspects of management are being integrated into university curricula throughout the United States and Canada, as well as in other countries. The American Association of Collegiate Schools of Business (AACSB) has formally recognized the need for a greater international focus at the university level, and academic institutions are actively pursuing an increased international emphasis.

There are many teaching approaches that can be effective in pursuing this emphasis — among them are lectures, readings, library research, field research, case studies, and various types of simulations and exercises. Some teaching approaches focus on the study of theories and concepts; others focus on the real world and how theories and concepts apply in practice. Many instructors incorporate a blend of approaches into their classes.

This book presents a number of experiential exercises and projects for use in class and as homework. They illustrate some of the complexities of international management decisions and may be used in combination with the other teaching methods mentioned above. They have been designed to be fun, yet realistic; and students find they add an interesting and enjoyable dimension to classes.

An Introduction to Experiential Learning

Experiential learning broadly refers to learning that occurs from experience. If you cross the street without looking and get hit by a car, and if you learn from the experience to look both ways before crossing, then you have encountered experiential learning. Much of our learning is experiential, and we engage in experiential learning every day. In a classroom setting we attempt to achieve the same learning through the use of exercises that simulate a portion of the real world; we ask students to pretend the situation is real and make decisions in that context.

The overall learning process has been described in terms of four modes: concrete experience, reflective observation, abstract conceptualization, and active experimentation (see Kolb, 1984, for a detailed discussion of these learning styles). People use all four of these styles, but different individuals may emphasize one or another and learn more effectively through that approach.

Effective teaching incorporates opportunities to use all four learning styles. The most difficult to incorporate into the traditional classroom is concrete experience; the aim of the exercises and projects presented here is to provide an opportunity for some concrete experience learning in the classroom.

The Benefits of Experiential Learning

The exercises and projects in this text are intended to increase variety and interest in the classroom, while providing an effective learning environment. Proponents of experiential learning believe that:

- Learning is intensified when the process is interesting and fun.
- Learning generates involvement and interest when it provides active experience of concepts.
- Learning is effective when it is an active rather than a passive process.
- Learning is most effective when thought, action, and feedback are integrated.

- Learning that involves two-way communication is most effective.
- Learning is enduring when it is problem-centered.

These exercises and projects are designed to take advantage of these benefits. They have been tested with student groups to ensure that students find them interesting and learn from them.

What Students Should Expect

Some of the exercises and projects presented in this book are intended for larger groups, some for smaller; some are done individually, others in groups; some are done entirely in class, some involve limited outside work, others may be prepared entirely outside class; some involve class presentations, others written assignments; some are short, others can take several hours. The author's intent has been to prepare a variety of exercises and projects so the instructor can choose those that are most appropriate for a particular course and group of students; therefore, he or she will probably assign only some of the exercises or projects. These will be the exercises that the instructor feels are most meaningful for students, given the other learning experiences to which they will be exposed.

I would encourage students to read and think about all the exercises and projects, even though some may not be assigned. They will add to an overall appreciation of the challenges and complexities of international management.

Organization of the Book

The book is divided into several parts. Part 1 contains a series of exercises that are designed primarily for in-class use; Part 2 is made up of projects designed primarily for use with individual, company, and country profiles; Part 3 consists of profiles for use with the projects in Part 2.

The profiles are of ten individuals, three companies, and twelve countries. The companies and individuals are fictitious; however, they are realistic and incorporate characteristics that are drawn from the real world. These profiles were developed specifically for this text to represent a variety of company and individual situations. The countries are real countries, and the information is the most current available as of 1988. Country data is based on secondary sources, not firsthand information; this type of information would be readily available to decision makers in the real world. The countries chosen are varied in terms of geography, religion, language, race, political system, economic development, and so forth, in order to give a sense of the diversity of situations found in the real world.

The projects that use the profiles involve outside research and decision making. Two focus on updating country information and developing additional country profiles; the update project is important because country information changes constantly, and the development of additional country profiles provides an opportunity for students to study countries of particular interest. The decision-making projects mirror decisions that multinational companies frequently make and deal with the companies, individuals, and countries in order to make them realistic.

The exercises in Part 1 can be viewed in terms of the management process— planning, organizing, staffing, directing, and controlling—as well as in terms of their functional focus. Exhibits I.1 and I.2 identify the focus of each exercise and project.

Exhibit 1.1 Summary of Exercises

Exercises legend (No. — Title — Page):

1. Defining an International Company — 29
2. Benefits of Trade — 29
3. Trade Considerations — 33
4. Choosing a Supplier — 34
5. Friendly Negotiations — 35
6. How Do You Negotiate? — 36
7. Would You Give a Bribe? — 38
8. A Question of Foreign Exchange — 38
9. Choosing a Global Structure — 39
10. An Advertising Campaign — 43
11. Expatriate Assignment and Repatriation — 44
12. Social Responsibility: It All Depends on Your Point of View — 47
13. Japanese Management Practices — 48
14. How About Stereotypes? — 57
15. What Is Culture? — 58
16. Managing Political Risk — 63
17. The Stakeholders' Views — 63
18. How Well Did They Do? — 68

Section	Category	1	2	3	4	5	6	7	8	9	10	11	12	13	14	15	16	17	18
Management process	Controlling				•		•	•					•					•	•
	Directing						•						•	•		•		•	•
	Staffing										•					•	•		
	Organizing				•	•			•								•		
	Negotiating		•	•	•	•	•												
	Planning	•	•	•	•	•					•		•					•	•
Functional activity	Production and operations			•	•	•	•						•					•	•
	Organizational behavior and theory						•				•				•	•	•		•
	Policy and strategy	•	•	•	•	•							•				•	•	•
	Finance					•		•											•
	Marketing and sales			•	•	•					•								•
Type of assignment	Outside required work	•										•							
	Combined individual and group	•																	•
	Group		•	•	•	•	•			•	•	•	•						•
	Individual							•	•					•	•	•	•		

Exhibit 1.2 Summary of Projects

Projects			Management process						Functional activity					Type of assignment			
No.	Title	Page	Controlling	Directing	Staffing	Organizing	Negotiating	Planning	Production and operations	Organizational behavior and theory	Policy and strategy	Finance	Marketing and sales	Outside required work	Combined individual and group	Group	Individual
1	Update of Country Information	73						●			●			●			●
2	Additional Country Profiles	73						●			●			●			●
3	Export Decisions	74						●			●			●		●	
4	Investment Decisions	75						●	●		●	●	●	●		●	●
5	Case Studies	76	●	●	●	●		●	●	●	●	●	●	●		●	
6	PCNs, HCNs, or TCNs	79		●	●	●			●	●		●	●	●		●	
7	Choice of Expatriate Managers	80			●					●				●		●	
8	Fitting In	89			●					●				●			
9	Cross-Cultural Organizational Behavior	90				●				●				●	●		
10	Designing Projects	101	●	●	●	●	●	●	●	●	●	●	●	●	●	●	●

There are many other issues faced by international companies that could ha been included in this book; these exercises and projects, however, should give you an appreciation of the complexity of decisions in companies that are international.

Student Participation and Learning

Learning is always partially a function of participation, but this is particularly true with experiential learning. If a student participates with enthusiasm, learning can be substantial for everyone involved and enjoyable, as well. In contrast, if a student chooses not to participate, there will be little benefit for that individual; further, this makes learning more difficult and less enjoyable for classmates.

Some students are uncomfortable with this method of learning because they find it unstructured and wonder how much real information can be gained in exercises. If you feel uncomfortable and concerned about this as a means of learning, why not try to "suspend your disbelief," relax, and enjoy the process, then reevaluate it at the conclusion.

An Overview of International Management

The following brief description of the major characteristics of international management will give students a preliminary overview of the context in which the exercises in Parts 1 and 2 take place.

Managing a business in the environment of the 1990s will almost certainly involve international management. This can range from the small manufacturer, which may employ a cross-cultural workforce, to the global company, which may view the world as a market for both inputs and sales. The scope of these two examples is different, but both face an international environment, and neither can overlook its implications.

Corporations are developing a global perspective to survive and prosper in this international environment. This is a challenge for the organizations of the late twentieth and early twenty-first century. Many will succeed or fail on the basis of their ability to deal with this dynamic environment.

International business itself is not new; international companies have existed for a long time. If one goes back to the earliest records of the Egyptians, the Greeks, the Phoenicians, or the peoples of the Far East, there are references to business having been transacted across borders. The difference today stems from rapid advances in transportation and communications technology that have resulted in relatively fast and easy global movement and communication. This means that virtually all business has some international aspects. Anyone who is involved in the management of a business organization, therefore, needs to be concerned with the international nature of his or her business.

Historical Overview

The post–World War II era has seen a rapid expansion of international business. This internationalization of business has been described by Robinson (1981) in terms of the "actors" participating in the process. There are four major phases, as follows.

to take advantage of perceived opportunities

Exhibit **I.3**   Proactive Reasons for Engaging in International Business

Advantage/opportunity sought	Explanation
Additional resources	Various inputs, including natural resources, technologies, skilled personnel, and materials, may be easier to obtain outside the home country.
Lowered costs	Various costs, including labor, materials, transport, and financing, may be lower outside the home country.
Incentives	Incentives may be available from the host government or the home government to establish operations in, or trade with, foreign countries.
New/expanded markets	New and different markets may be available outside the home country; excess resources, including management, skills, machinery, and money, may be utilized in foreign countries.
Exploitation of firm-specific advantages	Technologies, brands, and recognition can all provide opportunities in the global environment.
Taxes	Differing corporate and income tax systems in different countries provide opportunities for companies to maximize their worldwide after-tax profits.
Economies of scale/synergy	National markets may be too small to support efficent production, while sales from several national markets combined are more efficient. Synergy can be obtained from transferring learning across national boundaries.

business decisions to justify international activities, therefore, there must be per-ceived benefits that outweigh the risks. International operations generally can be seen as either proactive or reactive. Proactive international ventures are undertaken to take advantage of perceived opportunities; reactive ventures are undertaken in response to actions taken by other parties or to defend against perceived threats.

Exhibits I.3 and I.4 summarize the major proactive and reactive motives that account for companies becoming international in their operations. Proactive motives include resource availability, lower costs, incentives, new markets, exploiting firm-specific advantages, and international tax advantages. Reactive motives include react-ing to trade barriers, responding to international customers or competitors, and seeking to avoid home country regulations.

Proactive Explanations   International differences in customs and cultures, as well as differing factor endowments, provide many opportunities for companies outside of their home borders, as the following illustrates:

- Resources are available in some locations and not in others, they are easier to access in certain locations, or they can be cheaper and subject to fewer restrictions. This is true of natural, human, and technological resources.

- Costs are lower in some locations than in others. Natural resources are less expensive in locations where they are plentiful, and labor costs are lower where labor is abundant. In addition, transportation and energy costs may differ depending on the location of production and markets. The costs of doing business, including interest rates and taxes, vary from country to country.

- Many governments offer incentives to encourage companies to do business with or in a particular country or region. Incentives offered by host governments include such things as provision of industrial buildings, insurance, tax exemptions, tax holidays, and interest-free loans. Incentives offered by home governments include trade assistance, subsidies, low-interest loans, and risk insurance. These incentives can increase profits and decrease risks, making foreign operations very attractive.

- Different levels of economic development and different life-styles, customs, and conditions throughout the world all provide opportunities for new markets in foreign locations. A mature product in a declining market at home may be an innovative product in a growth market somewhere else. Outdated technology at home may be welcomed elsewhere. Skills developed in the home market may be transferred to other locations. The opportunities are almost endless.

- Company strengths that originate at home can be equally advantageous in the global environment. A well-known brand name, a technological lead, and a recognized company image are all potential global strengths.

- Tax differentials among countries are important to companies that operate internationally. A company can minimize the corporate taxes that it pays glob-

in response to actions of other parties or to defend against perceived threats.

Exhibit **1.4** Reactive Reasons for Engaging in International Business

Outside occurrence	Explanation
Trade barriers	Tariffs, quotas, buy-local policies, and other restrictive trade practices can make exports to foreign markets impractical; local operations in the foreign location thus become desirable.
International customers	If the customer base becomes international and the company wants to continue to serve it, local operations in foreign locations may become necessary.
International competition	If the competition becomes international and the company wants to remain competitive, foreign operations may become necessary.
Regulations	Regulations and restrictions imposed by the home government may increase the costs of operating at home; it may be possible to avoid these by establishing foreign operations.

ally by locating its various operations in appropriate countries. A company seeking to maximize its after-tax profits will seek out these opportunities.

- Economies of scale that are not available in a single country may be possible on a larger international scale. In addition, integrated operations may offer a form of synergy through learning from different locations.

Reactive Explanations Many companies do not actively seek international involvement; this can be because the risks and costs are seen as too high, the payoffs are seen as relatively low, or the company does not have adequate resources to pursue international opportunities actively. These companies, nevertheless, often find that internationalization is forced on them because of events outside of their control. The following issues illustrate reactive internationalization:

- Trade barriers imposed by trading partners who are customers for a company's product or services often force a company to initiate international operations. These trade barriers can make a product or service too expensive for customers in the export market. However, if the product or service is produced locally, it ceases to be subject to the trade barriers. Many companies react to the imposition of trade barriers by setting up operations to serve foreign markets locally.

- If a company's customers choose to become international, the company may have to follow their lead in order to retain them as customers. Many international companies prefer to deal with one supplier worldwide; thus, if a supplier cannot supply their needs in foreign locations, it may lose them as domestic customers as well.

- If the competition becomes international, a company may have to follow this lead in order to remain competitive. If international competitors become well established in foreign environments, this may put them in a position to attack a competitor's domestic market with lower cost products or services. In addition, if competitors become well established in international markets, the domestic company may find it very difficult to compete in these markets at a later stage. Many companies, therefore, follow the international lead of their competitors.

- Home governments can impose regulations and restrictions that increase the costs of operating. These include environmental, health and safety, and insurance regulations, among others. If less rigorous regulations and restrictions exist elsewhere, other factors being equal, companies may decide to operate in the less restrictive environment.

Forms of Entry into Foreign Locations

A company that has decided to become international can make its entry into foreign markets in a variety of forms ranging from exports and imports, through licenses and contracts, to ownership of foreign operations. The nature of the business activities that a particular company undertakes are a function of that company's specific situation.

A simplified way of looking at the decision regarding the form of entry that is appropriate for a particular company is in terms of the following three dimensions:

1. degree of perceived risk in a particular location
2. degree of perceived attractiveness of a particular location
3. the company's ability to undertake international operations.

In a positive situation, where risk is perceived as relatively low, the location is perceived as attractive, and the company believes it has the ability to undertake the international operation, the company would wish the maximum involvement allowed by law. This would differ from country to country because laws and regulations differ.

In a negative situation where risk is perceived as high, the location is perceived as relatively unattractive, and the company is unsure of its ability to expand internationally, the company would decide to avoid this international possibility completely.

In mixed situations, decisions reflect strengths and opportunities as well as weaknesses and potential threats. For example, in a risky but attractive environment, a company wants to minimize its exposure while exploiting the market; exports or a licensing arrangement might be appropriate. In a safe but unattractive environment, exports of surplus production might be all a company should consider. In a safe and attractive situation, where the company considers its abilities weak, a joint venture to augment its resources would be appropriate, as would a program to strengthen its own resources prior to expansion.

Ownership and Partners

Many international ventures involve shared ownership and the choice of partners. Foreign companies may be required by local regulations to have local owners, or they may choose to do so because of the perceived benefits associated with having local input. In addition, companies may choose to share ownership with other foreign companies.

In general terms, the benefits from sharing ownership are the sharing of risks and the addition of needed resources.

Sharing ownership with locals is generally desirable from a local political viewpoint and thus may be less risky. A foreign company may be more accepted because locals are seen as part of the decision-making process and thus more responsive to local interests. In addition, local ownership ensures retention of some of the benefits of the operation for a host country. Many companies seek local partners because this input provides valuable local information and insight, which allows the foreign company to be more responsive to local needs.

Sharing ownership with other foreigners is also desirable from the company's viewpoint because it spreads the risk and supplements resources. The financial burden of international investment can be shared among partners, and host governments may be more unwilling to antagonize many foreigners than one. Other foreign partners are often sought to supply complementary resources, such as special skills, capital, machinery, and so forth, that a company lacks. Foreign partners as described here may be other companies from the home country or companies from a third country.

Shared ownership, in addition to its benefits, has some drawbacks. Of most concern to companies is the potential loss of control that accompanies shared ownership. In addition, the objectives of the several partners often differ and can lead to conflicts that can be costly. International communication among partners is often difficult, particularly where language differences exist, and getting things done can take a long time.

If shared ownership is necessary or desirable, then the degree of ownership is an important consideration. Ownership in foreign subsidiaries can range from a minority share on the part of the home company to 100-percent ownership. Partners can range from silent (sharing ownership but not decision making) to fully participating. A company can choose to share ownership with one partner or many. The various options need to be weighed carefully because there are benefits and risks involved in each. To some extent, the choice will be a function of what is legal and practical in a given country; but within these limits there will still be options available.

In essence, the choice among these options must be made in light of protecting a company's particular strategic advantages. This means that protecting and retaining control over certain aspects of a company's business will be of paramount importance to management, and ownership decisions should reflect this. Ownership and control, while interconnected, are not identical. It is important to recognize that host countries can retain control of a subsidiary, through regulation and a host country's sovereign rights, even if the subsidiary is wholly owned by a foreign company. Equally, a company can retain control of a subsidiary in which it has a minority ownership share through its control of technology, markets, supplies, capital, and so forth.

A decision to share ownership also implies the necessity for choosing partners. In some situations, this can involve a relatively simple share offering on local stock markets. In most situations, it involves selecting one, or a small number, of partners.

Joint ventures have been likened to marriages; if they are to be successful, partners must be chosen with care. The cost of a joint-venture breakup is high; therefore, companies need to plan carefully to avoid this outcome. Perhaps the most useful advice on choosing a joint-venture partner is to go slowly; consider several partners, consider how well resources complement each other, consider both parties' objectives, and consider the relationship of corporate culture and national culture. Once a partner has been chosen, be specific about the following:

- each party's contribution to the project
- each party's expectations of the project
- management arrangements
- goals and objectives
- performance evaluation
- time frames
- conflict resolution mechanisms.

Perhaps most important, ask what happens if things do not go well. Like a marriage, there is often euphoria associated with signing the joint-venture agreement; companies must look beyond this, and contracts should include specific provisions for dissolving the partnership.

Managing International Operations

The increasingly complex international environment affects all aspects of business. It affects decision making in terms of corporate planning and organizing, as well as corporate staffing and management of human resources. All the functions of a business—for example, marketing, personnel, finance, and operations—are also changed in an international environment.

The movement of goods and services, money, and people across national borders makes the management of international operations complex. Operational decisions are made in the context of the national and cultural characteristics of the varying environments in which a company operates.

There is no clear distinction between national and cultural characteristics, but national characteristics are considered to be the more concrete and observable ones that distinguish nation from nation. National characteristics include laws and regulations, economic conditions, and political ideology. They are generally used to describe an entire nation. Cultural characteristics are more abstract and subjective and include values, attitudes, and beliefs. These are often thought of as pertaining to an entire nation, but they may be shared with other peoples and there may be different cultures within any nation.

The Role of Culture in International Management

The abstract nature of culture makes it difficult to identify and analyze; any examination of culture is therefore simplistic and must be understood in this context.

The model in Exhibit I.5 is useful in understanding the relationship between cultural antecedents, values, and manifestations. This model suggests that both national and societal variables contribute to societal culture, which is expressed in terms of individual values; these values in turn influence individual behavior. Individual behavior is important to the organization in all of its operations; thus, the organization that operates internationally must try to understand the various cultures within which it operates.

A useful method for analyzing cultures is in terms of their relative similarity or dissimilarity. Exhibit I.6, using information presented by Ronen and Shenkar (1985), presents clusters of countries based on the similarities of their cultural values; cultural values, in this context, are the shared preferences of a national grouping. Exhibit I.7, using information presented by Punnett and Ronen (1985), presents similarities and differences in cultural antecedents among these clusters of countries; cultural antecedents, in this context, refers to the national and cultural variables that are believed to shape cultural values (see page 18).

In general, operations in culturally similar countries can be expected to be relatively easy, whereas operations in culturally dissimilar countries can be expected to be relatively difficult. Operations in similar countries can incorporate many of

Exhibit **1.5** Simplified Model of Cultural/National Variables and Organizational Behavior

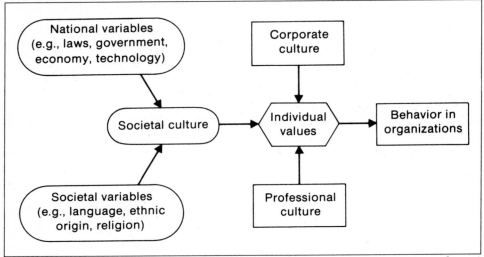

Societal culture is a function of both national and societal variables; individual values are a function of societal culture, as well as corporate and professional culture; individual behavior in organizations depends, at least partially, on the values held by these individuals.

the home country procedures, while operations in dissimilar countries will have to adapt procedures or develop new ones.

Decisions regarding the standardization or adaptation of management procedures need to be made in light of particular cultural values. One of the most useful models that has been developed for assessing cultural values proposes four cultural value dimensions (Hofstede, 1980). These dimensions are described as follows.

Individualism–Collectivism (IDV): The degree of emphasis given to the individual compared with the degree of collectivity that prevails in a society. In a society that is high on individualism, there is an emphasis on individual achievement, leadership, and decision making; individuals have a right to their own opinions, want autonomy on the job, and owe their basic allegiance to themselves. In contrast, in a society that is low on individualism, or high on collectivism, the emphasis is on group achievement and decision making; social needs are high and the group provides support for the individual.

Uncertainty Avoidance (UAI): The degree to which ambiguity and uncertainty are accepted and tolerated by society. In a society high on uncertainty avoidance, there is a lack of tolerance for uncertainty or ambiguity; people prefer and need formal rules and structure, and do not readily accept deviance. In contrast, in a society low on uncertainty avoidance, uncertainty and dissent are accepted; there are fewer rules, they are less conservative, change is accepted readily, and generally they are risk-takers.

Power Distance (PDI): The degree of acceptance and formalization of inequality in society. In a society high on power distance, the order of inequality is well defined,

Exhibit **1.6**   Country Clusters Ranked on Similarities of Values

---

Cluster 1—Anglo
  Canada, Australia, New Zealand, United Kingdom, United States

Cluster 2—Germanic
  Austria, Germany, Switzerland

Cluster 3—Latin European
  Belgium, France, Italy, Portugal, Spain

Cluster 4—Nordic
  Denmark, Finland, Norway, Sweden

Cluster 5—Latin American
  Argentina, Chile, Columbia, Mexico, Peru, Venezuela

Cluster 6—Near Eastern
  Greece, Iran, Turkey

Cluster 7—Far Eastern
  Hong Kong, Indonesia, Malaysia, Philippines, Singapore, South Vietnam, Taiwan

Cluster 8—Arab
  Bahrain, Kuwait, Saudi Arabia, United Arab Emirates

Independent (Not closely related to other countries)
  Japan, India, Israel

Note: Countries within a cluster are considered similar with regard to their cultural values. Clusters are arranged in an approximate order of cluster similarity; i.e., the Anglo cluster is more similar to the European clusters (Germanic, Latin European, and Nordic) than it is to the Latin American, Near Eastern, Far Eastern, and Arab clusters.

Source: Based on information presented by Ronen and Shenkar, 1985.

one's place in society is known and accepted; society and organizations are hierarchically structured with a clear hierarchy of power. In contrast, in a society low on power distance, equality is seen as desirable and all people have equal rights; while power differences exist, they are seen as changeable.

Masculinity–Femininity (MAS): The degree to which traditional male values are accepted by society. In very masculine societies, the male values of assertiveness, money, and possessions predominate; sex roles are clearly defined and ostentatious manliness is admired. In feminine societies (societies low on MAS), female values of nurturance, sympathy, and service predominate; sex roles are fluid and both manliness and femininity are admired.

This value framework has been used in a number of research studies, and data exist for a wide variety of cultures and nations for comparative purposes. Exhibit I.8 summarizes the data presented by Hofstede for countries grouped according to the clusters previously identified. Countries are described as being high (H), moderately high (MH), moderately low (ML), or low (L) on each of the value

Exhibit **1.7** Cultural Antecedants Among Clusters Relative to Anglo Culture

	Germanic	Latin European	Nordic	Latin American	Near Eastern	Far Eastern	Arab	Independent
Anglo								
Language (English)	*	x	x	x	x	x	x	India ?[a]
Religion (Judeo-Christian)	*	*	*	*	x	x	x	x
Race (Caucasian)	*	*	*	?	x	x	x	x
Economy (Industrial)	*	*	*	x	x	x	x	Japan

Similarities are indicated by an *, differences by an x, and some overlap by a ?

[a]English is a commonly spoken language in India.

Source: Based on information presented by Punnett and Ronen, 1984.

Exhibit **1.8** Cultural Value Indices for Countries, Grouped by Cluster

Cluster	IDV	UAI	PDI	MAS
Anglo				
Australia	H	ML	ML	MH
Canada	H	ML	ML	MH
Ireland	MH	L	L	MH
New Zealand	H	ML	L	MH
South Africa	MH	ML	ML	MH
United Kingdom	H	L	ML	MH
United States	H	ML	ML	MH
Germanic				
Austria	MH	MH	L	H
Germany (East and West)	MH	MH	ML	MH
Switzerland	MH	ML	ML	H
Latin-European				
Belgium	MH	H	MH	MH
France	MH	MH	MH	ML
Italy	H	MH	ML	H
Portugal	ML	H	MH	ML
Spain	MH	MH	MH	ML
Nordic				
Denmark	MH	L	L	L
Finland	MH	ML	ML	L
Norway	MH	ML	L	L
Sweden	MH	L	L	L
Latin American				
Argentina	ML	MH	ML	MH
Chile	L	MH	MH	L
Columbia	L	MH	MH	MH
Peru	L	MH	MH	ML
Venezuela	MH	MH	L	H
Far Eastern				
Hong Kong	L	L	MH	MH
Philippines	ML	ML	H	MH
Singapore	L	L	H	ML
Taiwan	L	MH	MH	ML
Thailand	L	MH	MH	ML
Near Eastern				
Greece	ML	H	MH	MH
Iran	ML	ML	MH	ML
Pakistan	L	MH	MH	MH
Turkey	ML	MH	MH	ML
Independent				
Brazil	ML	MH	MH	ML
India	ML	ML	H	MH
Israel	MH	MH	L	ML
Japan	ML	H	MH	H

Note: H = high (1st quartile); MH = moderately high (2nd quartile); ML = moderately low (3rd quartile); L = low (4th quartile)

dimensions. These descriptions were derived by dividing the Hofstede scores into quartiles.

This information on cultural values is useful in understanding different cultures in which a company operates. It is, however, only one model of culture and is not intended to be comprehensive. In addition, this societal framework is not meant to imply that all people of a culture will be alike. Organizations can use this cultural information as a starting point, but they will need to complement this information with more detailed, culture-specific information.

One approach that incorporates culture-specific information into the management process takes situations considered to be universally encountered by managers (for example, discipline, evaluating performance, leadership, motivation) and asks host-country managers to identify, from their cultural perspective, the most effective means of dealing with such situations. This approach, while time-consuming and costly, can pay off for international companies (Punnett, 1989).

Summary

The complexity of international management decisions means it is often difficult to understand them, from a practical point of view, within a classroom setting. The purpose of this book is to give students an opportunity to address international decisions in a simulated real-life setting. The exercises included here encompass the major management processes in international management, as well as the various business functions. These exercises are limited in number, and, therefore, there are many subtleties of international management that they do not cover. The intent of these exercises is not to cover all aspects of international management but, rather, to give students an appreciation of decision making in an international environment.

The suggested readings that follow will give the student a broader appreciation of the issues faced by international managers. These readings are only a fraction of those available on each of the topics, and the interested student is encouraged to seek out additional readings. These readings have been selected from a variety of sources and represent a variety of viewpoints, both theoretical and practical. It is the author's hope that these readings, combined with the exercises in Parts 1 and 2 and the profiles in Part 3, will serve to increase students' readiness to work in the international environment of the 1990s.

References

Hofstede, G., *Cultures Consequences: International Differences in Work Related Values* (Beverly Hills: Sage, 1980).

Kobrin, S., *International Expertise in American Business* (New York: Institute of International Education, 1984).

Kolb, David A., *Experiential Learning: Experience as the Source of Learning and Development* (Englewood Cliffs, N.J.: Prentice-Hall, 1984).

Punnett, B. J., "International Human Resource Management," in A. Rugman (ed.), *Canadian Dimensions in International Business* (Toronto: Prentice-Hall Canada, 1989).

Punnett, B. J., and S. Ronen, Tables 5.3, 5.4, 5.5, from "Operationalizing Cross-Cultural

Variables," paper delivered at 44th Annual Meeting of the Academy of Management (Boston, 1984), in S. Ronen, *Comparative and Multinational Management* (New York: John Wiley & Sons, 1986), pp. 157–60.

Robinson, R. D., "Background Concepts and Philosophy of International Business from World War II to the Present," *Journal of International Business Studies* (Spring–Summer 1981).

Ronen, S., and O. Shenkar, "Clustering Countries on Attitudinal Dimensions: A Review and Synthesis," *Academy of Management Review* 10 (3) (1985): 435–54.

Suggested Readings

Overview

Ball, D. A., and W. H. McCulloch, Jr., "Appendix A: Sources of Economic and Financial Information," and "Appendix B: Alphabetical List of the Names, Acronyms, or Initials by Which Some of the More Important International Organizations Are Known," and "Glossary," in *International Business: Introduction and Essentials* (Plano, Tex.: Business Publications, 1988).

Fayerweather, J., "A History of the Academy of International Business from Infancy to Maturity: The First 25 Years," *Essays in International Business,* South Carolina, 6, 1986.

Grosse, R., and D. Kujawa, "Glossary," in *International Business — Theory and Managerial Applications* (Homewood, Ill.: Richard D. Irwin, 1988), pp. 717–43.

Kindleberger, C. P., and D. B. Audretsch (eds.), *The Multinational Corporation in the 1980s,* (Cambridge, Mass.: MIT Press, 1983).

Kobrin, S., *International Expertise in American Business* (New York: Institute of International Education, 1984).

Punnett, B. J., "Sources of Information for International Business," in *Handbook of International Business,* I. Walter (ed.) (New York: John Wiley & Sons, 1982).

Robinson, R. D., "Background Concepts and Philosophy of International Business from World War II to the Present," *Journal of International Business Studies* (Spring–Summer 1981).

United States Council for International Business, *Corporate Handbook to International Economic Organizations and Terms* (New York: U.S. Council for International Business, 1985).

Vernon, R., "The Product Cycle Hypothesis in a New International Environment," in H. Vernon Wortzel and L. H. Wortzel (eds.), *Strategic Management of Multinational Corporations: The Essentials.* (New York: John Wiley & Sons, 1985), pp. 16–27.

Culture

Graham, J. L., The Influence of Culture on the Process of Business Negotiations," *Journal of International Business Studies* 16, no. 1 (Spring 1985): 81–96.

Hall, E. T., *Beyond Culture* (Garden City, N.Y.: Anchor Press, 1976).

Hall, E. T., *The Hidden Dimension* (Garden City, N.Y.: Anchor Books, 1969).

Hall, E. T., *The Silent Language* (Garden City, N.Y.: Anchor Books, 1973).

Hall, E. T., "The Silent Language in Overseas Business," *Harvard Business Review* (May–June 1960): 87–95.

Hofstede, G., "Motivation, Leadership, and Organization: Do American Theories Apply Abroad?" *Organizational Dynamics* (Summer 1980): 42−63.

Kolde, Endel-Jakob, "Socio-Cultural Environment of International Business," in *Environment of International Business,* 2nd ed. (Boston: Kent, 1985), pp. 416−30.

Ronen, S., and O. Shenkar, "Clustering Countries on Attitudinal Dimensions: A Review and Synthesis," *Academy of Management Review (1985): 435−54.*

Planning and Strategy

Caves, R. E., "Industrial Organization, Corporate Strategy and Structure," *Journal of Economic Literature* (March 1980): 64−92.

Contractor, F. J., "The Role of Licensing in International Strategy," *Columbia Journal of World Business* (Winter 1981): 73−81.

Contractor, F. J., "Strategies for Structuring Joint-Ventures: A Negotiations Planning Paradigm," *Columbia Journal of World Business* (Summer 1984): 30−39.

Contractor, F. J., and T. Sagafi-Nejad, "International Technology Transfer: Major Issues and Policy Responses," *Journal of International Business Studies* (Fall 1981): 121−35.

Daniels, J. D., R. A. Pitts, and M. J. Tretter, "Strategy and Structure of U.S. Multinationals: An Exploratory Study," *Academy of Management Journal* (1984): 292−307.

Doz, Y. L., "Strategic Management in Multinational Companies," *Sloan Management Review* (Winter 1980): 27−46.

Doz, Y. L., and C. K. Prahalad, "Headquarters Influence and Strategic Control in MNCs," *Sloan Management Review* (Fall 1981): 15−29.

Gladwin, T. N., "Conflict Management in International Business," in I. Walter (ed.), *Handbook of International Business* (New York: John Wiley & Sons, 1982).

Hamel, G., and C. K. Prahalad, "Do You Really Have a Global Strategy?" *Harvard Business Review* (July−August 1985): 139−48.

Kobrin, S. J., "Political Risk: A Review and Reconsideration," *Journal of International Business Studies* (Spring−Summer 1979): 67−80.

Root, F. R., "Entering International Markets," in I. Walter (ed.), *Handbook of International Business* (New York: John Wiley & Sons, 1982).

Simon, J. D., "Political Risk Assessment: Past Trends and Future Prospects," *Columbia Journal of World Business* (Fall 1982): 62−71.

Walters, K. D., and R. J. Monsen, "Managing the Nationalized Company," *California Management Review* (Summer 1983): 16−26.

Weigand, R., "International Investments: Weighing the Incentives," *Harvard Business Review* (July−August 1983): 146−52.

Weiss-Wik, S., "Enhancing Negotiators' Successfulness," *Journal of Conflict Resolution* 27, no. 4 (December 1983): 706−39.

Wells, L. T., "Negotiating with Third World Governments," *Harvard Business Review* (January−February 1977): 72−80.

Yaprak, A., and Sheldon, K. T., "Political Risk Management in Multinational Firms: An Integrative Approach," *Management Decisions* (1984): 53−67.

Organization

Business International Corporation, *New Directions in Multinational Corporate Organization* (New York: Business International, 1981).

Caves, R. E., "Industrial Organization, Corporate Strategy and Structure," *Journal of Economic Literature* (March 1980): 64–92.

Daniels, J. D., R. A. Pitts, and M. J. Tretter, "Strategy and Structure of U.S. Multinationals: An Exploratory Study," *Academy of Management Journal* (1984): 292–307.

Davis, S. M., "Trends in the Organization of Multinational Corporations," *Columbia Journal of World Business* (Summer 1976): 59–71.

Egelhoff, W., "Strategies and Structures in the MNC: An Information Processing Approach," *Administrative Science Quarterly* (1982): 435–58.

Hawkins, R. G., and I. Walter, "Planning Multinational Operations," in P. C. Nystrom and W. H. Starbuck (eds.), *Handbook of Organizational Design* (New York: Oxford University Press, 1981), pp. 253–67.

Killing, J. P., "How to Make a Global Joint-Venture Work," *Harvard Business Review* (1982): 120–27.

Finance, Marketing, and Production

Booth, L. D., "Hedging and Foreign Exchange Exposure," *Management International Review* (Spring 1982): 26–42.

Booth, L. D., "Capital Budgeting Frameworks for the Multinational Corporation," *Journal of International Business Studies* (Fall 1982): 113–23.

Buss, M. D. J., "Managing International Information Systems," *Harvard Business Review* (September–October 1982): 153–62.

Davidson, W. H., and P. Haspeslagh, "Shaping a Global Product Organization," *Harvard Business Review* (July–August 1982): 125–32.

Dunning, J. H., "Explaining Changing Patterns of International Production: In Defense of the Eclectic Theory," *The Oxford Bulletin of Economics and Statistics* (1979): 269–96.

Foulkes, F. K., and J. L. Hirsch, "People Make Robots Work," *Harvard Business Review* (January–February 1984): 94–102.

Garvin, D. A., "Quality on the Line," *Harvard Business Review* (September–October 1983): 64–75.

Goldar, J. D., and M. Jelinek, "Plan for Economies of Scope," *Harvard Business Review* (November–December 1983): 141–48.

Harris, Greg. "The Globalization of Advertising," *International Journal of Advertising* (1984): 223–34.

Levitt, T., "The Globalization of Markets," *Harvard Business Review* (May–June 1983): 92–102.

Nakane, J., and R. W. Hall, "Management Specs for Stockless Production," *Harvard Business Review* (May–June 1983).

Poynter, T. A., and A. M. Rugman, "World Product Mandates: How Will Multinationals Respond?," *Business Quarterly* 47 (October 1982): 54–61.

Ricks, D., *Big Business Blunders: Mistakes in Multinational Marketing* (Homewood, Ill.: Dow Jones-Irwin, 1983).

Sommers, M., and J. Kernan, "Why Products Flourish Here, Fizzle There," *Columbia Journal of World Business* (March–April 1967).

"Where Are Global Campaigns Going or Staying," *Advertising World* (April 1985): 30–31.

"Will New International Regulations Affect Advertising?" *Advertising World* (February 1985): 32–33.

Human Resource Management and Organizational Behavior

Adler, N. J., "Reentry: Managing Cross-Cultural Transitions," *Group and Organization Studies* (1981): 341–56.

Adler, N. J., "Women as Androgynous Managers: A Conceptualization of the Potential for American Women in International Management," *International Journal of Intercultural Relations* (1987): 407–36.

Bass, B. M., "Leadership in Different Cultures," in B. M. Bass (ed.), *Stogdill's Handbook of Leadership* (New York: Free Press, 1981), pp. 522–49.

Business International Corporation, *Worldwide Executive Compensation and Human Resource Planning* (New York: Business International Corporation, 1982).

Earley, P. C., "Intercultural Training for Managers: A Comparison of Documentary and Interpersonal Methods," *Academy of Management Journal* 30, no. 4 (1987): 685–98.

Heller, J. E., "Criteria for Selecting An International Manager," *Personnel* (May–June 1980): 47–55.

Illman, P. E., "Motivating the Overseas Workforce," in *Developing Overseas Managers and Managers Overseas* (1980): 107–13.

Jelinek, M., and N. J. Adler, "Women: World-Class Managers for Global Competition," *The Academy of Management Executive* (February 1988): 11–20.

Laurent, A., "The Cultural Diversity of Western Conceptions of Management," *International Studies of Management and Organization* (Spring–Summer 1983): 75–96.

Matsui, T., and I. Terai, "A Cross-Cultural Study of the Validity of the Expectancy Theory of Work Motivation," *Journal of Applied Psychology* (1979): 263–65.

Punnett, B. J., "Goal Setting: An Extension of the Research," *Journal of Applied Psychology* (February 1986).

Tung, R., "Expatriate Assignments: Enhancing Success and Minimizing Failure," *The Academy of Management Executive* (May 1987): 117–26.

Country-Specific Information

Adler, N. J., and J. L. Graham, "Business Negotiations: Canadians Are Not Just Like Americans," *Canadian Journal of Administrative Sciences* 4, no. 3 (1987): 211–38.

Beliaev, E., T. Mullen, and B. J. Punnett, "Cultural Influences on Commercial Negotiations Between U.S. and U.S.S.R. Executives," *California Management Review* (Winter 1985).

Budde, A., J. Child, A. Francis, A. Kieser, and R. Burgleman, "Corporate Goals, Managerial Objectives, and Organizational Structures in British and West German Companies," *Organizational Studies* 3, no. 1 (1982): 1–32.

Burger, P., and R. Doktor, "Cross-Cultural Analysis of the Structure of Self-Perception Attitudes Among Managers from India, Italy, West Germany, and the Netherlands," *Management International Review* 16, no. 3 (1976): 71–78.

Davidson, W. H., "Creating and Managing Joint-Ventures in China," *California Management Review* (Summer 1987): 77–109.

Deyo, F. C., "The Cultural Patterning of Organizational Development: A Comparative Case Study of Thailand and Chinese Industrial Enterprises," *Human Organization* (Spring 1978): 68–72.

England, G. W., "Managers and Their Value Systems: A Five Country Comparison," *Columbia Journal of World Business* (Summer 1978): 35–44.

England, G. W., and R. Lee, "The Relationship Between Managerial Values and Managerial Success in the United States, Japan, India, and Australia," *Journal of Applied Psychology* 59 (1974): 411–19.

Frankenstein, J., "Trends in Chinese Business Practice," *California Management Review* (Fall 1986): 148–60.

Gable, M., and P. Arlow, "A Comparative Examination of the Value Orientations of British and American Executives," *International Journal of Management* 3 (September 1986): 97–106.

Gillespie, K., "The Middle East Response to the U.S. Foreign Corrupt Practices Act," *California Management Review* (Summer 1987): 9–30.

Graham, J. L., "A Hidden Cause of America's Trade Deficit with Japan," *Columbia Journal of World Business* (Fall 1981): 5–15.

Hofstede, G., *Cultures Consequences: International Differences in Work-Related Values* (Beverly Hills: Sage Publications, 1980).

Jackofsky, E. F., J. W. Slocum, Jr., and S. J. McQuaid, "Cultural Values and the CEO: Alluring Companions?," *The Academy of Management Executive* 11, no. 1: 39–49.

Maher, T. E., "Condemning Japan While Imitating her Management Techniques: No Solution for America's Problems," *Advanced Management Journal* (Winter 1988): 31–35.

Melikian, I., A. Grinsberg, D. M. Guceloglu, and R. Lynn, "Achievement Motivation in Afghanistan, Brazil, Saudi Arabia, and Turkey," *Journal of Social Psychology* 83 (1971): 183–84.

Nath, R., (ed.), *Comparative Management: A Regional View,* (Cambridge, Mass.: Ballinger, 1988).

Orpen, C., "The Relationship Between Job Satisfaction and Job Performance Among Western and Tribal Black Employees," *Journal of Applied Psychology* 63, no. 2 (1978): 263–65.

Ostubo, M., "A Guide to Japanese Business Practices," *California Management Review* (Spring 1986): 28–42.

Pezeshkpur, C., "Challenges to Management in the Arab World," *Business Horizons* 21 (1978): 47–55.

Punnett, B. J., "Motivating Employees in the Caribbean: A Study in St. Vincent and the Grenadines," *Canadian Journal of Latin American and Caribbean Studies,* (1986).

Shenkar, O., and S. Ronen, "Structure and Importance of Work Goals Among Managers in the People's Republic of China," *Academy of Management Journal* 30, no. 3: 564–76.

Vardi, Y., A. Shiron, and D. A. Jacobson, "A Study on the Leadership Beliefs of Israeli Management," *Academy of Management Journal* 23 (1980): 367–74.

Wright, P., "Organizational Behaviour in Islamic Firms," *Management International Review* 21 (1981): 86–94.

Part 1 Exercises

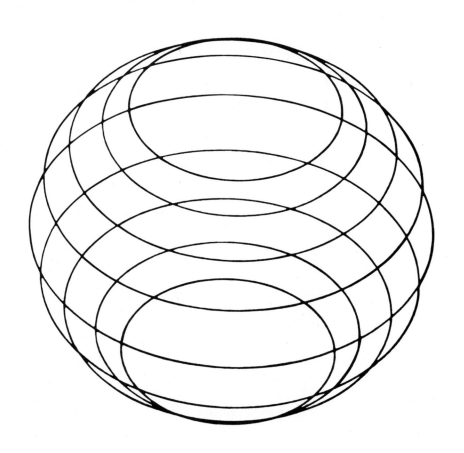

Exercise 1 How Do You Define an International Company?

Aim

This exercise can be a good introduction to the topic of international business. It also can be used to help you summarize what you have learned about international companies.

Time

This exercise should take students about thirty minutes of outside preparation and about one hour of in-class time.

Assignment

Imagine that you could categorize companies as "domestic" or "international." Prior to class, think about the differences that are likely to be found between domestic companies and international companies and make a list of the characteristics of an organization that would probably be different in the two groups; be as exhaustive and imaginative as possible. In class, you will discuss your list with others in a small group. The group will decide which characteristics are most useful and develop criteria to be used for judging whether a company is international. Please use the worksheet provided.

For example, your group might consider "ratio of foreign sales to domestic sales" an important distinguishing characteristic and decide that once a company reaches foreign sales of 20 percent of total sales it should be considered international.

Once your group has decided on a list of characteristics and criteria, move on to Part 2 of the exercise. Here you are asked to develop a definition of an international company and to consider whether there are degrees of internationalism; that is, do you feel it is helpful to distinguish between a multinational, an international, and a global company? Use the worksheet provided on pages 31 to 32 to address these issues.

Exercise 2 Benefits of Trade

Aim

This exercise demonstrates the potential benefits that can accrue from trade.

Time

The exercise takes about thirty minutes of class time.

Format

The class will be divided into five groups of three or four. Each group will begin with ten units of one good (labeled A, B, C, D, and E).

Assignment

Each group will attempt to increase its wealth by trading goods with other groups on a one-for-one basis; that is, if you give up one unit of A, you get one unit of B, or for two units of A you get two units of B, and so on. Your aim is to maximize your group's wealth. Calculate the value of goods as follows:

Good # Units	A	B	C	D	E
1	$ 5,000	2,000	6,000	4,000	3,000
2	9,000	3,900	11,000	7,500	5,500
3	12,000	5,400	15,000	10,000	7,500
4	14,000	6,600	18,000	11,500	9,000
5	15,000	7,600	19,000	12,500	10,000
6	15,800	8,400	19,900	13,200	10,800
7	16,400	9,000	20,700	13,700	11,500
8	16,800	9,400	21,400	14,000	12,100
9	17,000	9,600	22,000	14,200	12,600
10	17,100	9,700	22,500	14,300	13,000

Note that:

- The value of each unit of a good is a function of how much of that good you already own; that is, the more of any good that you have, the less each additional unit is worth. For example, one unit of A is worth $5,000; two units is worth $9,000, or $4,500 each.

- If your group gives up one unit you lose some value; this must be balanced against what you gain by trading. For example, if you have ten units of A and give one up you lose $100 (you go from ten units to nine, $17,100 to $17,000); if you trade for B and if you have no units of B you gain $2,000 (you go from zero units to one, $0 to $2,000). Your group gains $1,900. Alternatively, if you have six units of A and give one up, you lose $800 (you go from six units to five, $8,400 to $7,600); if you trade for B and if you have six units of B you gain $600 (you go from six units to seven, $8,400 to $9,000). Your group loses $200.

Your instructor will provide your group with ten units of a good to begin with; you should record the beginning value of the ten units your group has been assigned. Each good is represented by a different letter, A–E.

You will have five minutes to discuss your strategy as a group; you may decide to trade as individuals or as a group, but your gains or losses will accrue to the group. You will then trade, following your chosen strategy, with the other groups. Goods must be traded on a one-for-one basis only—if you give up one unit of a good you get one unit of another in return. Your objective is to maximize your group's wealth. Your instructor will tell you when to start trading and when to stop.

You will recalculate your wealth at the end of the trading period and determine your gains or losses.

Worksheet for Exercise 1

Name(s) _____

Date _____ Class _____

Part One: Distinguishing Between a Domestic and an International Company

Characteristics   Measurement criteria

1. _____
2. _____
3. _____
4. _____
5. _____
6. _____
7. _____
8. _____
9. _____
10. _____
11. _____
12. _____
13. _____
14. _____
15. _____
16. _____
17. _____
18. _____
19. _____
20. _____

Part Two: Definition

Definition of an international company:

_____

_____

_____

_____

_____

This definition should be a synthesis of the characteristics and measurement criteria identified in Part One.

Exercise **3** Trade Considerations

Aim
The purpose of this exercise is to examine various trade agreements between and among countries, given certain cultural characteristics.

Time
The exercise takes about forty-five minutes of class time.

Assignment
The class will be divided into five groups of three to six individuals. Each group will represent a specific country—A, B, C, D, or E. The following data describe the products, costs, objectives, and constraints for each country:

> **Country A**
> Product: Aircraft
> Cost: $5 million each
> Quantity available: 5
> Goal: Maximize profit
> Constraints: (1) Need cows—at least 8 herds
> (2) Must sell all aircraft; no domestic use

> **Country B**
> Product: Trucks
> Cost: $1.5 million
> Quantity available: 15
> Goal: Import advanced technology
> Constraints: (1) Need 3 aircraft urgently
> (2) Want 5 computers and 2 cows

> **Country C**
> Product: Cows
> Cost: $1 million per herd
> Quantity available: 20 herds
> Goal: Access to a variety of products (the more the better)
> Constraints: (1) Cows are sacred
> (2) Alcohol is forbidden

> **Country D**
> Product: Computers
> Cost: $2 million each
> Quantity available: 8
> Goal: Maximize exports
> Constraints: (1) Cannot trade with country B
> (2) Want 3 aircraft

> **Country E**
> Product: Wine
> Cost: $.5 million per shipment

Quantity available: 30 shipments
Goal: Maintain good relations with trading partners
Constraints: (1) Cannot produce beef locally
              (2) Must arrange transportation for purchases

Your assignment as a group is to trade with other groups in order to try and reach your objective, given your particular products, costs, and constraints. You may trade with one group and receive a product that you do not need in order to use it in trading with another group. You may barter goods or pay for them with your currency.

Each group will be provided with a stock of dollars, as well as a stock of goods. At the conclusion of the exercise, each group will evaluate its position in terms of its original goals and constraints.

Exercise 4   Choosing a Supplier

Aim

This exercise will give you the opportunity to assess a variety of options that might be available to a small company seeking international sources of supply.

Time

This exercise takes about thirty minutes of class time; no outside preparation is necessary.

Background

You represent a small North American company that wants to purchase supplies from a less developed country. Your company supplies fishnets and other fishing supplies to Great Lakes commercial fishermen; Mr. Perch, the president, started the company after several years as a commercial fisherman.

Mr. Perch recently visited a trade show where he had the opportunity to observe some nets manufactured in Korea. The price of these nets compared favorably with those made in North America—$4.00/sq ft versus $12.00/sq ft. The Koreans have not exported nets to the United States or Canada; thus, Mr. Perch sees an opportunity to gain a price advantage over the competition. He orders a small quantity of the nets on a trial basis; this involves considerable effort in terms of arranging letters of credit, transportation, clearing customs, and so on— but it seems well worth the effort if a cheap source of supply is the result.

The Korean company is excited about the prospect of a possible export market. Market research suggests that there is a large potential market for the products in the United States and Canada and that they enjoy a considerable cost advantage over competitors from North America.

The trial shipment arrives in North America and Mr. Perch finds that the nets are unsuitable for use in freshwater lakes—they were designed for use in the ocean. Mr. Perch is upset and angry; he contacts the Korean company to express his misgivings. In the meantime, he becomes aware of a variety of other potential sources of the supply, including the Philippines, Indonesia, and various Caribbean islands.

The Korean company is confused by this turn of events. The company is interested in pursuing this export opportunity but does not have the expertise necessary to manufacture nets that are appropriate for freshwater fishing. The Korean government is also interested in the export opportunity and has indicated a willingness to provide export incentives for the company.

Format

The class is divided into an even number of small groups. Half of the groups represent the North American company; half represent the South Korean company.

Assignment

Each group discusses the situation within their small group and decides on an appropriate course of action; each group then meets with a counterpart group—one representing the North American company, one the South Korean—to decide on a detailed agreement. A spokesperson for the joint groups is chosen to report the details of the agreement to the class.

Each group wants to maximize the benefits from its perspective; at the same time the groups are seeking a win–win solution that will be satisfactory to all parties.

You should consider the following issues:

- continuity of supply
- quality assurance and warranty
- transaction currency and method of payment
- exclusivity
- credit and financing.

Exercise 5 Friendly Negotiations

Aim

This exercise is intended to give you some experience at conducting international negotiations.

Time

The exercise will take about fifty minutes of class time.

Situation

Mongo, a large developing nation with friendly relations with the United States, has recently found that it has extensive reserves of PRT. PRT is a newly discovered mineral that cures certain types of cancer. PRT is available in a number of other locations worldwide, but it is difficult to mine in these areas; whereas Mongo's PRT appears to be relatively easy and cheap to obtain. Mongo is eager to make the best possible use of this mineral but does not have the local expertise necessary to mine, refine, and sell PRT effectively; thus it has been looking for a partner. A U.S. company—Global Pharmaceuticals—has extensive mining and pharmaceutical interests and has some experience mining and selling PRT. The U.S. company believes it has developed a fairly high level of expertise in PRT mining and would like to increase its involvement in PRT mining and selling. Both sides are anxious to reach an agreement regarding exploitation of Mongo's PRT for their mutual benefit. Estimates suggest that yearly sales could exceed US$400 million once full production is reached and that net profit margins could be as high as 10 percent of sales.

Assignment

The class is divided into an even number of small groups of three to five individuals. Half the groups represent the country of Mongo, half represent the Global Pharmaceuticals company. Meet as a small group for twenty minutes to discuss the situation described above and decide on your bargaining position. Then meet with a counterpart group for twenty minutes to negotiate an agreement. Each set of two groups will then describe their agreement to the rest of the class.

Exercise 6 How Do You Negotiate?

Aim

This exercise is intended to give you experience at conducting international negotiations.

Time

The exercise will take about one hour of class time.

Assignment

The class is divided into an even number of small groups of three to five individuals. Half the groups represent the country of Naire, half represent the Allcool Company. Meet as a small group for twenty minutes to discuss the situation described below and decide on your bargaining position. Then meet with a counterpart group for thirty minutes to negotiate an agreement. Each set of two groups will then briefly present their agreement to the rest of the class.

Background

Naire is a developing nation in Africa that has recently elected a socialist government. Allcool is the Nairean subsidiary of a large multinational company headquartered in the United States.

Allcool produces alcohol and tobacco products for local consumption. The company had operated profitably in Naire for ten years.

Following recent elections, the new government of Naire has nationalized all foreign-owned companies, including Allcool. A new state corporation has been created to run Allcool, and members of the political elite have been put in charge of operations; as this is based on their support of the new government rather than experience in the alcohol or tobacco industries, the company soon encounters difficulties.

Specific problems include:

- employment levels rising from 1,200 to 1,600 employees
- production falling from 4,000 to 1,000 cartons of cigarettes and from 3,000 to 900 cases of liquor
- decreasing quality—rejects up 15 percent and customer complaints up substantially
- lack of foreign exchange to purchase needed foreign supplies and machinery
- profits falling from 12 to -9 percent of sales.

Naire also encounters other difficulties, specifically:

- trade balance deficits
- lack of foreign exchange
- external debt arrears
- government instability
- high unemployment
- high inflation
- no real growth in GNP.

At the time of nationalization, the Allcool company was valued by its parent at US$4,000,000. The government of Naire offered to pay US$1,000,000 in compensation. The Allcool parent refused this offer but assumed an attitude of cooperation toward the government. The company felt it stood a better chance of reaching a reasonable settlement by pursuing a cooperative attitude and wanted to be ready to resume control if the opportunity presented itself.

Present

The government of Naire has expressed a desire to win back the confidence of foreign investors and has instituted new investment incentives in addition to making overtures to previous investors. The Allcool company believes there may be an opportunity to reestablish itself in Naire and has agreed to a meeting with the government.

Exercise 7   Would You Give a Bribe?

Aim
This exercise gives students an opportunity to consider the advantages and disadvantages of making a payment that appears to be a bribe.

Time
This exercise will take twenty to thirty minutes.

Background
Investment-U.S. is a company headquartered in the United States; the company has recently entered into a trading agreement with an Indian company. The Indian company has agreed to act as representative for the U.S. company on the basis of product information provided by Investment-U.S., as well as government incentives provided by the Indian government. Mr. Smith, marketing vice president of Investment-U.S., is in India to ensure the success of the project. He is surprised to find that the initial shipment has been held up in customs because government import restrictions have not been complied with due to insufficient data; this information had been supplied previously by the U.S. head office. The information is vital to the implementation of the agreement.

Mr. Smith is approached by a junior clerk in the Indian company who explains that his predecessor was very disorganized and that the material has probably been misfiled. The clerk suggests that if he were to work overtime he could probably find the material, but the Indian company does not pay for overtime and the clerk wants to be appropriately recompensed.

Assignment
You are Mr. Smith: you feel that you are being asked for an illegal payment. Would you agree to the payment or not? Justify your view briefly in writing.

Exercise 8   A Question of Foreign Exchange Rates

Aim
This exercise will give you an opportunity to examine the impact of changes in exchange rates on profits. It will also give you some practice at converting from one currency to another.

Time
This exercise will take a total of fifty minutes. You will need to spend about thirty minutes making the calculations and responding to the questions posed. This will be followed by twenty minutes of class discussion. Remember to bring a calculator.

Assignment

A situation is described below that involves different currencies. Please read the brief description and respond to the questions.

Situation

A small Canadian company has contracted to purchase 100,000 toys for £3.50 each from a British company. The Canadians have agreed to pay in sterling. The Canadians have also agreed to sell the toys to a U.S. company for US$5.50 per toy. The Canadian company has agreed to accept U.S. dollars but plans to convert these revenues to Canadian dollars. The Canadian company estimates its marginal costs (warehousing, travel, and so on) as C$0.75 per toy.

Exchange rates at the time of signing the agreements are as follows:

Canadian $1 = US$0.80

Canadian $1 = British £0.66

Questions

1. Is this a good deal for the Canadian company? Why or why not?

2. What impact would a devaluation of the U.S. dollar relative to the Canadian dollar have on the Canadian company's profits? What impact would a revaluation upward have?

3. What impact would a devaluation of the British pound relative to the Canadian dollar have on the Canadian company's profits? What impact would a revaluation upward have?

4. What impact would a devaluation of the British pound relative to the U.S. dollar have on the Canadian company's profits? What impact would a revaluation upward have?

5. If exchange rates changed to the following, what impact would this have on the Canadian company's profits?

Canadian $1 = US$0.90

Canadian $1 = £0.57

6. What could the Canadian company do to minimize its exposure to exchange-rate losses?

Exercise 9 Choosing a Global Structure

Aim

This exercise is intended to illustrate the relationship of certain strategic choices to appropriate structural choices.

Time

This exercise will take about twenty minutes of class time.

Format

This exercise takes the form of a game. The class will be divided into groups of five individuals (if the class does not divide equally into five, the instructor will form one smaller group and give separate instructions); each group will play the game.

Assignment

Each individual in the group represents one of the companies (A, B, C, D, or E) described below:

Company A
Pharmaceutical company with manufacturing operations in twenty-three countries and sales in forty-eight countries. The company manufactures and sells a major line of painkillers as well as a small number of specialty drugs.

Company B
Oil company conducting research and development (R and D), exploration, extraction, refining, wholesaling, and retailing operations worldwide.

Company C
Accounting firm with 20 percent of business outside of the United States through associates in five countries. Clients are mainly North American MNCs with overseas operations.

Company D
Manufacturing company with sales and manufacturing facilities in fifteen countries. The company manufactures a wide range of products, from electronic parts to sports equipment.

Company E
Retail company with stores specializing in fashion, sports equipment, hardware, and office furniture, located in the United States; exports to Canada.

Each individual has ten units that may be used to acquire the structure (L, M, N, O, or P) he or she feels is best for his or her particular company. Note that:

- Product refers to any product, service, or group of products or services
- NA = North America
- SE = South East
- LA = Latin America

Structure L:

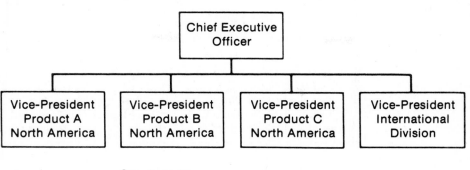

Structure M:

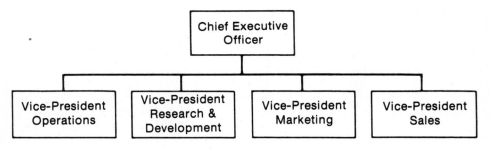

Structure N:

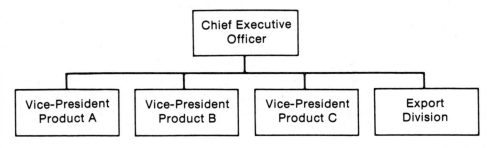

Structure O:

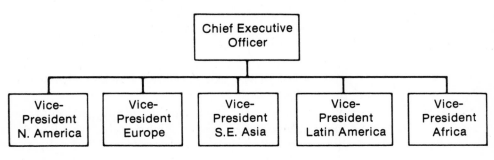

Structure P:

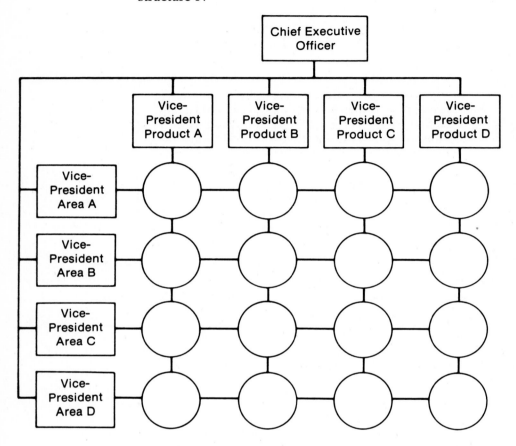

Step 1—Each individual in the group writes on a piece of paper a choice of structure and how much his or her company is willing to pay (of their ten units) for this structure.

Step 2—Within each group, structures are assigned on the basis of these choices as follows:

- If only one player has chosen a particular structure, he or she is awarded that structure and pays the stated number of units for it.

- If two or more players have chosen the same structure, the one paying most gets the chosen structure, the other(s) bid on the structures left.

- In the case of a tie, the parties get to bid again until the tie is resolved. If the tie cannot be resolved (that is, if the players bid all of their units) then the instructor acts as mediator and assigns the available structures at random.

Step 3—If you change your mind you may negotiate with one or more of the players in your group to trade structures.

Step 4—Your instructor announces the "winning solutions," and you calculate scores as individuals and as groups. Scores are based on "correct choices" as well as on unused points as follows:

- Individuals score +15 for having a company/structure match and add to this any unused units.
- Groups add together all individual scores for an overall group score.

Exercise **10** An Advertising Campaign

Aim

This exercise is intended to help students consider some of the cultural and national issues that affect an advertising campaign.

Time

This exercise will involve outside preparation and about one hour and forty minutes of in-class time.

Format

You will work in small groups of four to six. Your group will be assigned a particular country to consider in terms of an advertising campaign. Your group will develop an advertisement to be used in your country and you will present this to the class, explaining the rationale.

Assignment

You are a manufacturer of a line of sunglasses ranging from inexpensive to expensive. You are trying to expand your export sales and have identified the assigned country as a potential market. You must decide how to advertise the product; specifically, you should identify a target market, product price range, and positioning and media strategy, considering factors such as regulations, media availability, and cultural values. Once you have identified the factors you consider important, you will develop a specific advertisement to be used in promoting your product.

Your advertisement should be designed for a particular media—one that you have identified to be a major part of your advertising campaign; you should include slogans, drawings, voices, and so forth, as appropriate, and describe models, voice-overs, music, and so on, if they cannot be included in your presentation.

Each group will present their advertisement to the class with a brief explanation. The rest of the class will then be asked to evaluate the advertisement on a scale of one to five using the evaluation sheet provided on page 45. Your instructor will summarize these evaluations and provide feedback to each group in the following class. Each group will hand in a written assignment that consists of "copy" for their advertisement, backed up by an explanation of why this particular format was chosen; this should be brief—your aim is to persuade the instructor that your advertising copy will be effective in your country given your chosen target market, local customs, regulations, and so on.

Exercise 11 Expatriate Assignment and Repatriation

Aim

The purpose of this exercise is to demonstrate many of the complex issues that arise when choosing parent country nationals (PCNs) to send to other countries. This situation is examined both from the perspective of the company selecting candidates for a foreign assignment and from the perspective of the individual considering such an assignment.

Time

The exercise takes approximately one hour (or about eighty minutes when a written assignment is included).

Preparation

The instructor will assign selected countries to review prior to conducting the exercise. These countries will be used in the exercise.

Format

The class will be divided into an even number of small groups, with three or four students per group. Half of the groups represent a company choosing a manager for an expatriate assignment; their task is to design a package of transfer conditions that they will offer to the prospective expatriate. The other groups represent the prospective expatriate; their task is to decide what they would require to accept the overseas assignment.

Assignment

This exercise is designed to make you aware of the issues faced by companies when selecting and training candidates for overseas assignments, as well as the concerns of candidates accepting such assignments. There are many aspects of such assignments that should be considered if the foreign assignment is to be successful.

The company must consider such things as selection, training, compensation, evaluation, communication, and repatria-

Worksheet for Exercise 10

Name(s) _____

Date _____ Class _____

Evaluation Sheet

Try to put yourself in the position of the target market being addressed and evaluate the effectiveness of the advertisement presented on a scale of 1 to 5 where 1 = excellent, 2 = very good, 3 = good, 4 = fair, and 5 = poor. Please make brief comments following your evaluation to indicate what you liked most and least about the particular advertisement being evaluated.

Group	Country	Evaluation	Comments
1		1 2 3 4 5	
2		1 2 3 4 5	
3		1 2 3 4 5	
4		1 2 3 4 5	
5		1 2 3 4 5	
6		1 2 3 4 5	
7		1 2 3 4 5	
8		1 2 3 4 5	

tion, among others. The company will want to ensure that the assignment is successful and minimizes the cost associated with the transfer, as well.

The candidate will want to consider the implications of the move from both career and personal points of view. He or she will want to maximize the net benefits associated with the transfer.

You are asked to make decisions regarding a transfer. These decisions, corporate and individual, are often made by people with little international experience—people like you. There are no right or wrong choices so feel free to suggest anything your group deems appropriate.

The instructor will provide you with specific countries to examine prior to class and specific discussion questions in class.

Exercise 12 Social Responsibility: It All Depends on Your Point of View

Aim

This exercise is designed to illustrate the complexity of "socially responsible" decision making. Students will recognize that two groups may take opposing views on the same issue and each justify its view as socially responsible.

Time

This exercise takes about forty-five minutes of class time.

Background

The XYZ Company—a North American company—has extensive and profitable operations in a country—LMN—that is seen as violating basic human rights (from a North American perspective) of a large section of its population. The company is faced with the decision of whether it should continue its operations in LMN. The decision is similar to that faced by American companies with operations in South Africa in 1987.

Format

The class will be divided into three groups. One group represents the board of directors of XYZ; they must make a decision regarding operations in LMN. A second group represents management in LMN, a mix of North Americans and local LMN managers; they believe that XYZ should maintain operations in LMN. The third group represents an activist group in North America; they believe that XYZ should pull out of LMN.

Some individuals may be assigned to observe the process.

Assignment

Each group has a specific assignment:

Group 1—Board of Directors You are to develop criteria that you will use to make your decision. You will listen to the arguments presented by the other two groups and make a decision on the basis of the criteria you develop.

Group 2—Management of XYZ in LMN You are to develop arguments to present to the XYZ board of directors to persuade the board to continue its operations in LMN. You will also have the opportunity to respond to the activist group; therefore, you should consider your response to the arguments it is likely to present.

Group 3—Activist Group You are to develop arguments to present to the XYZ board of directors to persuade the board to pull out of LMN. You will also have the opportunity to respond to the local management group; therefore, you should consider your response to arguments they are likely to present.

Observers You are to observe one group; note the decision-making process and the dynamics of the group during its discussions. Complete the worksheet provided (page 49) and be prepared to report to the class on your observations.

Procedure

The discussion will proceed as described below:

1. Each group will have fifteen minutes to discuss its position internally and develop its arguments.

2. The management group and the activist group will then be called on to present their positions to the XYZ board; they will have five minutes each. The board may ask for expansion of points if it wishes, in which case it may be permitted an additional five minutes.

3. There will be a five-minute period for each group to reconvene and review what has been presented.

4. The board will then call on each of the two groups for responses to the other's arguments.

5. The board will meet briefly to make a decision.

6. The board will explain its decision criteria to the two groups and present its final decision.

7. Observers will report on their observations.

Exercise **13** Japanese Management Practices

Aim

Japanese management practices have received much attention in recent years. The economic success of Japan since the Second World War has led North Americans to ask "what can we learn from them?"; in addition, their management practices often

Worksheet for Exercise 12

Name(s) _____

Date _____ Class _____

Observer's Report

Group Observed _____

Conflict

(In general, was there much conflict? What specific issues caused conflict?)

Decisions

(How were decisions reached—for example, by consensus, majority vote, and so on?
Did everyone agree? How long was the decision-making process?)

Group Dynamics

(Was there a leader of the group? What other roles were evident—for example,
facilitator and information provider? Did everyone participate in the discussion?)

appear to be very different from our own, thus we feel a need to study them carefully. This exercise is designed to make you more familiar with Japanese management practices, as well as to illustrate how your management choices might differ from theirs.

Time

This exercise will take about forty-five minutes of in-class time.

Assignment

Begin by examining Exhibit E13.1, which summarizes some management practices that have been identified in literature as differentiating Japanese and North American managers. You will then find on the following pages nine work scenarios and answer options. Read each of the scenarios and choose the appropriate response from your viewpoint. After choosing your own response, based on your beliefs about Japanese management and North American management, indicate what response you think a Japanese manager would make and what response you think a North American manager would make.

Management Scenarios

Scenario 1. A junior employee has been hired for a probationary period of three months during which time the company may dismiss the employee without cause. After six weeks the employee's supervisor is dissatisfied with the employee's work habits (tardiness) and overall performance.

What would you do? _____

a. Dismiss the employee immediately.

b. Allow the employee to complete the probationary period; if performance has not improved, dismiss the employee at that point.

c. Reprimand the employee pointing out that he or she is on probation and will not be retained unless his or her performance improves.

d. Discuss specific issues with the employee and set improvement targets to be reviewed before the end of the probationary period.

What option do you think a *Japanese* manager would choose? _____

What option do you think a *North American* manager would choose? _____

Scenario 2. A supervisor consistently performs well and has received good yearly performance appraisals. Recently the supervisor has worked overtime to design a system that may improve productivity. You are pleased by the enthusiasm and initiative and want to encourage it.

Japanese	*North American*

Career Development

Japanese	*North American*
• Life-time employment, rare dismissal, nonspecialized career path	• Short-term employment, frequent dismissal, specialized careers
• In-house training as generalist, for all employees	• Specific skill training useful in many companies, seen as perk
• Early career emphasis on following directions, team skills; later, quantifiable objectives, team leadership in decision making	• Early career quantifiable objectives; later, individual decisions and inspiring followers
• Job rotation for all to develop generalists	• Transfers for middle managers to broaden views
• Evaluation on proficiency at tasks, team-work skills, ability to contribute to development of others	• Evaluation on achievement of quantifiable objectives
• Promote on seniority, training	• Promote for doing something beyond the job paid for
• Entry directly from school, promote from within	• Fill top levels from outside—gives "fresh blood"
• Emphasis on group cooperation	• Emphasis on accomplishments, ability
• Outstanding performance not equated to fast movement up ranks/rapid salary increases; instead, additional responsibility/recognition—"elite track"; hiring based on education not skills, low wages consistent through industry, bonuses, fringe benefits, allowances tied to company performance	• Performance must be rewarded quickly with promotion/pay increases or the employee will leave; hiring based on skills of immediate use to company, high wages in top companies, bonuses tied to achievement of objectives, perks due to status;
• Relative pay equality workers/ management, pay increases with age and seniority	• Wide salary discrepancies, based on position and level in company
• Payment-by-results based on group performance	• Payment-by-results based on individual performance

Conflict Resolution

Japanese	*North American*
• Resolution involves long-term perspective	• Short-term perspective, immediacy
• Cooperation based on team spirit, individual subordinated to group	• Spirit of competition and rivalry
• Disagreement with superior often but polite	• Disagreement with superior seldom but violent
• Disputes settled through conferral and trust, no detailed contracts, flexibility and compromise stressed;	• Disputes settled through contracts, binding arbitration, direct and confrontative, adversarial
• Takes time, process is important, solved by adjustment—win–win	• Time is money, conflict solved by orders, coercion—win–lose

Decision Making

Japanese	*North American*
• Subordinates' ideas and suggestions encouraged; obligation to include all people; effective implementation	• Decisions fixed, bounded in time; definite point of reference; alternatives selected before action; decisions

Japanese	*North American*
requires reconciliaton of competing interests	separate from implementation, effective implementation may involve a winner and a loser
• Collective decisions, use "Ringi" system; everyone feels their view heard and will support; groups responsible for outcome, use of "action behind the scene"	• Individual decisions; implementation involves lobbying or coercion; individuals responsible for outcome, use announcements
• Top management coordinates decisions and middle management formulates	• Top management formulates decisions middle management feeds information to top
• Solutions formulated by those close to the problem; information flows bottom-up and horizontal; information channels link clusters of decision points	• Solutions formulated by those with authority; information flows top down
• Middle managers impetus and shapers of solutions to problems; coordinate and assure functional areas in agreement; implementation immediate	• Middle managers functional specialists who carry out bosses' orders; unanimity based on win–lose;
• Emphasis on information flows; CEO improves on initiative of others, creates atmosphere in which subordinates motivated to seek better solutions;	• CEO makes key decisions, sets policy; welfare of organization depends on his or her actions
• Top management facilitates decisions, objectives implicit	• Top management issues edicts; objectives explicit
• Process important, question framed by group; consensus, maintaining harmony, right spirit considered; indirect speech and subtle nuances used	• Executives gather relevant information, ask for advice, evaluate on basis of efficiency and effectiveness

Attitude Toward Employees

Japanese	*North American*
• Personal well-being, housing, recreation, and security considered	• Personal matters left at home; ratings on performance
• Organization a system of personal relationships, values, social interactions	• Organization a system of roles
• Business paternalistic; emphasis on status security and harmony; preservation of group most important	• Business mechanistic; emphasis on smoothly functioning parts; realization of profits most important
• Quality control circles based on belief that cause of poor performance unknown and workers will find causes and remedy if given opportunity	• Layers of inspectors based on belief that workers holding back, need to be checked on
• Concern with person	• Concern with product
• Feeling of caring about people; use of open office facilitates communications	• Care about output and meeting profit objectives; private offices limit communications
• Corporate task to attend to whole person—economic, social, spiritual, and psychological needs	• Employees seen as objects, units of production; corporate task to attend to economic needs

What would you do? _____

a. Use the regular year-end performance in three months to note the supervisor's behavior.

b. Make no special note as it is clear that the supervisor is performing well, thus there is no need to draw particular attention to this.

c. Discuss the extra work immediately giving positive feedback and praising the extra effort.

d. Note performance at the year-end review and reward the extra effort with a bonus.

What option do you think a *Japanese* manager would choose? _____

What option do you think a *North American* manager would choose? _____

Scenario 3. A manager is to be assigned to his first overseas post. He or she has been with the company for ten years, is well-liked by subordinates, and is technically competent. His or her overseas assignment begins in three months.

What would you do? _____

a. Allow the manager an extended vacation because the move will be stressful.

b. Provide language and cultural training to help make the transition smooth.

c. Provide language and cultural training for both the manager and his or her family.

d. Assume that his or her management and technical skills will allow him or her to make the transition smoothly and that an overemphasis on the change will do more harm than good.

What option do you think a *Japanese* manager would choose? _____

What option do you think a *North American* manager would choose? _____

Scenario 4. An employee who generally performs well has asked you for special business training at company expense.

What would you do? _____

a. Immediately grant permission.

b. Consider how this training relates to the employee's job; if directly related, grant permission.

c. Consider the impact on others in the organization; if there is no apparent negative impact, grant permission.

    d. Encourage the employee to undertake the training but at his or her own expense.

What option do you think a *Japanese* manager would choose? _____

What option do you think a *North American* manager would choose? _____

Scenario 5. Your company employs a large accounting staff to perform bookkeeping functions manually. A younger member of this staff has approached his or her supervisor with an idea for computer automation.

What do you think the supervisor should do? _____

    a. Ask him or her to write up a proposal for the installation and requirements of the system for presentation to upper management.

    b. Suggest that this is really not of concern to the employee and that such issues are better dealt with by the technical staff.

    c. Suggest a meeting of the entire accounting staff to discuss the idea.

    d. Thank the employee and mention the idea to his or her own supervisor as soon as the opportunity presents itself.

What option do you think a *Japanese* manager would choose? _____

What option do you think a *North American* manager would choose? _____

Scenario 6. Several employees have complained about a coworker. They find this individual difficult to work with and uncooperative; nevertheless, the group as a whole performs well. You believe the employee in question works hard and performs well but has difficulty relating to others.

What would you do? _____

    a. Encourage the employee to seek psychological counseling.

    b. Transfer the employee to a position where group interactions were minimized.

    c. Meet with the entire group to discuss the problem and attempt to resolve the issues.

    d. Ignore the issue because the group is performing at its expected level.

    e. Work with the employees who have complained to help them understand their coworker better.

What option do you think a *Japanese* manager would choose? _____

What option do you think a *North American* manager would choose? _____

Scenario 7. You have observed that a group of employees in your department have not been performing up to their previous productivity levels. It seems that a personality conflict over an event outside the workplace is the cause.

What would you do? _____

a. Wait and see if the conflict subsides; if it does not, issue a formal warning to the individuals involved.

b. Talk to the group about their productivity but assume that they will resolve the conflict internally.

c. Separate the individuals involved by transferring them to other divisions.

d. Talk to the group about their productivity and work with the individuals involved to resolve the conflict.

What option do you think a *Japanese* manager would choose? _____

What option do you think a *North American* manager would choose? _____

Scenario 8. As a result of a promotion, an upper-level management position is available for a suitable candidate. One potential candidate is bright, intelligent, and gets on well with people but dislikes the operations side of the business.

What would you do? _____

a. Consider him or her for the upper-level position.

b. Eliminate him or her from consideration.

c. Consider him or her for such a position only after a period spent working in operations.

d. Assess the need for operational know-how in this position and consider the candidate in this light.

What option do you think a *Japanese* manager would choose? _____

What option do you think a *North American* manager would choose? _____

Scenario 9. Your superior has asked you to fill a position in another department temporarily while a permanent replacement is found; you held this position before being promoted to your present position.

What would you do? _____

a. Agree to a temporary change in duties.

b. Recommend a subordinate who you believe would fill the position adequately on a temporary basis.

c. Suggest that the position would be better filled by someone in the other department.

d. Say that you would be willing to do both jobs on a temporary basis if adequately compensated for the additional work.

What option do you think a *Japanese* manager would choose? _____

What option do you think a *North American* manager would choose? _____

These scenarios were developed with input from Canadian and Japanese managers in Canada to represent realistic situations and choices of action. A mail survey and interviews were conducted to examine how similar or different their choices of action would be. This particular study focused on managers in Canada; of course, managers in the United States might react differently to these situations. You should take this into account when comparing your responses and guesses to the actual responses received. Students in the United States should consider their similarities and differences relative to Canadian responses, as well as to Japanese responses.

Your professor will provide you with a summary of the actual responses for you to compare your responses with. Were your guesses regarding Japanese and North American responses close to the actual results? How do your own beliefs correspond to or differ from those expressed by the managers in this study?

If you look closely at the results of this study, you will note that in spite of the significant differences between the responses of the two groups, there is also a substantial similarity in responses. In all cases except Scenario 5, the majority of managers in both groups favored the same response. Can you suggest some reasons for these similarities?

Do you think the differences in responses correspond to the differences one would expect to find?

Exercise 14   How About Stereotypes?

Aim

This exercise is based on a funny joke heard in Europe. It illustrates the fact that stereotypes can be both positive and negative; you may find it amusing.

Time   This exercise will take about ten minutes of class time.

Format   This exercise takes the form of a game. As individuals you are asked to match nationalities and tasks in the context of the European Economic Community (EEC).

Assignment   Several countries of the EEC are trying to decide what role each should play in the community. There is some disagreement among the countries so they decide to play a game—first they will assign tasks as they would be assigned in Heaven, then they will assign tasks as they would be assigned in Hell. You are asked to put yourself in this position and create the assignments using the worksheet provided on page 59. Your instructor will provide you with the view of "Heaven" and "Hell" as seen by the Europeans.

The countries are:	The tasks are:
Britain	government
France	engineers
Germany	cooks
Italy	lovers
Switzerland	policemen

Exercise 15 What Is Culture?

Aim   This exercise is intended to familiarize students with the concept of "culture."

Time   This exercise may be assigned as homework or it can be completed in class. It should take about eighty minutes to complete.

Format   This exercise may be assigned as an individual exercise, a small group exercise, or a class brainstorming session.

Assignment   The following issues will be addressed (the worksheet on pages 61 to 62 will be helpful in addressing them):

1. formulation of a definition of culture
2. identification of aspects of culture of interest to an international company
3. comparison of the concept of "culture" with that of "nation"
4. exploration of similarities and differences between a culture and a nation.

This exercise can be completed without outside reading, but readings on culture can be helpful and your instructor may assign specific readings in preparation.

Worksheet for Exercise 14

Name(s) _____

Date _____ Class _____

Country	Assigned task
Heaven	
Britain	
France	
Germany	
Italy	
Switzerland	
Hell	
Britain	
France	
Germany	
Italy	
Switzerland	

Worksheet for Exercise 15

Name(s) _____

Date _____ Class _____

1. How would you define a culture?

2. What specific aspects of a culture are particularly important to an international company? Can you think of examples to illustrate their importance in work situations?

Important aspects of a culture:

Examples to illustrate their importance:

3. Do you think a culture is basically the same as a nation? Explain why or why not using an example.

4. Identify similarities and differences between a culture and a nation.

Similarities:

Differences:

Exercise **16** Managing Political Risk

Aim

This exercise is intended to familiarize you with various aspects of international operations that are generally classed as managing political risk.

Time

This exercise may be assigned as homework or it can be completed in class. It should take about eighty minutes to complete.

Format

You will complete this exercise on your own; this will be followed by a class discussion where individuals will be called upon to contribute their ideas on the various topics.

Assignment

You will use the worksheet provided on pages 65 to 66 to:

1. formulate a definition of political risk
2. identify specific aspects of political risk
3. identify characteristics of a country that make it risky
4. identify characteristics of a company that might make it politically risky
5. suggest ways for the company to manage risk.

This exercise can be completed on your own without outside reading, but readings on political risk are helpful. Your instructor may assign specific readings in preparation for the exercise.

Exhibit E16.1 summarizes some recent thoughts on risk reduction or managing political risk (see Gregory, 1987, for a complete discussion of this topic). How do your suggestions for minimizing risk fit into this framework?

Exercise **17** The Stakeholders' Views

Aim

The purpose of this exercise is to demonstrate an international strategic decision that involves more developed and less developed countries (LDCs) and that is influenced by ethical considerations. Students are asked to consider their personal moral convictions in the context of a particular company decision and from different stakeholders' perspectives.

Time

The exercise takes approximately sixty minutes.

Exhibit **E16.1** Managing Political Risk

Virtually all international operations involve some exposure to political risk. The challenge from a management viewpoint is not to avoid risk but to manage risk so it is reduced to as low a level as possible.
Risk management falls into two broad categories:

1. *Integrative techniques,* which aim to integrate the foreign firm into the host society
2. *Protective/defensive techniques,* which aim to minimize the integration of the firm into the host society.

   Integrative techniques (see Exhibit E16.2) generally result in decreased likelihood of encountering unwelcome political action but increased severity of loss to the company if such action occurs.
   Protective/defensive techniques (see Exhibit E16.2) generally result in increased likelihood of encountering unwelcome political action but decreased severity of loss to the company if such action occurs.

Exhibit **E16.2** Integrative and Protective/Defensive Techniques of Political Risk Management

Examples of Integrative Techniques
   Local strategy determination
   Local R and D
   Local sourcing and distribution
   Employment and training of locals
   Local management
   Shared ownership
   Use of local firms and services
   Consideration of host government objectives
   Careful choice and training of parent managers
   Maintenance of local contacts

Examples of Protective/Defensive Techniques
   R and D located outside
   Crucial segment of operations outside
   Control of supply, distribution, market by parent
   Limit local participation
   Locals limited to nonstrategic positions
   Raise capital from varied sources—both local and
      international
   Limit financial exposure

Worksheet for Exercise 16

Name(s) _____

Date _____ Class _____

1. I would define political risk as:

2. In assessing political risk, I would consider the following factors:

3. I think of a country as risky if the following things are true of that country:

4. I think a company is subject to political risk if the following things are true of that company:

5. If your company were involved in a situation that you felt to be risky, how would you minimize your exposure to the risk?

Preparation   Students might want to review material on government objectives in less developed countries prior to class. The instructor will decide whether this preparation is necessary for your class.

Background   Imagine the following situation: Both the United States and Canada have simultaneously banned production and use of the pesticide, ABC; the ban is the result of demonstrated harmful effects to certain species in the wild and an apparent potential for causing cancer in humans. ABC is very effective in controlling certain pests that do extensive damage to crops.

The production and sale of ABC has been profitable for the XYZ company, and the company has stocks of ABC that can no longer be sold in North America.

The XYZ company has been approached by a lesser developed country, LMN, with two propositions. First, LMN is willing to buy the existing stocks of ABC at a reduced price; second, LMN is willing to offer incentives for the XYZ company to manufacture ABC locally in LMN.

There are many options available to XYZ. The appropriate choice among options is a function of the cost–benefit tradeoff as perceived by various constituencies and according to the individual's subjective assessment of the situation. You are asked to express your own reaction to the situation as a member of a particular group concerned with the company's decision.

Format   The class will be divided into five stakeholder groups. Group 1 represents shareholders, group 2 represents the interests of the company employees, group 3 represents the potential LDC customer, group 4 represents a concerned citizen group in North America, group 5 represents a concerned citizen group in LMN.

Assignment   Consider the company's options—be exhaustive—and how each option could affect your group. You should decide as a group which option you wish the company to choose, then formulate a series of arguments that could be used to persuade the company to adopt your choice. Finally, consider how your choice will be affected if XYZ is struggling for profitability and ABC is its main product.

This exercise will give you a feeling for how different stakeholder groups may view the same situation and how individual, personal views can affect strategic decisions.

You will have a period of about thirty minutes to discuss and formulate the position of your group. Each stakeholder group will then be asked to present its position, chosen course of action, and arguments for following that course of action. When each group has presented its decision and arguments, a second round of discussion will be conducted. There will be a brief discussion, within each group, of the various positions that have been presented; then each group will have the opportunity to respond to the suggestions of the other groups and raise counterarguments.

Exercise **18**   How Well Did They Do?

Aim
This exercise will give you an opportunity to consider some of the problems associated with evaluating subsidiary operations and management.

Time
This exercise will take about forty-five minutes of in-class time.

Preparation
Prior to class you should read the case study presented below and identify concerns that you have about evaluating the management of the subsidiary described in the case.

Assignment
Your professor will give you the details of your assignment in class.

Case Study

A large multinational company, International Products, Limited (IPL), has its headquarters in New York City. IPL has a wide variety of affiliations with other companies in other countries as well as a number of subsidiaries. Top management at headquarters is almost entirely American.

IPL recently established a majority-owned subsidiary—Offshore Products—in a small developing country. The company owns 60 percent of the subsidiary; the other 40 percent is owned by a wealthy local businessman. Offshore Products assembles electronic components, which it sells to other subsidiaries of IPL; assembly materials are provided by headquarters and billed to Offshore Products. IPL also provides Offshore Products with machinery and supplies that are not available locally, as well as management assistance.

Management at Offshore Products consists of three locals and two Americans. The expectation is that the two Americans will remain until they are confident that the local managers are capable of running operations on their own. It was initially hoped that the Americans would be there for one year, but after a year of operations they have indicated that they believe they will have to remain for a second year. The local partner is not involved in the day-to-day operations of Offshore Products but provides advice and assistance on local matters when requested.

Offshore Products has completed its first year of operations and its performance is being reviewed by a top-management group in New York. Costs have been substantially higher than anticipated, and Offshore Products is losing money (see Exhibit E18.1).

The headquarters (HQ) management group must consider:

1. the performance of the U.S. managers at Offshore Products

2. the performance of the local managers at Offshore Products

3. evaluation of overall operations.

The loss incurred by Offshore Products is small relative to IPL's other operations; nevertheless, it is unexpected and raises a number of issues that headquarters must resolve. IPL must decide how, and indeed if, operations at Offshore Products should continue.

The issue is complicated by the fact that there was a change in government in the country six months ago and IPL is unsure of its relationship with the new government. Further, there are rumors of a forthcoming devaluation of the country's currency.

Exhibit **E18.1** Offshore Products Income Statement for the Year Ending February 28, 1988

	Actual	Projected
Net sales	1,200,000	1,000,000
Less:		
Materials	540,000	400,000
Direct labor	300,000	200,000
Import duties[a]	90,000	—
Depreciation	50,000	50,000
	980,000	650,000
Gross profit	220,000	350,000
Administrative expenses		
Management salaries and expenses	230,000	200,000
Staff expenses[b]	100,000	75,000
Other expenses	100,000	75,000
	430,000	350,000
Net loss	(210,000)	

[a] A request is being considered by the government for a refund of import duties.
[b] The local partner received $50,000 consultation fee; the balance was for services from headquarters.

Part 2 Projects

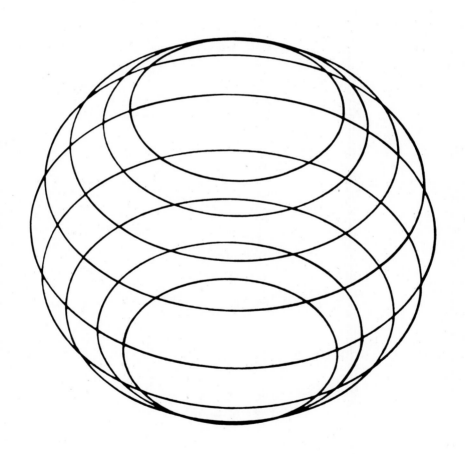

Project **1** Update of Country Profile Information

Aim This project will familiarize students with sources of country information and serve to ensure that students are using current information in their decision-making process. It is important to recognize that countries often change and that country information can become outdated quickly; this exercise gives students an opportunity to understand the need for monitoring and updating country information systematically.

Time This involves work outside of class almost exclusively. Students will be required to provide their updated information to classmates; this may take the form of a brief class presentation or it may be a written assignment.

Assignment Students will be assigned one or more of the countries profiled in Part 3 of this text and asked to update the information. You should follow the format in the text and make sure your updated profiles are the most current available. Where information has changed in a dramatic way, this should be highlighted and explained. A list of suggested sources of information follows Project 2.

Project **2** Additional Country Profiles

Aim This project gives students valuable practice at finding information on countries and putting this information into a useful format. This project also gives students the opportunity to investigate countries that may be of particular interest.

Time This project involves work outside of class almost exclusively. Students will be required to provide their country profiles to classmates; this may take the form of a brief class presentation or it may be a written assignment.

Assignment Students will choose one or more countries to investigate; these should be countries that are not profiled in the text. Students can use the format in the text as a guide but should not feel constrained by it; any information that is potentially relevant to international management decisions should be included in the profiles. The suggested sources that follow can be used, but, again, do not feel limited to these sources only. Be sure, however, to document all sources used in obtaining information.

Sources

The following are suggested sources of information for Projects 1 and 2:

Academic American Encyclopedia

Business International Comparative Statistics

Encyclopedia Americana

Hofstede, G., *Cultures Consequences*

Micropedia Ready Reference

Moody's International Manual

Price Waterhouse Information Guide

The New Encyclopedia Britannica

United Nations Economic Surveys

World Book Encyclopedia

World Tables

Yearbook of International Trade Statistics

Yearbook of National Accounts Statistics

Project **3** Export Decisions

Aim

The purpose of this project is to give students an opportunity to examine potential export markets and make decisions in regard to approaching such a market.

Time

This project will involve outside work. Your instructor may have you present your findings and conclusions orally to the class; this can be either a brief presentation lasting about ten minutes or a more lengthy presentation of up to half an hour. Your instructor will decide which format to follow.

Assignment

Each group will be assigned a product or group of products to investigate and a country to consider as an export market. Each group will compile information on its product(s), as well as the potential market, and make a decision regarding the viability of exporting to that market. In addition, each group will decide which export route would be most appropriate for its product(s) and market(s) (see Exhibit P3.1).

Groups should consider the following factors in making decisions:

- potential market size and attractiveness
- export and import tariffs and quotas
- policies encouraging the purchase of local products and services

Exhibit **P3.1** Potential Export Routes

> The exporting company can go directly to the customer or through **home country agents,** such as:
>
> - export houses
> - resident foreign buyers
> - export commission houses
> - export associations
> - export brokers
>
> The exporting company, the home country agent, or both can go directly to the customer or through **foreign agents,** such as:
>
> - individuals
> - import brokers
> - import houses
> - distributors
> - sales branches
> - sales subsidiaries
>
> Some combination of the above can be used, such as: export company to resident foreign buyer to export broker to import broker to import house to distributor to final customer.

Source: Adapted from Robinson, R. D., *International Business Management: A Guide to Decision Making* (Hinsdale, Ill.: The Dryden Press, 1978), p. 73.

- transportation and distribution channels
- advertising and media
- exchange rates and currency fluctuations

Your discussion should answer the following questions:

1. Who will be your customer(s)?
2. How attractive is this as a potential export market and why?
3. What payment arrangements would you accept?

Each group should prepare a written summary of its analysis and decision to back up the oral presentation.

Project **4** Investment Decisions

Aim

The purpose of this project is to give students an opportunity to apply theories and models regarding investment decisions to a realistic situation.

Time   This project involves substantial outside work. Students will
                         have half an hour to present their findings and conclusions to
                         the class.

Assignment   Each group will be assigned a multinational company to inves-
                         tigate. Information on the company may be available in the
                         form of a published case study, or you may research the com-
                         pany in the library.

                         Each group is also assigned two countries to be considered
                         for investment. Each group is asked to decide which market it
                         wishes to enter and how it proposes to enter (joint venture,
                         wholly owned subsidiary, license, contract, and so on). The
                         presentation to the class should take the form of a task force
                         presenting findings to a top-management group. Each group
                         will also prepare a written document to back up its oral
                         presentation.

                         Exhibit P4.1 presents an outline of an international expan-
                         sion decision that can be used to help you make this investment
                         decision.

Project **5**   Case Studies

Aim   This project gives students an opportunity to analyze the
                         strengths and weaknesses of companies and to identify oppor-
                         tunities and challenges in a global environment.

Time   This project involves outside preparation and about half an hour
                         of in-class discussion for each of the companies in Part 3, "Com-
                         pany Profiles." Your instructor may wish to cover all three
                         profiles on the same day or may wish to discuss each on a
                         different day.

Assignment   Students should read carefully the profile(s) assigned and then
                         answer the questions below. Remember to think in interna-
                         tional terms; a domestic strength sometimes can be a liability
                         internationally, or a domestic weakness may be turned into an
                         advantage globally. Similarly, different opportunities and chal-
                         lenges exist in a global environment.

Questions   1. What do you see as the company's major strengths from
                            an international perspective?
                         2. What do you see as the company's major weaknesses from
                            an international perspective?
                         3. What global opportunities would you identify for the
                            company?

Exhibit **P4.1** Outline of International Expansion Decision

Questions to Answer

1. *Should we be international?* Consider the potential advantages and drawbacks, e.g.,

   - effect on home market
   - competitors' activities
   - customers' needs
   - potential markets
   - potential suppliers
   - cost differences.

2. *Are we capable of becoming international?* Consider strengths and weaknesses, e.g.,

   - management
   - money
   - products
   - marketing
   - equipment.

3. *How attractive is the location?* Consider market potential, e.g.,

   - size
   - per capita income
   - income distribution
   - accessibility
   - degree of competition
   - stability.

4. *How risky is this situation?* Consider factors of importance to your company, e.g.,

   - economic stability
   - government stability
   - friendliness
   - restrictiveness
   - government–business relations.

5. *How much involvement is desirable?* Consider location attractiveness versus perceived risk:

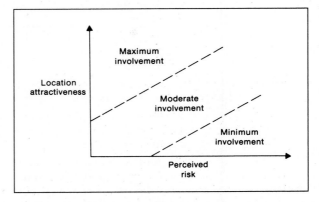

6. *What specific form of entry is appropriate?* Consider the limiting factors, e.g.,

   - legal situation
   - regulations
   - incentives
   - degree of control desired

Exhibit **P4.1** continued

Final Choice
Some form of:

- exports   • contract
- licensing   • turnkey
- franchise   • equity investment

Each possible form of entry can be considered in terms of desired degree of involvement

Decision Matrix
Involvement increases as:

- location attractiveness increases
- capability increases
- perceived risk decreases

Eight possibilities:

1. High location attractiveness High capability High risk	5. Low location attractiveness High capability High risk
2. High location attractiveness High capability Low risk	6. Low location attractiveness Low capability High risk
3. High location attractiveness Low capability Low risk	7. Low location attractiveness Low capability Low risk
4. High location attractiveness Low capability High risk	8. Low location attractiveness High capability Low risk

Cell 2 is most attractive—you want to maximize involvement given the limiting factors; that is, if full ownership is allowed this would be your choice.

Cell 6 is least attractive—you want no involvement or minimal involvement; that is, if you are approached by someone who wishes to buy your products and will take all the risk you would agree, but you would not go after this market otherwise.

Cells 1, 3, 4, 5, 7, and 8 are mixed—you must decide what degree of involvement will maximize the advantages and limit the effect of the drawbacks.

4. What challenges does the company face globally?

5. What changes, if any, would you suggest for this company with regard to:

- stated strategy
- ownership policy
- makeup of management
- selection and training of management and employees
- organizational structure
- communications and control
- other issues.

Please be as specific as possible in your answers to the questions above. The three assignment sheets on pages 81 to 86 should be used for your written responses.

Project 6 Parent Country Nationals, Host Country Nationals, or Third Country Nationals?

Aim

The purpose of this project is to decide on the appropriate nationality for managing a subsidiary in a particular location.

Time

This project will involve limited library research, an outside group meeting, and about thirty minutes of in-class time.

Format

The class will be divided into groups of four or five. Each group will be assigned two or three countries to consider. You should use the information provided in the "Country Profiles" in Part 3, supplemented by additional information from your library, as is appropriate.

Assignment

You have three broad choices: parent country nationals (PCNs), host country nationals (HCNs), and third country nationals (TCNs). You are asked to make a general assessment of which group(s) would be most appropriate for various management levels for your particular countries.

Your assessment should consider:

- host country regulations and laws
- availability of potential managers
- training of managers
- acceptance of foreigners
- cultural gaps

- religious, racial, ethnic, or other biases
- headquarter control over policies and practices.

Based on the above information, your group should decide which nationalities would be most appropriate for top, middle, and supervisory management in your assigned countries. Please use the worksheet provided on pages 87 to 88 to prepare the assignment. A brief summary of your recommendations, and reasons for these recommendations, will be presented to the class and a written summary handed in. Your class presentation should be about five minutes in length.

Project 7   Choice of Expatriate Managers

Aim

This project gives students the opportunity to try to match individuals to different countries. The student will consider the general characteristics that are desirable in candidates for overseas assignments, as well as specific individual circumstances that may make a particular candidate more or less desirable for a specific country.

Time

This project takes forty to sixty minutes of class time.

Preparation

Prior to class, students should read the "Individual Personal Profiles" provided in Part 3 and review information on the countries assigned by the instructor.

Format

The class will be divided into groups of three to five individuals. Each group represents a team reviewing ten candidates for a variety of overseas posts.

Assignment

Assume that all of the candidates are equally desirable from a technical perspective. Your task is as follows:

1. Decide if any candidates should be eliminated from consideration. If so, why?

2. Choose one or two likely candidates for each country. Why are they suited to that assignment?

3. Identify additional information that you would want to have before making a final decision. Why is this information important?

4. Make a final choice of one individual for each country. If you make assumptions, make them explicit and explain why they are necessary and how they affect your decision. Given your choice of candidates, what individual

Worksheet for Project 5

Name(s) _____

Date _____ Class _____

Major strengths of _____, from an international perspective:

Major weaknesses of _____, from an international perspective:

Global opportunities for _____:

Global challenges for _____:

Suggested changes for _____:

Worksheet for Project 5

Name(s) _____

Date _____ Class _____

Major strengths of _____, from an international perspective:

Major weaknesses of _____, from an international perspective:

Global opportunities for _____:

84

Global challenges for _____:

Suggested changes for _____:

Worksheet for Project 5

Name(s) _____

Date _____ Class _____

Major strengths of _____, from an international perspective:

Major weaknesses of _____, from an international perspective:

Global opportunities for _____:

Global challenges for _____:

Suggested changes for _____:

Worksheet for Project 6

Name(s) _____

Date _____ Class _____

Chief Executive

(Check the appropriate column and give reasons)

Country	PCN	HCN	TCN	Reasons
1.				
2.				
3.				

Middle Management

(Check the appropriate column and give reasons)

Country	PCN	HCN	TCN	Reasons
1.				

2.

_____

3.

_____

Supervisory Management

(Check the appropriate column and give reasons)

Country	PCN	HCN	TCN	Reasons
1.				

2.

3.

programs of training and compensation would you recommend?

Use the worksheet provided on pages 91 to 93 in assessing and choosing candidates for various countries.

You will have about forty minutes to discuss the above questions, then each group will present and explain its decisions.

Project 8 Fitting In

Aim

This project will give students the opportunity to make decisions about organizing a subsidiary so that it fits into an existing organization.

Time

This project will involve some outside work, including an outside group meeting, and about thirty minutes of in-class time.

Preparation

Prior to meeting with your group, you should read the profile for your assigned company and country.

Assignment

Each group will be asked to consider one of the companies in "Company Profiles" setting up a new subsidiary operation in one of the countries in "Country Profiles" (see Part 3). The instructor will assign you a company and country to consider. You are asked to decide on an appropriate structure for this subsidiary in different ownership situations and which ownership option would be preferred. The ownership possibilities are:

1. The subsidiary is wholly owned.
2. The subsidiary is a joint venture (JV); your company owns a majority share.
3. The subsidiary is a joint venture (JV); your company owns a minority share.

You should consider the following factors in making your decision:

- present structure of the organization
- parent company policies toward subsidiaries
- geographic location of the subsidiary
- cultural differences between head office and subsidiary.

Your decision should include:

- relationship to headquarters and other subsidiaries
- reporting relationships

- degree of autonomy and decision-making authority
- functional responsibilities
- functions and services provided by headquarters

Use the worksheet provided on pages 95 to 97 to summarize your discussion and decisions; these will be handed in. Your instructor may require a brief presentation to the class.

Project 9   Cross-Cultural Organizational Behavior

Aim

This project gives students the opportunity to consider some factors that might affect the motivation of people in different countries. Students will consider specific organizational behavior theories and their impact in specific countries.

Time

The assignment will take about fifty minutes of class time.

Preparation

Some individual outside preparation is required for this exercise.

- Some students will be asked to prepare a motivation plan based on a particular theory (these students represent a North American manager).
- Other students will be asked to react to a theory in a specific country (these students represent a local employee).

The theories to be investigated are:

1. Maslow's hierarchy of needs
2. equity theory
3. expectancy theory
4. goal setting
5. reinforcement.

The countries to be considered will be assigned by the instructor, selected from "Country Profiles" in Part 3.

Assignment

Prior to class you will prepare by reviewing the theory, country, or both that you have been assigned. You will meet in class in assigned groups to discuss the motivation theory from the various country perspectives. You will then report your insights to the rest of the class.

You should use the assignment sheet provided on pages 99 to 100 to prepare for this exercise. Your instructor will give each student a specific assignment.

Worksheet for Project 7

Name(s) _____

Date _____ Class _____

Candidate name: _____

| | Selection Factors | |
| Country | For | Against |

1.

2.

3.

4.

5.

Conclusion: _____

Candidate name: _____

Country	Selection Factors	
	For	Against
1.		
2.		
3.		
4.		
5.		

Conclusion: _____

Summary of Final Decisions

Assignment   **Key Reasons**

Country

Candidate

Country

Candidate

Country

Candidate

Country

Candidate

Country

Candidate

Candidate Not Assigned   **Key Reasons**

1.

2.

3.

4.

5.

Worksheet for Project 8

Name(s) _____

Date _____ Class _____

Name of company: _____

Location of subsidiary: _____

1. Relationship to HQ and other subsidiaries

Wholly owned:

Majority JV:

Minority JV:

2. Reporting relationships

Wholly owned:

Majority JV:

Minority JV:

3. Degree of autonomy and decision-making authority

Wholly owned:

Majority JV:

Minority JV:

4. Functional responsibilities

Wholly owned:

Majority JV:

Minority JV:

5. Functions and services provided by HQ

Wholly owned:

Majority JV:

Minority JV:

Worksheet for Project 9

Name(s) _____

Date _____ Class _____

North American Manager

Theory to be investigated:

Main aspects of theory:

Reservations (if any) regarding theory:

Putting the theory into practice:

Local Employee

Theory to be investigated:

Country to be investigated:

Main aspects of theory:

Assessment of this theory in this country and aspects of the theory that are compatible with the country:

Aspects that are not compatible:

Project **10** Designing Projects

The profiles provided in Part 3 can be used in a variety of combinations that result in interesting projects. Your instructor may design such projects and assign them to you; alternatively, you may be asked to design a project of interest to you.

There are three sets of profiles: a set of individual personal, company, and country profiles. Projects can be developed around one set of profiles, or they can incorporate information from more than one set. Projects can be functionally oriented (for example, marketing, finance, personnel, and so on), they can focus on a management activity (for example, planning, organizing, and so on), or they can do both.

The following will serve as thought starters:

- A profiled company develops marketing programs for different countries.
- An individual is assigned to different countries.
- A country develops programs to attract foreign direct investment.
- New export industries are developed for one of the countries profiled in Part 3.

Part 3 Profiles

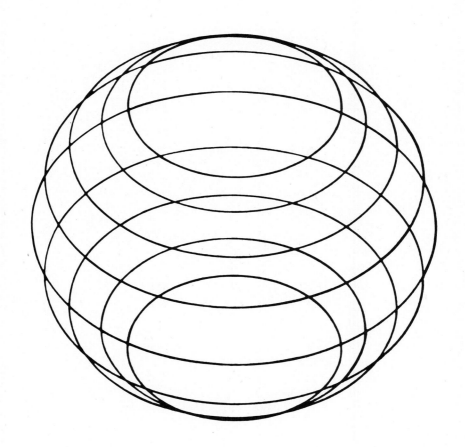

Individual Personal Profiles

The individuals depicted in these profiles are fictitious. They represent people who might work for the same company—a fictitious company, identified as BJP—in a variety of positions and at various levels. The profiles are summary descriptions that might have been prepared from information the company has on file, plus individuals' statements of interest in foreign postings and comments from fellow employees. They are intentionally brief but not unrealistically so; in making international assignment decisions, one often begins with fairly limited information.

The information in the profiles includes age, marital status, family, education, religious affiliation, and experience with the company and prior to joining it. Some comments regarding personality and reasons for considering the individual for an overseas assignment are also included. Because the information is limited, in some cases you may wish to make inferences or assumptions about a particular individual.

The profiles do not include detailed information on the individual's job-related or technical skills. You should make the assumption that the individuals are technically competent for a particular assignment and base your assessment on other factors that might affect individuals in various foreign assignments.

Profile 1   Sandy Merrifield

Name	Sandy Merrifield	**Sex**	Female
Marital Status	Single	**Age**	Twenty-five

Religious Affiliation   Practicing Roman Catholic.

Family   Parents run motel in Florida; Sandy lives alone in an apartment in New York City.

Education   B.A. in English literature.

Languages   Has studied and "understands" but does not speak Spanish.

Experience   Joined BJP's Packaging Division on graduation from college three years ago. Worked as secretary to the marketing manager for two years. Promoted to assistant to the marketing manager eleven months ago.

International Experience   Belonged to an international students' organization while at college; spent six months as a volunteer social worker in Ethiopia.

Personality	Outgoing, well liked by fellow workers.
Hobbies	Skiing, hiking, bicycling. She is a member of a local synchronized swimming team.
Additional Information	Has not traveled internationally other than to Ethiopia. She expresses a particular interest in an overseas position because it will give her an opportunity to see the world.

Profile 2 Clarke Jenkins

Name	Clarke Jenkins	**Sex**	Male
Marital Status	Married	**Age**	Thirty-six

Religious Affiliation	Active member of Baptist Church; expresses deep religious values.
Family	Black Guyanese parents live in England; wife is Canadian of British descent, actively involved in volunteer work with several community charitable organizations; two children, ages seven and nine.
Education	British high-school education with A-level qualifications; Bachelor of Commerce from major Canadian university, M.B.A. from small college in New York state.
Languages	Speaks French and Swahili.
Experience	Joined BJP's head office two years ago as assistant to the vice-president of Finance; prior to this, he worked with an accounting firm in Canada for five years.
International Experience	Worked with a consulting firm in Jamaica (West Indies) for four years.
Hobbies	No information available.
Personality	Described by supervisor as open to new ideas. Describes himself as sensitive to cultural differences.
Additional Information	Was born in Guyana, moved to England at the age of six, emigrated to Canada at nineteen, and moved to New York for M.B.A. studies at age thirty-two. Has traveled extensively in Africa, Asia, and Europe as well as in North America.

Profile **3** Bambi Totts

Name	Bambi Totts	**Sex**	Female
Marital Status	Single	**Age**	Twenty-three

Religious Affiliation No affiliation expressed.

Family Lives at home with parents.

Education B.A. in French.

Languages Speaks French fluently; some Spanish and Italian. Picks up foreign languages easily.

Experience Joined BJP two years ago as a clerk in the Translation Department. Has been promoted to a junior translation position.

International Experience None.

Personality Cheerful, outgoing, and talkative; well recommended by her superior.

Hobbies Music, dancing, aerobics.

Additional Information Has traveled throughout Canada and the United States. Expresses an interest in a foreign assignment as providing an opportunity to meet new people and experience different ways of life.

Profile **4** Karl Goss

Name	Karl Goss	**Sex**	Male
Marital Status	Married	**Age**	Forty-five

Religious Affiliation No affiliation expressed.

Family Three children, ages twenty-three, eighteen, and twelve; the eldest is married, the second has just entered college. Wife was born in Germany and moved to the United States when she was very young; she is currently employed as a social worker.

Education	B.S. in engineering.
Languages	Speaks some German.
Experience	Joined BJP's Engineering Division ten years ago; prior to that he worked as director of engineering for a small manufacturing company.
International Experience	None.
Personality	Serious, reliable, energetic; those who work with him think highly of him.
Hobbies	Chess, classical music.
Additional Information	German roots; has traveled in Europe on several vacations. Owns a home in the country and devotes spare time to his home and family.

Profile 5 Luis Alvarez

Name	Luis Alvarez	**Sex**	Male
Marital Status	Single	**Age**	Twenty-six
Religious Affiliation	Nominally Roman Catholic.		
Family	Lives alone.		
Education	B.A. in chemistry; M.B.A.		
Languages	Speaks some Spanish and Russian.		
Experience	Joined BJP's Research and Development Department two years ago.		
International Experience	None.		

Personality Works hard but is easygoing and well liked. He enjoys meeting people of different ethnic backgrounds and is tolerant of different views.

Hobbies Basketball.

Additional Information Describes himself as "fascinated by languages"—as a child he would listen to foreigners and try to figure out what languages they were speaking. He has made a point of learning as many languages as possible—although he is not fluent in any foreign languages, he is familiar with several. He has traveled in the British Isles and has visited Mexico and Brazil. He believes his tolerance for different views will serve him well in unfamiliar overseas environments.

Profile **6** Katherine Wilson

Name	Katherine Wilson	**Sex**	Female
Marital Status	Divorced	**Age**	Thirty-eight

Religious Affiliation No strong religious affiliation.

Family Lives alone; devotes much of her free time to her elderly mother.

Education Joint M.B.A./law degree.

Languages Speaks no foreign languages but has often worked with interpreters.

Experience Joined BJP's Legal Department seven years ago and has risen steadily in the department.

International Experience Has traveled extensively for the company and is familiar with overseas operations.

Personality Reserved, strong, controlled personality. Respected by colleagues and subordinates, but she does not socialize much and they feel they do not know her well.

Hobbies Tennis, reading.

Additional Information She is highly regarded by managers in foreign affiliates.

Profile **7**   Peter Scwarz

Name	Peter Scwarz	**Sex**	Male
Marital Status	Married	**Age**	Thirty-five

Religious Affiliation   No affiliation expressed.

Family   Married to a financial analyst; two children, ages five and seven.

Education   Undergraduate business degree in accounting.

Languages   Speaks no foreign languages.

Experience   Has worked for BJP for fifteen years, starting on a part-time basis when he was still in college.

International Experience   None.

Personality   Hard worker; usually arrives at the office a at 7:00 A.M. and stays late if there is work to be done.

Hobbies   Avid nature photographer; spends much of his outside time on this hobby and has had some photographs published.

Additional Information   He and his wife have made a point of visiting different countries each year when vacationing, and they are enthusiastic about spending an extended period in a foreign location. They are concerned, however, about his wife's career and the children's education.

Profile **8**   Jean Bade

Name	Jean Bade	**Sex**	Male
Marital Status	Married	**Age**	Forty-two

Religious Affiliation   Practicing Catholic; religion described as playing a relatively minor role in his life.

P
E
R
S
O
N
A
L

P
R
O
F
I
L
E
S

Family	Wife is an elementary school teacher; one child, age fourteen.
Education	No college degree.
Languages	Speaks no foreign languages fluently.
Experience	Has worked for BJP for ten years; has risen through the company ranks to become vice-president of Sales.
International Experience	Has traveled extensively as a sales representative in Australia, Singapore, and Hong Kong.
Personality	Colleagues describe him alternately as "hot tempered" and "adaptive." He makes friends easily.
Hobbies	Coaches a Little League baseball team.
Additional Information	Gets along in foreign locations even when he does not speak the language—he has a knack for picking up a few words and appropriate gestures that make his hosts comfortable.

Profile **9**   Richard Capwell

Name	Richard Capwell	**Sex**	Male
Marital Status	Engaged	**Age**	Twenty-five

Religious Affiliation	Protestant upbringing.
Family	His parents live in the suburbs; he has an apartment in the city, but sees a lot of them. His fiancée has just graduated from college and is seeking employment; she speaks several foreign languages.
Education	Undergraduate business degree in accounting.
Languages	Speaks no foreign languages.
Experience	Recently joined BJP after working for a large public accounting firm for three years. He has had a great deal of responsibility early in his career and has performed well.
International Experience	Organized and ran European biking tours during summers at college.

Personality	Described as relaxed and easygoing, yet he produces at a very high level.
Hobbies	Sports.
Additional Information	His father is Lebanese, his mother British; they live in the United States, where Richard was born. He has not traveled much but describes himself as being culturally adaptable because of his mixed parentage. He sees his fiancée's language ability as a plus in an overseas assignment.

Profile 10   Karen Coombs

Name	Karen Coombs	**Sex**	Female
Marital Status	Married	**Age**	Thirty
Religious Affiliation	No affiliation expressed.		
Family	Husband is high school teacher; no children.		
Education	B.A. in Russian; M.B.A., major in international business.		
Languages	Speaks Russian.		
Experience	Joined the BJP Personnel Department as a specialist in international relations two years ago; previously worked with an international consulting company.		
International Experience	Has visited a variety of foreign locations for brief periods; has worked with foreign companies setting up operations in Canada and the United States.		
Personality	Described as an enthusiastic, hard working, and dedicated employee.		
Hobbies	Reading (science fiction and Russian novels), walking.		
Additional Information	She is of Eastern European parentage but has always lived in North America. She looks forward to the opportunity to spend an extended period overseas because she has enjoyed her previous visits to new countries.		

Company Profiles

The companies described in these profiles are fictitious. They do, however, represent companies that might well exist; the descriptions draw on information about existing companies, and they have been developed to be realistic. The profiles are in the form of summary descriptions; these descriptions might have been prepared from information in the companys' annual reports and supplemented by interviews with managers and employees. They are brief but contain a good deal of information.

The profiles include information on ownership, business, locations, worldwide sales, size, structure, management, training, communications and control, company strengths, company concerns, corporate strategy, and competition. This information gives you a basis for assessing the companys' strengths and weaknesses and their opportunities and challenges, and for making decisions in a realistic framework. Because the information is limited, you may find it necessary to make assumptions about the companies for certain decisions; be sure to make these assumptions explicit in your discussions.

Profile **1** Forms, Incorporated

Name	Forms, Incorporated (FI)
Ownership	FI is globally owned with shares sold on all of the major stock markets of the world. FI was founded by a wealthy European family in 1926; this family retains control of the company with the largest holding in the corporation (10 percent). Almost all subsidiaries are wholly owned, and FI prefers 100 percent ownership in foreign operations. Joint ventures have been established where required locally when the location has been seen as strategically important to FI. In these situations, FI prefers local partners who do not wish to be actively involved in decision making.
Business	FI produces and markets business forms and computer software worldwide. Business forms represent 78 percent of sales, software 20 percent, and the final 2 percent is provided by a variety of related mechanical products (for example, storage racks and other forms-related equipment).
Locations	FI headquarters are in Belgium, although only 3 percent of sales are in Belgium. The company has sales in over one hundred countries and production operations in fifteen.
Worldwide Sales	Approximately US$2 billion in 1987; 40 percent of sales are in Europe, 10 percent in Africa, 15 percent in the Middle East, 5

percent in the Communist bloc, 10 percent in Japan and the Pacific rim, 10 percent in Latin America and the Caribbean, and 10 percent in Canada and the United States.

Size

Approximately 25,000 employees worldwide; over 600 sales offices.

Structure

The company is organized around two main streams of activity: production and after-sales service, and marketing and sales; these are seen by top management as equally important aspects of the organization. Each is operated as a profit center with regional coordinating committees serving as liaisons between the two. Both production and sales are organized regionally; however, the regions are not necessarily contiguous.

Regional Production Centers   Regional production centers have been identified on the basis of efficiency and integration of operations. Five production-center regions have been established: (1) the United States and South and Central America, (2) Western Europe, (3) Southern Europe, (4) the Middle East and Africa, and (5) the Far East. Production facilities are located as follows:

Area 1—United States, Mexico, Barbados, Brazil

Area 2—Belgium, France, Switzerland

Area 3—Greece, Italy, Spain

Area 4—Nigeria, Zambia, Saudi Arabia

Area 5—Australia, Malaysia.

Regional Sales Centers   Sales centers have been identified on the basis of local variation in customer needs and buying habits as follows: (1) the United States and Canada, (2) South America, (3) Central America and the Caribbean, (4) the European Economic Community, (5) Communist bloc countries, (6) Japan, (7) South Africa, and (8) Africa (except South Africa).

Coordinating Committees   These committees have been established to overcome some of the difficulties presented by the different makeup of the two types of regional centers as follows: (1) the Americas, (2) Europe, (3) the Middle East and Africa, and (4) the Far East.

Management

Top management is entirely European, and salespeople are also largely European. Production personnel and management are almost entirely local once operations are established, but there is always one "home office" representative. This representative

C
O
M
P
A
N
Y

P
R
O
F
I
L
E
S

is expected to oversee operations and quality control, and provide a communication link between the subsidiary and the home office. These home office representatives have extensive international experience as they generally do not spend more than three years in one location.

Training

Salespeople receive extensive training not only technically but also culturally. Cultural training includes films and lectures on the host culture, intensive language instruction, and interaction with host nationals and foreigners who have lived in the host country. Salespeople generally stay in one region for several years and work with their replacements for several months when leaving. Management receives similar training for overseas posts.

Communications and Control

Top management believes in personal communications and visits subsidiaries regularly. The philosophy is "you have to know your people personally if you expect them to work hard." In addition, regional meetings are held regularly and subsidiary managers visit the home office once a year. Social functions are held regularly to celebrate local achievements. Personal interaction and supervision constitutes a large part of the control system—things are done the FI way. There is also a formal system of written reports; these are sent to the home office by the subsidiary management on a weekly, biweekly, and monthly basis.

Company Strengths

The company has been very successful; this can be attributed to its product innovation, as well as efficient manufacturing. Efficiency has been achieved through standardized production processes. Manufacturing operations are identical wherever they are located. The buildings are built to the same specifications—the layout and the machinery are the same; thus, an operator from Spain could be flown to Barbados and immediately find his or her way around the factory.

Product innovation has been achieved through localization, that is, through responsiveness to local needs, customs, and so on. Sales and marketing personnel provide customized approaches for their customers; they monitor changing needs in different locations and respond to them. In addition, however, they are trained to look for similarities in different situations and to capitalize on them to increase the use of standard forms.

Company Concerns

"Trade-offs" best summarizes the company's concerns. The two arms of the company—production and sales—are often in conflict regarding short-term objectives. In addition, local man-

C
O
M
P
A
N
Y

P
R
O
F
I
L
E
S

agement is often in conflict with headquarters over objectives, reports, and evaluations. Communication throughout the organization is difficult, and overseas personnel often feel out of touch with the organization as a whole. The organization structure is complex and results in delays as coordinating committees go from one location to another, attempting to integrate operations and sales. These delays have often resulted in directives from top management in Belgium, which at times add to intracompany conflicts.

Corporate Strategy

Rapid expansion is planned for the next five years. Top management believes it can increase sales dramatically in the Pacific rim, Latin America, and North America. This will require an expanded sales force in these locations, as well as increased production facilities. Top management is currently examining the operating and profit potential in Communist countries.

Competition

Globally there are two other competing firms that produce and sell throughout the world; one is Canadian, the other British. At the local level, there are small printing companies in virtually every country offering some products similar to FI's.

Profile 2 Black Beauty Corporation

Name

Black Beauty Corporation (BBC)

Ownership

BBC is controlled by the Carter family who own 51 percent of outstanding shares; 20 percent is owned by management and employees; the balance is traded publicly on the New York Stock Exchange. The Carter family established the company in 1955 in Detroit as a small family-run operation. Growth in sales during the 1960s led to a public offering of shares in 1968, and in 1970, an employee-ownership program was initiated.

Business

BBC produces and sells cosmetics and makeup for black consumers. The business began in the 1950s when Mrs. Carter found it impossible to obtain cosmetics and makeup suitable to her own dark complexion. She experimented with a variety of combinations and developed several products that she and friends felt were acceptable. From this small beginning, BBC has grown to be one of the largest suppliers in the world of cosmetics and makeup for black consumers.

Locations

BBC's head office is in Detroit, but it operates decentralized production facilities throughout the United States. Seventy-five percent of sales are in the United States, with the majority in the South and Northeast. In 1981, BBC entered the world market by establishing a plant in Jamaica to serve Caribbean countries; currently, approximately 10 percent of its sales is to the Caribbean, half of this supplied by products produced domestically in Jamaica. In 1982, BBC opened a second overseas production facility in Zimbabwe to explore the African market; currently, approximately 5 percent of its sales is to the African market, supplied entirely from the Zimbabwe facility. In 1984, BBC opened a third foreign facility in England to serve British and European locations; currently, 10 percent of sales is to Britain and Europe, supplied entirely from the British facility.

Sales

Total sales for 1987 were US$40 million. Sales rose dramatically during the 1960s at close to 15 percent a year; during the 1970s they continued to rise, but growth slowed to about 5 percent a year; in the 1980s growth in the U.S. market has stopped and there even appears to have been a declining trend.

Structure

The company is organized into geographic divisions in the United States; an international division is responsible for all foreign operations, including exports. Within the United States, each division is a profit center responsible for sales and production of all products. These divisions enjoy a fair amount of autonomy, with overall strategy determined by the head office. All of the foreign subsidiaries report to the vice-president of International Operations, an American.

Profitability

U.S. profits have declined from a high of 30-percent return on equity in 1970 to a low of 1.6-percent in 1985. Overseas operations have consistently lost money. The Jamaican facility showed small profits in its third and fourth years of operation but is now operating at a loss; this is attributed to low quality levels and supply inconsistencies due to strikes that have resulted in customers ordering directly from U.S. suppliers. The Zimbabwean operation has experienced many difficulties and projected sales have never materialized. The British operation has lost money but appears to have turned the corner and is expected to be profitable in the coming year.

Management

Top management are all citizens of the United States; all are black. Foreign production facilities are staffed by a mixture of Americans and locals. Top management would like to increase the percentage of locals in management positions in subsidiaries but has had difficulty finding qualified locals in Jamaica and Zimbabwe; qualified locals in Britain are generally white, and this is felt to conflict with BBC's overall image as a "black company." Managers have been sent from the United States to establish overseas operations and train local managers; initially, the intention was that they should remain for a maximum of three years, but in all cases, the U.S. managers have remained and are still operating the facilities on a day-to-day basis.

Company Strengths

The company produces a wide range of well-known products of high quality; these products are unique in many parts of the world. The company spends a competitive percentage (2 percent) of its sales dollar on research and development, and a substantial percentage (15 percent) on advertising and promotion. The company's image as a "black company" is believed to be important to its customers, as well.

Company Concerns

BBC is losing market share, and the total U.S. market is declining; it appears that many black consumers are using products primarily designed for white consumers and find these satisfactory. Overseas operations have not filled the gap created by a declining U.S. market, as hoped.

Corporate Strategy

BBC intends to expand its foreign markets but is still in the process of formulating an operational policy to achieve this objective. The company is examining the possibility of increasing its target market to include other nonwhite races. There appears to be substantial potential in the Pacific rim countries.

Profile 3   Beverages, Inc., International

Name

Beverages, Inc., International (BII)

Ownership

BII is a holding company with its head office in New York and subsidiaries in ten countries. The ownership is difficult to describe: its principal shareholders, accounting for 30 percent of ownership, are two other large multinational companies—one based in the United States and one in France; the balance of shares in the holding company are widely owned. Ownership in subsidiaries ranges from 100-percent ownership to fifty–fifty joint ventures to minority ownership, depending on the situation and particular products to be manufactured or sold. The company believes that each foreign subsidiary should be approached as a new project and structured according to the needs of the specific situation.

Business

BII's main business is distilling; it is the world's largest producer of distilled spirits. In addition, it produces an extensive line of

C
O
M
P
A
N
Y

P
R
O
F
I
L
E
S

wines. BII's major products are recognized worldwide and include products that are of high quality and expensive, as well as those that are moderately priced.

In addition to its major business as a distiller and wine producer, BII comprises various unrelated businesses such as hardware retailing, fashion boutiques, and computer software. All of these businesses contribute to a profitable consolidated income statement, but distilling remains its major business.

Locations

The company has distilling operations in ten of the industrialized countries of the world (the United States, Canada, Britain, France, Germany, Australia, New Zealand, Japan, Sweden, and Denmark) and sells its products throughout the world. The company produces and sells identical products worldwide, but certain product lines are more popular in certain locations.

Sales

Sales in 1987 totalled US$3 billion worldwide. Sales in the United States account for 55 percent of total, sales to Canada 10 percent, sales in the EEC 20 percent, and the rest of the world 15 percent. The company employs about 15,000 people worldwide. New products are first developed for the U.S. market then test marketed in other locations once accepted in the home market.

Structure

The company has a global regional structure for its distilling business. Production and sales are organized into geographic groups, each reporting to its own regional vice-president, located in New York. These groups correspond to sales as follows: United States and Canada, the EEC, and other foreign operations. Although the company considers itself global and theoretically considers all markets important, the dominance of its domestic market means that this tends to dominate top-management thinking.

Management

Top management is a mix of Americans, Canadians, and Europeans; the company has made a specific effort to diversify the makeup of its board of directors, as well as its executives. Management in subsidiaries is also generally mixed, the majority being local, then some Americans, and then others from third countries. BII's motto in this regard is "The best person for the job regardless of nationality." Despite efforts to "globalize" management's thinking, middle management still thinks of the United States as "home" and as its major market; and upper management tends to view foreign assignments as possibly detracting from, or prohibiting, career advancement. In addition, the failure rate of foreign assignees (about 15 percent of foreign assignments become defined as "failures") has been a concern to the company.

C
O
M
P
A
N
Y

P
R
O
F
I
L
E
S

Training

American personnel who are going abroad participate in a two-week training program prior to leaving the home country; this program focuses on cultural differences and ways of doing business. Proposed local managers of foreign operations spend a two-week period in a U.S. distilling facility and two weeks at the head office in New York prior to undertaking management responsibilities; it is believed that this helps them understand the need for following the company's prescribed policies and procedures.

Communications and Control

Both production and marketing are standardized globally. Although some production and marketing adaptations are made for local conditions, the same products are made worldwide and marketed with the same message. Consequently, production and marketing decisions are made almost entirely at the head office. These decisions are communicated to the divisions in writing; foreign subsidiaries, as well as U.S. operations follow through on them, providing periodic reports on progress. The head office provides specific goals, objectives, policies, and procedures, but it is then left up to local management to decide how best to achieve goals and objectives and implement policies and procedures.

Company Strengths

The company's size and worldwide recognition in the distilling industry are its basic strengths. Its accumulated international experience serves as a basis for further international expansion. Diversification into unrelated businesses has served to cushion the company from negative shocks to the distillery business.

Company Concerns

The company's focus remains domestic in spite of efforts to globalize. The domestic market is seen as a mature market, while many overseas markets are growth markets; the company must capitalize on these now or lose international market share to competitors. The failure rate of expatriate managers is also a concern; this may be related to the company's lack of global view.

Corporate Strategy

BII intends to capitalize on its strengths to expand globally; it intends to push its quality image with a global advertising program and to back this up with increased foreign production. Currently, BII is examining the feasibility of establishing production facilities in a wide variety of locations throughout the world.

Competition

There are several large global companies in the distilling business and many small local companies; thus, BII faces a wide variety of competition. The large, global companies are recognized worldwide, just as BII is; the small, local companies generally enjoy local government protection. Alchoholic beverages have traditionally been subject to high import tariffs and duties, as well as high local taxes; thus, local competitors can prove to be serious competition.

Country Profiles

The countries described in these profiles are real countries. They represent a wide range of governments, locations, economic situations, and so forth, even though only a limited number could be included.

The profiles have been assembled from information that is available to the public; this information was obtained from libraries and representatives of the various countries located in the United States and Canada. Although the profiles are quite lengthy, only a limited amount of information could be included; this means that additional information will usually be required for making specific decisions.

The profiles include information on the geography, history, economy, government, business sector, and life-style of each country. The data are the most recent available at the time of writing but the specific years presented may differ from country to country; this must be noted when comparing countries. It is also important to note that some countries provide gross domestic product (GDP) figures, while others provide gross national product (GNP) figures. GNP includes income received by locals from production abroad, GDP does not. GDP does include returns on foreign capital invested in the home country but excludes income received by locals from foreign production; thus, GDP is felt to give a more accurate picture than GNP of a country's domestic economic performance. (A note on reading geographical and economic figures: 1 km = .62137 mi; 1 sq km = .3861 sq mi; and '000 means "thousands of," e.g., 2,635 covered by the notation '000 = 2,635,000.)

This information will give students a basis for considering different countries in the context of making decisions regarding business activity in those countries. Because the information is limited, students may find it necessary to make assumptions about countries for making certain decisions; be sure to make these assumptions explicit in your discussions.

The country profiles do not include much specific information on the cultural values of the countries discussed. Students should consult additional sources when making management decisions that need to consider cultural values. Two very helpful sources of information are:

Hofstede, G., *Cultures Consequences: International Differences in Work Related Values* (Beverly Hills, Cal.: Sage, 1980).

Ronen, S., *Comparative and International Management* (New York: John Wiley & Sons, 1986), particularly Part 11.

All of the maps presented in the Country Profiles are from the U.S. Department of State, Bureau of Public Affairs, *Background Notes* series.

C
O
U
N
T
R
Y

P
R
O
F
I
L
E
S

Profile 1 Brazil

This report has been prepared from information provided by:

> Department of State, Bureau of Public Affairs, *Background Notes—Brazil* (Washington, D.C.: U.S. Government Printing Office, September 1985).
>
> *The New American Desk Encyclopedia* (New York: Signet Books, 1984).
>
> *The Europa Yearbook 1985—A World Survey,* vol. 1 (London: Europa Publications, Limited, 1985).
>
> *The Changing Brazilian Economy,* Catalogo Brasiliero das Industries da Alimentacao, Brazil, distributed by the Brazilian Embassy, Ottawa, 1987.

Geography

Location   Occupying almost one-half of South America, Brazil borders every country on that continent except Ecuador and Chile. Latitudinally, the country extends from just north of the equator to almost 36° south; longitudinally, it runs from 36° east of Greenwich to 72° east. With an area of 3,286,000 sq mi (8,512,000 sq km), Brazil is the fifth largest country in the world and has an Atlantic coastline of more than 4,500 mi (7,200 km).

Population Dispersion   More than 90 percent of the people live on 10 percent of the land, a 200-mi-(320-km-) wide zone bordering the south Atlantic Ocean. Approximately two-thirds of the country's population is urban. There are four topographic regions:

1. the densely forested northern lowlands covering about one-half of the interior and containing the undeveloped Amazon River basin

2. the semiarid scrubland of the northeast

3. the rugged hills and mountains interspersed with gently rolling plains of the central west and south

4. a narrow coastal belt.

Although one-half of Brazil is less than 650 ft (194 m) above sea level, most populous areas are higher. Many of the highest areas are located close to the coast, and many rivers have their sources not far from the Atlantic Ocean. About one-half of Brazil is covered by forests. The largest rain forest in the world is

C
O
U
N
T
R
Y

P
R
O
F
I
L
E
S

Exhibit **C1.1** Map of Brazil

located in the Amazon River basin and is so impressive in its
character and extent that the entire Amazon region is identified
with it. Eastern Brazil has tropical, semideciduous forests and
soil of limited agricultural value. The soft-wood forests of the
southern highlands provide most of the construction timber
used in Brazil. Fears that these forests are being cut down so

fast that they are in danger of extinction within the next few decades have led to the emergence of a small but increasingly vocal environmental movement. The thorn forests of the north-eastern interior are made up of dry, cactus-infested, drought-resistant vegetation; their sparseness is due to overgrazing and overcultivation, and to the unreliability of rain.

Central Brazil consists of the states of Mato Grasso, Goias, and parts of Minas Gerais and São Paolo—all of which are largely grassland, with only scattered trees. Unlike the grassy plains of North America, the Brazilian grasslands are sterile, and only grass flourishes there.

Brazil's northern and coastal regions have a warm, humid climate with moderate to heavy rainfall. June through August is normally cool and dry; the remaining months are warm and wet. Freezing temperatures occur occasionally in the south-ernmost part of the country. The west-central region—containing the capital, Brasilia—is warm and dry much of the year but also has a wet season.

Demography

Urban growth has been rapid; this increasing trend toward urbanization has aided economic development, but, at the same time, it has created serious social stresses in the major cities. National pride is strong, but, in spite of class distinctions, racial friction is not significant.

Brazil's people are largely descended from immigrants, and São Paolo has the largest Japanese community outside of Japan. Indigenous full-blooded Indians, located mainly in the northern and western border regions and in the upper-Amazon basin, constitute less than 1 percent of the population. Their numbers are rapidly declining as contact with the outside world and commercial expansion into the interior increases.

Economy

The official exchange rate as of July 1985 was 6,420 cruzeiros (C$) = US$1. At September 1984, the official exchange rate was 2,329 cruzeiros (C$) = US$1. The average exchange rate (cruzeiros per US$) was 577. 04 in 1983, 179.51 in 1982, and 93.12 in 1981. In 1986, Brazil introduced a new currency, the cruzado (Cz$), in an attempt to deal with devaluated cruzeiro.

Trade (1984): Exports—$27 billion; manufacturers 67.5 percent; primary products 32.5 percent. Imports—$13.9 billion; crude oil 48 percent.

Natural Resources: Iron ore, manganese, bauxite, nickel, uranium, gemstones.

Agriculture: Coffee, soybeans, sugar cane, cocoa, rice, beef, corn, oranges.

Industry: Steel, chemicals, petrochemicals, machinery, motor vehicles, consumer durables, cement, lumber, shipbuilding.

COUNTRY PROFILES

Exhibit **C1.2** Demographic Data

Nationality: Noun and adjective—Brazilian(s)

Population (1985): 135 million; the most populous country in South America, sixth in the world

Annual Growth Rate (1982): 2.3%

Population Density (1985): 41 people per sq mi (15.9 per sq km)

Cities (1983 estimates): Capital—Brasilia (population 1.4 million); other cities—São Paolo (8.5 million), Rio de Janiero (5.1 million), Belo Horizonte (1.86 million), Salvador (1.5 million), Fortaleza (1.3 million), Recife (1.2 million), Porto Alegre (1.1 million), Novo Iguacu (1.1 million), Curitiba (1.0 million)

Ethnic Groups: Portuguese, Italian, German, Japanese, African, American Indian; 55% white, 38% mixed, 6% black, remainder Indian or Asian

Religions: 90% Roman Catholic; also Protestantism and spiritualism

Languages: Portuguese (the only Portuguese-speaking nation in the Americas); English

Education: Literacy in 76% of the adult population

During the 1950s, the GDP grew at an annual rate of more than 6 percent. It slowed from 1963 to 1965, but averaged above 11 percent annually during the "Economic Miracle" from 1968 to 1973. Growth slowed again to an annual rate of 6 percent between 1974 and 1980, largely as a result of oil

Exhibit **C1.3** Education

	Institutions	*Teachers*	*Students*
Preprimary	23,098	81,049	1,866,868
First Grade	205,445	970,213	23,802,950
Second Grade	8,454	203,676	2,874,505
Higher	879	123,167	1,407,655

Exhibit **C1.4** National Accounts (Cr$'000 million)

	1980	1981	1982
GDP at factor cost	11,929.6	23,120.1	45,713.7
Income paid abroad	404.3	1,015.4	2,590.4
GNP at factor cost	11,525.3	22,104.7	43,123.3
Indirect tax less subsidies	1,234.2	2,511.7	5,101.6
GNP at market prices	12,759.5	24,616.4	48,224.9
Private	11,436.8	22,061.8	42,997.3
Governmental	1,322.7	2,554.6	5,227.6
Total domestic expenditure	13,442.1	25,724.8	51,150.7
Private consumption expenditure (incl. increase in stocks)	9,424.6	17,998.2	35,296.4
Government consumption expenditure	1,153.2	2,285.2	5,056.7
Gross fixed capital formation	2,864.3	5,441.4	10,797.6
Balance of exports and imports of goods and services	− 278.3	− 93.0	− 335.4
GDP at market prices	13,163.8	25,631.8	50,815.3

Annual Growth Rate (1984) + 4%

Per Capita GDP (1984) $1,645

price increases. From 1981 to 1983, real growth was either negative (− 3.5 percent in 1981; − 3.2 percent in 1983) or negligible (1 percent in 1982). In 1984, the economy began to pick up, and the GDP grew by an estimated 4 percent. Brazil has the eighth largest economy among non-Communist countries.

The agricultural sector employs 35 percent of Brazil's population and accounts for about 12 percent of its GDP and almost 40 percent of the country's exports. The country is the world's leading exporter of coffee; the second largest exporter of cocoa and soybeans; and a major exporter of meat, sugar, and cotton. Brazil is one of the world's largest agricultural exporters.

Exhibit **C1.5** Currency in Circulation and Gold Reserves (at 31 December)

	1979	1980	1981
Currency in circulation (million cruzeiros)	183,719	320,281	574,463
Gold Reserves (kilograms)	52,987	68,571	68,566

Currency in circulation (Cr$ million): 1,094,305 in 1982; 2,021,298 in 1983

Exhibit **C1.6** Overseas Investments in Brazil, 1983 (US$ '000)

Countries of origin	Investments	Reinvestments	Total
Belgium	163,997	90,228	254,225
Canada	719,925	295,693	1,015,618
France	422,794	281,716	704,510
Germany, Federal Republic	2,089,847	758,011	2,847,858
Japan	1,805,750	231,118	2,036,868
Luxembourg	377,090	65,252	442,342
Netherlands	326,956	119,472	446,428
Netherlands Antilles	338,440	108,175	446,615
Panama	483,594	353,047	836,641
Sweden	289,073	97,712	387,685
Switzerland	1,120,198	817,903	1,938,101
United Kingdom	570,198	563,073	1,133,271
United States	4,504,053	2,694,154	7,198,207
Others	2,334,982	278,778	2,613,760
Total	15,547,797	6,754,332	22,302,129

Brazil's power, transportation, and communications systems have improved substantially in the past few years, providing a necessary base for economic development. The country has a large and increasingly sophisticated industrial base, ranging from basic industries such as steel, chemicals, and petrochemicals to finished consumer goods and an infant informatics industry. Within the past decade, industry has been the greatest contributor to economic growth, accounting for almost 35 percent of the GDP and 60 percent of exports in the mid-1980s.

Brazil is one of the world's leading producers of hydroelectric power, with a total potential of 106,500 megawatts. Already existing hydroelectric plants provide 90 percent of the nation's electricity. Mineral resources are extensive and are increasing with additional exploration; exploration of new petroleum sources continues. Evidence of Brazil's interest in alternative energy sources is its commercial nuclear reactor industry (the first reactor began operations in 1982). Imported oil previously accounted for more than 70 percent of the country's oil needs; by 1985 it provided only 50 percent. In addition to developing hydroelectric, nuclear, and coal resources, Brazil has become a world leader in the development of alcohol fuel, derived from sugar cane. Brazilian gasoline is a mixture containing up to 22 percent ethyl alcohol; more than 80 percent of all vehicles (and 94 percent of all passenger cars) sold in 1984 were alcohol

C
O
U
N
T
R
Y

P
R
O
F
I
L
E
S

powered. By 1985, the substitution of alcohol for petroleum had saved Brazil nearly $6 billion since 1975.

Brazil has long had a battle with high inflation rates: 90 percent in 1964, 25 percent in 1967, 40 percent in 1978, and a record 223 percent in 1984. The primary external causes of inflation have been large increases in the price of imported oil and high world interest rates, but Brazilian government actions, including large wage settlements, monetary expansion, deficit spending (especially by government-owned companies and state governments), and large federal subsidies have also contributed to the problem. The Brazilian government has relied heavily on external financing for the country's economic growth. The country's foreign debt has risen rapidly and is today the largest of any developing country. It is, at approximately $115 billion, the world's third-largest debtor (roughly one-quarter is owed to U.S. banks). (See Exhibit C1.7.)

Brazil's rapid industrialization and impressive mineral and other resources mean the country has much that augurs well for the future; a 1987 survey by one of Brazil's major banks, the National Bank for Economic and Social Development, forecasts that by the end of the twentieth century the GDP will be at $700 billion (at 1986 price levels), with the per capita GDP at roughly $4,000. Further, the survey predicted economic growth at 8 percent per annum (p.a.) for 1988–1990, and thereafter, for the balance of the 1990s, at 7 percent p.a. (The survey's findings were based on growth of 2.5 percent p.a. for developed countries, world trade growth rates of 4 percent p.a., and general world economic stability).

Brazil has had in place, unchanged since the mid-1960s, a generally liberal policy toward foreign direct investment, which has been particularly effective in attracting new investment

Exhibit **C1.7**   Cost of Living in Brazil (consumer price index, Rio de Janeiro, base: 1977 = 100)

	1981	*1982*	*1983*
Foodstuffs	899.3	1,746.0	4,772.6
Clothing	434.4	788.6	1,660.4
Housing	533.6	1,012.1	2,047.4
Household articles	678.0	1,341.3	3,060.6
Medicines and hygiene products	796.4	1,709.5	4,214.8
Personal services	895.7	1,913.8	4,555.8
Utilities and urban transport	975.2	1,876.0	3,920.4
All items	795.9	1,575.7	3,812.9

from Western Europe and Japan. The Brazilian government has established special policies to channel investment into priority areas including petrochemicals and telecommunications, as well as the more traditional areas of minerals and capital goods. Recently, there have been major moves to reserve markets for domestic producers in certain high technology areas, with the objective of promoting domestic development.

Government

Brazil is a federated republic with broad powers granted to the federal government. At the national level, the (1967) constitution has established a presidential system with three "independent and harmonious powers"—executive, legislative, and

Exhibit **C1.8** Government Data

> *Type:* Federal Republic; independence: 7 September 1822
>
> *Constitution:* 24 January 1967
>
> *Branches:* Executive—president (chief of state and head of government elected to a single 6-year term); legislative—Senate (69 members elected to 8-year terms and Chamber of Deputies (479 members elected to 4-year terms; and judicial (Supreme Federal Tribunal)
>
> *Suffrage:* Compulsory over 18
>
> *Subdivisions:* 23 states, 3 territories, federal district (Brasilia)
>
> *Defense:* 7% of government budget (1985)
>
> *Flag:* A yellow diamond on a green field, a blue globe with 23 white stars and a band with "Ordem e Progresso" centered on the diamond; globe represents the sky and the vastness of the states and capital, and green and yellow signify forest and mineral wealth
>
> *Membership in International Organizations:* UN and some of its specialized agencies; Organization of American States (OAS); Rio Pact; Latin American Integration Association (ALADI); International Cocoa Organization (ICCO); INTELSAT; Group of 77

COUNTRY

PROFILES

judicial—and provides for a series of checks and balances. The constitution provides for popular election of the president, who is assisted by a vice-president (elected with the president), a cabinet (presidentially appointed), and specialized administrative and advisory bodies.

The bicameral National Congress consists of sixty-nine senators (three for each state) elected at large in each state and territory to four-year terms on a basis of proportional representation weighted, however, in favor of less populous states. The apex of the judicial system is the Supreme Federal Tribunal. Its eleven justices, including the chief justice, are appointed by the president to serve until age seventy.

The framework of state and local governments closely parallels that of the federal government. Governors, elected for four-year terms, have somewhat limited powers. This is due to the highly centralized nature of the Brazilian system and to a constitution that reserves to the central government all powers not specifically delegated to the states. The limited taxing authority granted to states and municipalities, the only territorial subdivisions of the states, has tended to further weaken their powers.

Brazil's domestic economy has grown and diversified, and the country has become increasingly involved in international politics and economics. An indication of Brazil's broader role is increased trade with other developing countries (from 9 percent of the total in the 1970s to nearly 30 percent in 1983).

Business

Economically active population (1984): 50 million

Agriculture: 35 percent

Industry: 25 percent

Services: 40 percent

Trade union membership: About 6 million

Industry

See Exhibit C1.10.

Infrastructure

See Exhibits C1.11 and C1.12.

Life-Style and Travel Notes

The Portuguese navigator Pedro Cabral was the first European to discover Brazil (in 1500); from then to 1808, Brazil was ruled as a colony from Lisbon. In 1808, the Portuguese royal family settled in Salvador, Brazil, after fleeing Napoleon's army. Later the seat of government was moved to Rio de Janeiro. Brazil's independence was declared in 1822 under an emperor, and imperial rule lasted until 1889 when a federal republic was established.

Exhibit **C1.9** Economically Active Population (persons aged 10 years and over, 1980 census)

	Males	*Females*	*Total*
Agriculture, hunting, forestry and fishing	11,050,510	1,610,507	12,661,017
Manufacturing	5,276,417	1,663,004	6,939,421
Construction	3,112,600	58,446	3,171,046
Other industrial activities	599,681	62,315	661,996
Wholesale and retail trade	2,927,605	1,110,312	4,037,917
Transport and communications	1,660,565	139,678	1,800,243
Services (incl. restaurants and hotels)	3,057,153	3,974,973	7,032,126
Social services	850,150	2,120,950	2,971,100
Public administration	1,353,517	368,767	1,722,284
Other activities (not adequately described)	877,961	396,415	1,274,376
Persons seeking employment	626,827	337,359	964,186
Total economically active	31,392,986	11,842,726	43,235,712

Brazil's culture reflects much from this early period of its history, plus the influences of later immigrants from Africa (as slaves), other European countries, and Asia.

Brazil is home to a melting pot of peoples and is world famous for its pre-Lenten carnival, where resident and tourist

Exhibit **C1.10** Product Information

Selected products	1981	1982	1983
Asphalt ('000 metric tons)	888	982	na
Electric power (million kWh)	142,198	151,999	161,970
Coke ('000 metric tons)	3,741	3,930	4,642
Pig iron ('000 metric tons)	10,796	10,827	12,945
Crude steel ('000 metric tons)	13,230	12,996	14,671
Cement* ('000 metric tons)	26,051	25,644	20,870
Tires ('000 units)	18,022	19,350	20,093
Synthetic rubber (metric tons)	222,871	228,142	220,920
Passenger cars (units)	612,349	474,692	546,356
Commercial vehicles (units)	374,785	385,901	319,926
Tractors (units)	40,485	37,566	26,627
Fertilizers ('000 metric tons)	1,432	1,398	1,465
Sugar ('000 metric tons)	8,266	8,496	9,027
Newsprint ('000 metric tons)	118	121	106†
Other paper and board ('000 metric tons)	2,985	3,208	3,320†

Note: *Portland cement only. †Estimate

Exhibit **C1.11** Transportation Data

	1981	1982	1983
Railways			
Passengers ('000)	450,850	461,009	499,484
Passengers (km millions)	13,132	13,265	13,796
Passenger revenue (Cr$ millions)	10,351	19,528	37,852
Freight ('000 metric tons)	174,275	173,991	171,177
Freight tn (km millions)	79,448	78,022	74,966
Freight revenue (Cr$ millions)	84,533	180,555	428,322
Shipping			
Brazilian fleet (vessels)	1,625.0	1,788.0	1,878.0
Capacity ('000 dwt)	8,928.0	9,385.0	9,230.0
Freight (million metric tons):			
Total shipping	171.8	163.5	155.0
Brazilian share (percentage)	46.4	48.4	44.5
Road traffic (motor vehicles in use at 31 December)			
Passenger cars	8,526,984	8,800,365	9,274,613
Trucks	964,699	972,043	989,305
Buses	126,733	129,731	133,110
Commercial vehicles	839,736	844,953	879,466
Civil aviation (embarked passengers, mail, and cargo)			
Number of passengers ('000)	13,680	14,084	13,918
Freight (metric tons)	209,883	438,271	490,186
Mail (metric tons)	7,885	9,195	30,305

Exhibit **C1.12** Communication Data

Telecommunications: Telephone, telex, and television links with the rest of the world

Telephones (1983): 10.5 million telephones (7.9 per 100 residents; 2.4 per 100 residents in 1972, long distance direct dialing available in 50% of the country's municipalities

Satellite Communications (1983): A member of the INTELSAT system since 1965; Brazil operates 21 land stations and has signed agreements to launch 2 of its own satellites

revellers annually join to express themselves. Perhaps best characterized by the rhythmic beat of its indigenous Samba music, Brazil has also achieved world fame through its soccer prowess (boasting such notables as Pele and a host of other World Cup championship team participants).

Brazil is a country in the process of industrialization within the framework of its Latin culture—a culture known for its spontaneity and the value it places on interpersonal relationships. Foreign investors, and others negotiating with Brazilians, would be well advised to take heed of the challenges and opportunities posed by the peculiarities of this culture. In particular, personal trust is of prime importance in the negotiating climate. This trust is built on full knowledge of one's associates outside the business milieu—a process that can seem overly time-consuming and the value of which (if not recognized and appreciated by the non-Brazilian) may be underestimated, perhaps at the expense of the mission being negotiated.

Brazilian society, with its history of welcoming and assimilating newcomers into its midst, is freely accessible to foreigners. Further, government incentive schemes are geared toward inviting non-Brazilian investor participation.

Brazilian cities can be extremely crowded (Rio de Janeiro is, at 81,000 people per sq mi, the world's most densely populated city) and are home to many poor residents seeking alleviation from rural unemployment (as much as 30 percent of some city dwellers live in *favelas* (slums); however, the foreigner can find accommodations at any desired living standard.

Entry Requirements   Visas are required of U.S. citizens. No inoculations are required for entry.

Climate and Clothing   In most parts of the country, days range from warm to hot. Wear spring or summer clothes. The rainy season extends from November through February.

Health   Sanitation facilities in many places are being expanded. Carefully prepared and thoroughly cooked foods are safe for consumption. Tap water is not potable. Yellow fever, rabies, gamma globulin, typhoid, and polio shots are recommended.

Telecommunications   Telegraph and long-distance telephone services are good. Brasilia is two time zones ahead of eastern standard time.

Transportation   Direct air service is available. Rio is the normal point of entry, but São Paolo, Manaus, Recife, and Belem also have international flights. Intracountry air connections are expensive; trains are limited. Intercity buses run frequently and are inexpensive but crowded. Metered taxis with red license plates have relatively low rates that are raised after 11 P.M. Tipping is the same as in the United States. The highway system in southeastern Brazil and as far north as Salvador is good.

Profile **2** Canada

This report has been prepared from information provided by:

> Department of State, Bureau of Public Affairs, *Canada—Background Notes* (Washington, D.C.: U.S. Government Printing Office, March 1987).
>
> *Canada Handbook,* Statistics Canada, Ministry of Supply and Services, 1986.
>
> *Canada Yearbook,* Statistics Canada, Ministry of Supply and Services, 1985.
>
> *OECD Economic Surveys 1985/86,* Paris, July 1986.
>
> "The Canadian Edge," *Investment Canada,* Ministry of Supply and Services, June 1986.

Geography

Canada shares a 5,335-mi (8,892-km) border with the United States, unfortified for more than a century. There are five major geographic regions:

1. The Appalachian region encompasses the Atlantic provinces and part of southeastern Quebec and consists of rounded hills and rolling plains.

2. The St. Lawrence lowlands consist of fertile, low-lying plains bordering the Great Lakes and St. Lawrence River in southern Quebec and Ontario.

3. The Canadian shield is an area of pre-Cambrian rock extending from Labrador to the Arctic islands and cov-

Exhibit **C2.1** Geographic Data

Area: 3.8 million sq mi (9.92 million sq km); second largest country in the world

Terrain: Varied

Climate: Temperate to arctic

---

ering most of eastern and central Canada. The northern area of the shield is a moss-covered, treeless plain with permanently frozen subsoil. The shield is thickly forested in the south.

4. The interior plains extend from the U.S. border to the Arctic Ocean. In the south, they are unforested and form the breadbasket of Canada. North of the prairies, the plains are forested and contain large deposits of oil, gas, and potash.

5. The Cordilleran region is a strip of mountains (500 mi wide) that includes most of British Columbia, the Yukon, and part of western Alberta.

The climate varies greatly, from arctic to mild, but Canada may be described generally as having moderate summers and long, cold winters.

Demography   Of Canada's 25.5 million people, 80 percent live within 100 mi (160 km) of the U.S. border, and more than 60 percent of the population lives in the south central part of the country near the Great Lakes and the St. Lawrence River. Canadian and U.S. citizens, however, are not as similar as casual observers frequently assume. The Canadian character and outlook have been forged from a distinctive historical and social background. Canada's almost seven million French-speaking citizens are primarily descendants of colonists who settled the country three centuries ago; the English-speaking community has been built up mostly by immigration from the United Kingdom; the largest influx from the United States occurred during the American Revolution when thousands of "Empire Loyalists" fled to Canada. Canadians of neither British nor French origin are generally of German, Ukrainian, Scandinavian, Italian, Dutch, Polish, indigenous Indian, or Inuit (Eskimo) origin.

Religions   The three dominant Christian denominations are Roman Catholic, United Church of Canada, and Anglican. Medium-size denominations are Presbyterians, Lutherans, and Baptists. Smaller Christian denominations, notably the Adventists, Jehovah's Witnesses, Mennonites, Mormons, Pentecostals, Christian Reformed, Orthodox, Ukrainian Catholic, and Salvation Army are also part of Canada's religious community.

Education   Each province and territory is responsible for its own education system. Consequently, organization, policies, and practices differ. Each province has a department of education headed by a minister who is an elected member of the provincial cabinet. Despite such variations as the ages of com-

Exhibit **C2.2** Map of Canada

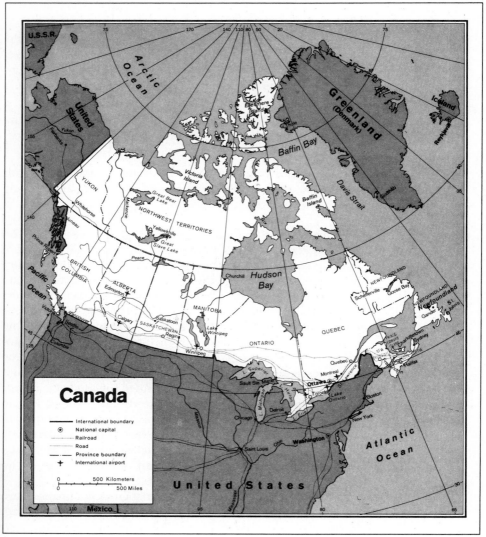

C
O
U
N
T
R
Y

P
R
O
F
I
L
E
S

pulsory attendance, course offerings and graduation prerequisites, the education systems that evolved in each province
basically consist of three levels: elementary, secondary, and
postsecondary. The number of years required to complete each
level and the dividing lines between them differ from province
to province. At the elementary and secondary levels, public
schools, including private Protestant and Roman Catholic

Exhibit **C2.3** Demographic Data

Nationality: Noun and adjective—Canadian

Population (1986): 25.5 million

Annual Growth Rate (1975–86): 1.2%

Cities: Capital—Ottawa (pop. 740,000); other cities—Toronto
(3.1 million), Montreal (2.9 million), Vancouver (1.3
million)

Ethnic Groups: 40% British, 27% French, 23% other
European, 1.7% indigenous Indian and Eskimo

Religions: 46% Roman Catholic, 18% United Church, 12%
Anglican

Languages: English, French

Education: Literacy in 99% of total population

---

schools, are operated by local education authorities according to public school acts of the provinces. Private schools are operated and administered by individuals or groups. Schools for the handicapped, most under direct provincial government administration, provide special facilities and training. Federal schools are administered directly by the federal government and include schools operated by the defense department for dependents of servicemen, and Indian schools operated by the Indian and northern affairs department. School attendance is compulsory for about ten years in every province—the starting age is six or seven, and the minimum leaving age, fifteen or sixteen. Several types of degree-granting institutions exist in Canada. Universities have, as a minimum, degree programs in arts and sciences; liberal arts colleges are smaller institutions with degree programs, usually only in arts; theological colleges grant degrees exclusively in theology; other specialized colleges offer degree programs in a single field, such as engineering, art, or education. There are more than sixty degree-granting institutions in Canada. Technical and trades training varies between and within provinces; they are offered in public and private institutions such as community colleges, institutes of technology, trade schools, and business colleges, as well as on the job, in apprenticeship programs, or in training programs of industry.

COUNTRY PROFILES

Population Density   At 6.7 persons per sq mi (2.6 per sq km) in 1981, Canada's average population density still ranks among the lowest in the world. However, Montreal has 3,566.1 persons per sq km, and Toronto has 3,392.2 persons per sq km. The highest density of any province is that of Prince Edward Island with 21.6 persons per sq km.

Urban–Rural Dispersion   At 3 June 1981, 67.4 percent of the population lived in 2,123 centers classified as incorporated cities, towns, and villages. In 1981, 75.7 percent of Canada's population lived in an urban environment with the degree of urbanization ranging from 36.3 percent in Prince Edward Island to 86.3 percent in Ontario.

Economy

Canada ranks seventh in the world in GNP and is one of the world's largest producers of a wide variety of minerals; the mineral industry has been a major factor in Canada's economic development. Canada's lakes contain more than 50 percent of the world's fresh water, and 75 percent of the country's power needs are met by hydroelectric energy. Canada exports substantial amounts of hydroelectric energy. Since 1984, Canada has registered one of the highest rates of economic growth and job creation among Organization for Economic Cooperation and Development (OECD) countries. In 1985, real GNP increased by 4.5 percent; growth in 1986 was in the 3.3 percent range; and growth in 1987 is projected at 3.7 percent. The spectacular growth of Canadian manufacturing, particularly since

Exhibit **C2.4** Economic Data

GNP (1986): C$367.2 billion

Annual Real GNP Growth Rate (1986 est.): 3.3%

Per Capita GNP (1984 est.): C$13,000

Natural Resources: Metals and minerals, fish, forests, wildlife

Agriculture: Wheat, livestock and meat, feed grains, oilseeds, dairy products, tobacco, fruits, vegetables

Industry: Motor vehicles and parts, fish and forest products, petroleum and natural gas, telecommunications, processed and unprocessed minerals

the 1950s, has transformed the nation from a rural, agricultural society into one primarily industrial and urban. Industry is now the leading segment of the nation's economy, employing one-third of the work force.

In total volume of trade, Canada ranks sixth in the world, after the United States, the Federal Republic of Germany, the United Kingdom, France, and Japan. In 1986, the value of goods traded between Canada and the United States was C$120 billion, more than that between any other two countries in the world. In 1986, roughly 22 percent of all U.S. merchandise exports went to Canada, and Canada supplied an equal part of total U.S. merchandise imports. Almost one-third of U.S.–Canadian trade occurs under the terms of the U.S.–Canada Automotive Agreement (Auto Pact), which provides for relatively free trade between the two nations in cars, trucks, and auto parts. In 1987, Canada and the United States were negotiating a bilateral trade agreement intended to make trade between the two nations freer than previously. The inflation rate in 1981 was 12.5 percent; in 1982, 10.8 percent; and in 1983, 5.8 percent.

Government

Canada is a constitutional monarchy with a bilingual federal system, a parliamentary form of government, and strong democratic traditions. The constitution provides for a federal government to which are reserved specific powers, such as those relating to defense, foreign affairs, trade and commerce, banking and currency, criminal law, postal services, and certain taxes, as well as all powers not expressly granted to the provinces. The provinces have the authority to administer and legislate on such matters as education, property, health, and local affairs generally.

Exhibit **C2.5** Trade Statistics

Exports (1986): US$87.1 billion
Major Markets: United States 78%; EEC 8.7%; Japan 5%
Imports (1986): US$79.2 billion
Major Suppliers: United States 72%; EEC 8%; Japan 6%
Fiscal Year: April 1–March 31
Exchange Rate (Aug. 1986): C$1 = US$0.72

COUNTRY PROFILES

Exhibit **C2.6** Government Data

> *Type:* Confederation with parliamentary democracy; independence: 1 July 1867
>
> *Constitution:* Amended British North America Act patriated to Canada in 1982, charter of rights and unwritten custom
>
> *Branches:* Executive—monarch (chief of state, represented by a governor general), prime minister (head of government), Cabinet; legislative—bicameral parliament (104-member Senate, 282-member House of Commons), provincial and federal court systems; judicial—Supreme Court
>
> *Political Parties:* Progressive Conservatives, Liberal, New Democratic, Social Credit
>
> *Suffrage:* Universal over 18
>
> *Political Subdivisions:* 10 provinces, 2 territories
>
> *Flag:* A red maple leaf on a white background flanked by vertical red bands

The cabinet is led by the prime minister, who is the leader of the political party in power. The cabinet remains in office as long as it retains majority support in the House of Commons on major issues.

Criminal law, a federal prerogative, is uniform throughout the nation and is based largely on British law. Civil law is based on the common law of England except in Quebec, which has retained its own civil code. Justice is administered by federal, provincial, and municipal courts.

Government in the provinces is patterned much along the lines of the central government. Each province is governed by a premier and a single, elected legislative chamber. A lieutenant governor, appointed by the governor general, represents the Crown in each province.

The Progressive Conservative party won 211 Commons seats (out of 282) in the September 1984 election and formed a majority government with representation from every region in the nation. The Liberal party, now the official opposition, won forty seats; the New Democratic party (NDP) won thirty. New elections were expected to be held in late 1988 or 1989.

COUNTRY PROFILES

Federal–provincial relations are a central feature of Canadian politics. The relative autonomy of the provinces and Canada's cultural dualism are productive of a dynamic political process.

Fiscal Policy   For the first time since 1981, the growth of federal revenue in 1985 exceeded that of outlays—if only by a slender margin. The slowdown in expenditure was concentrated mainly in nonstatutory programs; generally speaking, the provinces have maintained the cautious fiscal stance adopted during recent years, which has helped reduce their combined deficit from C$3.3 billion in 1982 to C$0.3 billion in 1985. The authorities have moderated undue downward pressure on the Canadian dollar by encouraging higher interest rates; this makes it clear that any depreciation that does take place will be in the context of a monetary policy stance that will not readily accommodate any increase in inflation. No specific target value is set for the exchange rate, which in fact has fluctuated considerably around a downward trend since the end of 1983. High world real interest rates and a deterioration in Canada's terms of trade have contributed significantly to this trend.

Trade Policy   The cornerstone of Canadian trade policy is a commitment to an open, multilateral trading system, as embodied in the legal framework of the General Agreement on Tariffs and Trade (GATT). Canada has traditionally sought more secure and enhanced access to world markets through recurring rounds of GATT multilateral trade negotiations and has, when necessary, resorted to its GATT rights in defense of Canadian trading interests.

The investment relationship between the United States and Canada is extremely close. The United States is the largest foreign investor in Canada. At the end of 1985, U.S. direct investment stood at $46.4 billion, more than 75 percent of total foreign direct investment in Canada. Similarly, Canada's investment exposure in the United States is now quite substantial. At the end of 1983, Canadian direct investment in the United States stood at more than $11 billion, the single largest source of foreign direct investment in the United States. U.S. investment in Canada is primarily in the mining and smelting industries, petroleum, chemicals, the manufacturing of machinery and transportation equipment, and finance. Canadian investment in the United States is concentrated in petroleum, real estate, manufacturing, and trade.

Incentive Policies   The various levels of government in Canada offer many incentive programs to investors who are starting or expanding businesses. The basic objective of these programs

C
O
U
N
T
R
Y

P
R
O
F
I
L
E
S

is one of improving the economic health of the residents concerned. For the Canadian federal government, specific objectives include the following:

- To promote better distribution of economic activity or
  employment across the country
- To help increase productivity and efficiency
- To increase national defense capability and mobility of the
  work force
- To promote international trade and to encourage industrial
  innovation, development, and introduction of new products and processes.

Virtually all federal and provincial assistance programs are
designed as true incentives or levers, and are available only if
a viable, promising project or venture would not proceed otherwise. The federal government's incentives can be classified
in two general categories—general incentive programs and
incentives under the Income Tax Act. The latter are statutory
in nature and nondiscretionary. Any business that fulfills the
terms of the applicable income tax regulations is eligible for
these incentives and accordingly pays a reduced income tax.
The general incentives, on the other hand, are discretionary in
that a company is not automatically entitled to them; these
incentives are negotiated with the government department that
administers the program. Canada's provincial and territorial
governments also offer their own incentive programs, which
are often complementary to those of the federal government.
In addition to the federal and provincial programs and services,
there are numerous municipal incentives available to businesses.

Relations with Other Countries   Canada took an active role
in the creation of the United Nations, which it has strongly
supported. A member of the North Atlantic Treaty Organization
(NATO) since its inception, Canada shares responsibility, with
the United States and other allies, for the North Atlantic Treaty
area. Due to its membership in NATO, Canada is an active
participant in discussion stemming from the conference on
Security and Cooperation in Europe. Two other international
organizations of special interest to Canada are the Commonwealth and La Francophonie. The Commonwealth is an association of former British colonies that share similarities of
language, customs, and institutions. Because some 30 percent
of all Canadians are French speaking, Canada has sought to
broaden and strengthen ties with La Francophonie, an association of French-speaking countries that includes France and
former French colonies.

Canadian economic assistance to developing countries totals more than C$1.4 billion annually. The official channel for government overseas-aid programs is the Canadian International Development Agency. Canada also contributes substantially to international and regional development organizations and is a major supplier of food aid.

Canada views its relationship with the United States as crucial to a wide range of Canadian interests. The bilateral relationship is varied and complex. Although occasional differences inevitably occur (since Canadian interests are not identical to those of the United States), the basic characteristics of Canadian–U.S. relations are close friendship and cooperation in a wide range of fields. The two countries cooperate closely in resolving transboundary environmental issues, which are increasingly important in the relationship; a principal instrument of this cooperation is the International Joint Commission (IJC). The United States and Canada have the world's largest bilateral trading relationship. In September 1985, Prime Minister Mulroney proposed that the two countries negotiate a comprehensive Free Trade Agreement (FTA). The United States accepted the proposal, and negotiations were under way in 1987.

Business

Canada is one of the world's major grain producers and is the world's second largest exporter of wheat, which accounts for more than 20 percent of its global agricultural exports, and is the major source of U.S. agricultural imports. Forest covers 44 percent, or 1.7 million sq mi (4.4 million sq km), of Canada's total land area; forest product exports represent about 15 percent of total export trade. Canada is the world's leading producer of newsprint, accounting for 40 percent of the global output. The United States imports nearly 75 percent of Canada's total newsprint production. Commercial fisheries provide an annual catch of about 1.54 million tn (1.4 million metric tn), and approximately 76 percent of the catch is exported.

Canada ranks first in the world in mineral exports and third in mineral production, behind the United States and the Soviet Union. It is the world's largest producer of asbestos, zinc, silver, and nickel; the second largest producer of potash, gypsum, molybdenum, and sulfur; and a leading producer of uranium, titanium, aluminum, cobalt, gold, lead, copper, iron, and platinum. Mineral deposits are located in all regions of the country.

Canada is a major producer of hydroelectricity, oil, and gas, and unlike most of its industrial partners, is a net exporter of energy (mainly gas and electricity). Canada's exports and imports of oil are currently in approximate balance. In 1984, Canadian oil production was estimated at 1.75 million barrels; in addition, there are Arctic reserves and vast deposits in the Alberta tar

COUNTRY PROFILES

sands. Canada produces annually about 3 trillion cu ft (65 billion cu m) of natural gas. The United States imports about 4 percent of its natural gas requirements from Canada.

Labor   Membership in labor organizations in Canada totaled 3,650,504 in 1984. About 56 percent of the members were in unions affiliated with the Canadian Labour Congress (CLC); 19 percent were in unions affiliated with other federations, and the remaining 25 percent were members of unaffiliated groups. The unemployment rate in 1981 was 7.5 percent; in 1982, 11 percent; and in 1983, 11.9 percent.

Wage Rates   Average weekly earnings in Canadian industry in 1984 were as follows:

Mining	$664.57
Forestry	542.18
Transportation, communication, and other utilities	521.31
Public administration	512.93
Construction	490.95
Manufacturing	465.64
Finance, insurance, and real estate	417.69
Industrial aggregate	405.13
Community, business, and personal services	345.21
Trade	293.49

The Department of Regional Industrial Expansion (DRIE) is responsible for encouraging investment in viable industrial undertakings in manufacturing and resource processing, as well as in related service industries, tourism, and small business. The Industrial and Regional Development Program (IRDP) is delivered and administered regionally with particular attention to the needs of small- and medium-size businesses. Each Canada census division is assessed independently to ensure that the highest levels of assistance may be available to the neediest areas. Financial support includes grants, contributions, repayable contributions, participation loans, and loan guarantees. A Small Businesses Loans Act (SBLA) makes loan guarantees available to new and existing small businesses.

Infrastructure

Banks   Canada's central bank, the Bank of Canada, is charged with the responsibility to regulate credit and currency in the best interests of the economic life of the nation; to control and protect the external value of the national monetary unity; to mitigate fluctuations in the general level of production trade,

C
O
U
N
T
R
Y

P
R
O
F
I
L
E
S

prices, and employment, as much as possible; and, generally, to promote the economic and financial welfare of Canada. The provisions of the Bank of Canada Act enable the central bank to determine the total amount of cash reserves available to the chartered banks as a group, and thereby influence the level of short-term interest rates. Canada's chartered banks operate under the Bank Act, which regulates certain internal aspects of bank operations such as auditing accounts, issuing stock, setting aside reserves, and similar matters. Under the revised Bank Act, foreign banks are permitted to incorporate subsidiaries by letters patent. The banking system at 31 March 1984 consisted of thirteen Canadian-owned banks that had been chartered by Parliament and fifty-eight foreign-owned banks that had received their letters patent. The banks operated 7,084 banking offices in Canada, including 149 offices of the foreign banks' subsidiaries. Canadian banks generally accept various types of deposits from the public, including accounts payable on demand, both checking and nonchecking notice deposits, and fixed-term deposits. They hold a portfolio of securities and typically make loans under various conditions for commercial, industrial, agricultural, and consumer purposes. In addition to the savings departments of the chartered banks and trust and loan companies, there are provincial government financial institutions in Ontario and Alberta, and the Montreal City and District Savings Bank in Quebec, established under federal legislation and reporting monthly to the finance department. Cooperative credit unions also encourage savings and extend loans to their members. There were sixteen central credit unions in 1981; these are organized as centralized banking entities to serve the needs of local credit union members, mainly by accepting deposits of surplus funds from them and by providing a source of funds for them to borrow when they cannot meet the demand for local loans. Trust and mortgage companies are registered with either federal or provincial governments. They operate under the federal Loan Companies Act and the Trust Companies Act or under the corresponding provincial legislation.

Insurance   Insurance business is transacted in Canada by about 900 companies and societies. Total life insurance in force in Canada at the end of 1982 amounted to C$512.5 billion. There were 155 companies registered by the federal insurance department to transact life insurance. Direct premiums written in Canada for property and casualty insurance totaled C$9.3 billion in 1982. At the end of 1982, there were 240 companies registered by the federal insurance department to transact property and casualty insurance. The Canadian Deposit Insurance Corporation was established in 1967 to provide, for persons having deposits with a member of the corporation, insurance against the loss of deposits up to a maximum of C$20,000 for any one depositor. Membership in the corporation is obligatory for chartered banks.

Transportation   Transportation is a vital element in the social and economic structure of Canada. Although the country is second largest in physical size in the world, it is only twenty-eighth in population size. Most of the population is concentrated near the southern border, so transportation is almost entirely linear. Establishment of the more economic circular routes common in the United States is possible only regionally in Canada. Nevertheless, good transportation services and facilities need to be provided to remote areas including the Arctic, too. Development of efficient transportation systems in Canada is further hampered by problems inherent in geography and climate.

Under the Railway Act, the Canadian Transport Commission (CTC), through its railway transport committee, has jurisdiction over construction, maintenance, and operation of railways subject to the legislative authority of Parliament. In general, all railways operating in more than one province or territory, and U.S. railroads extending into Canada, are under federal jurisdiction. VIA Rail Canada, Inc., operates intercity passenger services over Canadian National and Canadian Pacific lines. Involvement in freight services is concentrated on grain transportation, through the provision of hopper cars and terminal facilities, as well as prairie branch lines.

Under the Aeronautics Act, the CTC through its air transport committee, also is responsible for the economic regulation of commercial air services in Canada and of foreign air services operating into and out of Canada, and participates in bilateral negotiations for the exchange of traffic rights. Air Canada, a Crown corporation incorporated in 1973, maintains passenger, mail, and commodity services over a network extending to some sixty destinations in Canada, the United States, Great Britain, Europe, Asia, and the Caribbean. Of the approximately 2,200 aerodromes in Canada, half hold operating licenses from Transport Canada, which itself owns some 160 aerodromes and operates 90. Toronto International airport is the busiest airport in Canada, followed by Vancouver International and Montreal International.

Every province across Canada has a network of highways, both freeways and scenic routes. The Trans-Canada Highway, completed in 1962, links major cities across Canada from Victoria on Vancouver Island to St. John's, Newfoundland. One of the principal highways in Eastern Canada is the MacDonald-

C O U N T R Y   P R O F I L E S

Cartier, or Highway 401; 401 extends from Windsor in south-western Ontario to Cornwall, then into Quebec to become the Cartier-MacDonald, or Highway 20, along the south shore of the St. Lawrence River through to Riviere-du-Loup. Completing the highway system are bridges, ferries, and causeways used to cross major waterways.

Almost 60 percent of all transportation activity in Canada is in urban areas, where 75 percent of the population lives. About 80 percent of all urban travel is by private automobile. In recent years, buses have essentially supplanted the train for relatively short journeys by public transportation between cities and in rural areas. In 1982, the Canadian intercity bus industry carried over 31 million passengers.

Each day an estimated 6.7 million Canadians travel to work in 5.6 million automobiles, according to a November 1983 survey. At that same time, 1.4 million persons commuted by public transportation, and 1.1 million walked or used other means of transportation such as bicycles or taxis.

The truck is the most versatile of the goods-carrying vehicles in that it is not bound by tracks or waterways and is as useful for door-to-door delivery in a city as for long-distance haulage. This is particularly important in a country the size of Canada. In addition, because of Canada's size, geography, and dependence on trade, water transport has always played a dominant role in the economic system. Water transport has continued to be a relatively cheap and easy means of moving raw materials and consumer goods. During 1982, revenues of C$1.8 billion were generated by 288 Canadian-domiciled for-hire, private, government, and sightseeing marine carriers, according to the 1982 annual survey of water transportation. Canada has 25 large deep-water ports and about 650 smaller ports and multipurpose government wharves on the east and west coasts, along the St. Lawrence Seaway and Great Lakes, in the Arctic, and on inland lakes and rivers.

Medical Facilities   In 1980, there were 1,275 public hospitals operating and 4,743 special care facilities such as nursing homes and homes for the elderly. The rate of public hospital beds per 100,000 people decreased 25 percent from 1970 to 1977 through 1978; but there was an increase in rated bed capacity in special care facilities, and by 1982 the total number of these facilities had increased to 5,289.

Media   The broadcasting system evolved to meet the needs of a comparatively small bilingual and bicultural population in a vast country. One problem has always been to provide an adequate broadcasting service for all Canadians, even those living in remote places. This problem has been compounded by the fact that the majority of Canadians live within 100 miles of the U.S. border, and Canadian broadcasters have always had to compete for audience and advertising revenue with a dynamic and better financed U.S. industry. The Canadian Broadcasting Corporation (CBC), which is government-owned and operated, operates several national services: a French television network; an English television network; English and French AM radio and FM stereo networks; a special medium- and shortwave radio service in the North; and an international shortwave and transcription service. The CBC owned and operated 29 television stations from 1982 to 1983 and 545 television network relays and rebroadcasters. Television programing was also carried by 32 affiliated stations, 95 affiliated rebroadcasters, and 261 private or community-owned rebroadcast transmitters. Its national radio service owned and operated 60 radio stations and 549 rebroadcasters and low-power relay transmitters. The service was carried by 38 private affiliated radio stations and 66 private or community-owned rebroadcast transmitters. The corporation had production centers in Montreal (French), Toronto (English), and many other centers. CBC radio presents popular and classical music, serious drama and light comedy, talk shows, analyses of politics and the arts, local news, current affairs, weather and traffic reports, and regional and network programming. The CBC radio service supports performers and writers and gives expression to the Canadian identity. The English and French CBC television services provide Canadian programs consisting of news, current affairs, drama, sports, religion, science, children's programs, consumer information, and light entertainment. CBC northern service provides radio and television to Yukon and Northwest Territories to meet the needs of Inuit, Metis, and nonnative northerners.

There are three private TV networks in Canada, to which most of the private originating stations belong. CTV is national; Global, the other English-language network operates only in Ontario; TVA, the only private French-language network, has originating stations and rebroadcast facilities in Quebec and a rebroadcast facility in the Atlantic provinces. Other private TV facilities are independent of the networks; eleven of them broadcast in English, one in French, and one is multilingual. Private radio stations, collectively, employed many more people and paid more in salaries and wages than the private television industry.

Daily newspapers published in Canada in 1982 numbered 120, counting morning and evening editions. Combined circulation was over 5.5 million—about 82 percent in English and 18 percent in French. There were 10 dailies published in French,

102 in English, and 2 in other languages. Chain ownership is a prominent feature of the Canadian newspaper industry. In 1982, the two largest newspaper chains were Southam Press, Inc. (15 dailies), and Thomson Newspapers, Ltd. (40). Both Southam and Thomson newspapers are publicly-owned companies with shares traded on Canadian stock exchanges.

Life-Style

Modern Canadian culture has been shaped by three major influences—multicultural heritage, sustained government funding of the arts, and proximity to the continental United States. Canadians view their country not as a melting pot but, rather, as a cultural mosaic. Inuit, Indian nations, Francophones, Anglophones, and immigrant groups have all sought to maintain their unique cultural identities. Such efforts have been encouraged by extensive government funding of the arts.

Canada has a colorful literary tradition and in the field of visual arts, Canadians are most proud of a school of painters known as "The Group of Seven." Canadian filmmakers such as Harry Rasky and Bill Mason are world leaders in the field of documentaries, and Canada has a number of world-class dance troupes, orchestras, and repertory theaters. In addition, numerous well-known musicians and other international performers claim Canada as their home.

Canada's overall standard of living ranks among the highest in the world. In terms of wealth, measured by 1983 per capita GDP, Canada ranked fourth, behind Switzerland, Norway, and the United States.

Canadians are a mobile people. With fair distances between major centers, 82 percent of Canadian households own automobiles, vans, or trucks (compared to 90 percent in the United States). Canada also ranks very high in the percentage of households owning other durable goods, such as refrigerators (99 percent), washing machines (77 percent), telephones (98 percent), televisions (98 percent), radios (99 percent), and videotape recorders (23.4 percent). Some 60 percent of Canadian families own their homes, the quality and size of which are among the highest in the world. Almost 100 percent of Canadian households have piped water and amenities such as flush toilets and fixed baths or showers. The majority of houses are generally well maintained and often surrounded by attractive lawns with flower and vegetable gardens, shrubs, and shade trees.

Canadians are a cultured and sophisticated people. In most of their major centers, there are professional and amateur theater, dance, and musical companies; excellent art galleries, museums, and zoos; abundant parks and gardens. Canadian restaurants are good, and Canadian chefs successfully compete at the Culinary Olympics, having won several gold medals in recent years. The diverse ethnic mosaic of the population creates culturally interesting and rewarding opportunities for both education and entertainment in just about any major Canadian location.

Profile 3   China

This report has been prepared from information provided by:

Department of State, Bureau of Public Affairs, *Background Notes—China* (Washington, D.C.: U.S. Government Printing Office, December 1983.)

He, G., and B. J. Punnett, "Canadian Business Attitudes Towards the PRC," Unpublished working paper, 1987.

Geography

The People's Republic of China (PRC), located in eastern Asia, is almost as large as the European continent. It is the world's third largest country in total area (369,452 sq mi; 9,571,300 sq km), after the Soviet Union and Canada. Countries sharing its 14,000 mi (24,000 km) border include Korea, the USSR, Mongolia, Afghanistan, Pakistan, India, Nepal, Bhutan, Burma, Laos, and Vietnam. Hong Kong and Macau are on China's southern coastline. The South China and East Seas are to the east and mountains and deserts to the southwest and north; within these frontiers are the country's three natural regions—the high plateaus and desert of the west, the fertile plains of the north, and the numerous hills and valleys of the south. The country's two main rivers, the Yangtze River and the Yellow River, flow from the Tibetan plateau.

Two-thirds of China's area is mountainous or desert; about one-tenth is cultivated. Ninety percent of the people live on one-sixth of the land, primarily in the fertile plains and deltas of the east. The country lies almost entirely in the temperate zone, with portions of the southernmost area—Yunnan and Guandong Provinces and the Guangxi-Zhuang Autonomous Region—in the tropics. The climate is affected by regional monsoons, and summers are hot and humid throughout much of

C
O
U
N
T
R
Y

P
R
O
F
I
L
E
S

Exhibit **C3.1** Map of China

the country; winters are dry and unusually cool or cold for the given latitude. In summer, heavy rains cause frequent flooding.

Demography

China's population is just over 1 billion, based on a census conducted in 1982. Government authorities have endorsed birth control since the 1950s; the present family planning program began in the early 1970s and has become fully mobilized, with strict guidelines, since 1979. Overall population growth dropped from 2.3 percent in 1973 to 1.5 percent in 1978. The Chinese government is aiming for a target family size of three and has introduced incentives to limit the number of children per family to one. It is forecast that one-child families will result in zero growth by the year 2000. Officials aim for a total population not to exceed 1.2 billion by that time.

The largest ethnic group, the Han Chinese, constitute 93.3 percent of the total population. The other ethnic groups are concentrated mainly along the Chinese frontiers.

The national language of China is Putonghua (standard Chinese), also known as Mandarin and based on the Beijing dialect. Other principal dialects include Cantonese, Shanghainese, Fujianese, and Hakka. Chinese is the only modern language written entirely in nonphonetic ideographs.

Religious activities have increased significantly in the past several years. There are about 4 million Christians and more than 13 million Muslims in China, according to official estimates. Several hundred mosques and many Buddhist and Lamaistic monasteries have reopened since the Communist Mao regime made atheism the official policy in the 1950s. Author-

Exhibit **C3.2**   Demographic Data

Nationality: Noun and adjective—Chinese (singular and plural)

Population (1982 estimates): 1,008,175,288

Population Density (1983): 2,728.84 per sq mi (107.1 per sq km)

Annual Growth Rate (1982 est.): 1.5%

Life Expectancy (unofficial est.): Males—66.43; females—69.35

Ethnic Groups: 93.3% Han Chinese; others include Zhuang, Uygur, Hui, Yi, Tibetan, Miao, Manchu, Mongol, Buyi, and Korean

Religions: Officially atheist, but there are Muslims, Buddhists, Lamaists, Christians, and adherents to Chinese folk religions (varying amalgams of Buddhism, Confucianism, Daoism, and ancestor worship)

Languages: Standard Chinese (Putonghua) or Mandarin (based on the Beijing dialect)

Education: Years compulsory—5; 1990 goal is universal elementary school education; first-grade enrollment—93%; adult literacy over 75%

---

ities are now permitting clerical training and domestic publications of bibles, hymnals, and other religious works.

Economy

Trends and Policies When the People's Republic of China (PRC), was established in 1949, China's economy was suffering from severe dislocations caused by decades of war and inflation. The new government's immediate concern was consolidation of power, restoration of public order, and elimination of widespread unemployment and starvation.

Most of these problems were resolved by 1952, and in 1953 China launched its first five-year development plan, focusing on the rapid buildup of heavy industry. Many facilities were imported from the Soviet Union and installed with the aid of Soviet technicians. Agriculture, which furnished the greater share of China's GNP, received little state investment. Since 1957, the economy has managed considerable growth (averaging 6.4 percent per annum) despite major disruptions stemming from political turmoil and poor planning.

The experiments of this Great Leap Forward resulted in a depression in the early 1960s; compounding domestic difficulties was the withdrawal of Soviet assistance and technicians in August 1960. Beijing responded to these traumas by reemphasizing its traditional determination to be "self-reliant" and began to direct a greater share of its investment toward agriculture. After a brief period of uninterrupted economic growth, the Cultural Revolution and its aftermath disrupted the economy by injecting its ideology into economic planning, changing training and educational systems, and interrupting foreign trade.

In 1975, Premier Zhou Enlai outlined a new set of economic goals designed to elevate China to the status of a "front rank" economic power by the year 2000. This multistaged effort, described as the "four modernizations" program, aimed at achieving ambitious levels of production in Chinese agriculture, industry, science and technology, and national defense. It echoed a century-long Chinese search for a means to restore the country to relative "wealth and power" in a world of technologically advanced civilizations. In 1976, the death of Chairman Mao Tse-tung, the arrest of the Gang of Four, and the gradual establishment of a new moderate government under Deng Ziaoping and Hua Guofeng reduced the role of ideology in Chinese economic policy. The stage was set for a more pragmatic look at the political and economic problems facing the country.

China's commitment to the "four modernizations" was reaffirmed in 1978. A ten-year plan assigned a major role to massive imports of complete plants and technology from the West. By the end of the year, China had signed contracts committing itself to foreign purchases totaling US $7 billion. Poor economic performance during 1978, however, produced a more sober appraisal by the Chinese leadership of the gap between China's capabilities and its ambitions. In late 1978, the ten-year plan was replaced by a more moderate, short-term program aimed at improving domestic conditions such as insufficient energy production, poor transportation, and other infrastructure gaps that constrained economic development. The period 1979 through 1981 was to be devoted to economic "readjustment"; hundreds of industrial capital construction projects were canceled or postponed, as resources were shifted away from heavy industry toward light industry and agriculture. At the same time, China's leaders attempted to decentralize economic decision-making to the local government and enterprise level.

Budget deficits, extensive capital construction (generated largely at the local and enterprise level), and problems in controlling inflation led, in 1981, to a strong austerity program. Capital investment was cut back sharply; many foreign contracts for imported plants and equipment were canceled or postponed, inefficient factories were closed, and acquisition of foreign technology was made more selective. Tighter central control was reintroduced to some aspects of economic planning granted earlier to local authorities. Indications began to appear that the original three-year period of readjustment would be extended for several more years.

Current Policies   Since 1978, the premise of China's economic policy has been that consumer welfare, economic productivity, and political stability are indivisible. Emphasis has been placed on raising personal income and consumption and on introducing new productivity incentive and management systems.

In August 1980, leaders pressed ahead with these plans. In an accelerated drive toward readjustment and reform, they endorsed a controversial reform package that would reduce the role of central management in favor of a mixed planned-market economy. Key elements were expanded self-management rights, introduction of greater competition in the marketplace, an easing of the tax burden on nonstate enterprises, and facilitation of direct contact between Chinese and foreign trading enterprises.

The sixth five-year plan (1981–1985), announced in December 1982, presents in detail the leadership's strategy for laying a solid economic base to support the planned high growth of the late 1980s and the 1990s. Exhibit C3.3 presents figures on target growth and actual growth, which suggest that China's growth has surpassed even government plans.

COUNTRY PROFILES

Exhibit **C3.3** Sixth Five-Year Plan and Performance
(% annual average growth in real terms)

	Target *(1981–1985)*	*Actual* *(1981–1985)*
Gross of industrial output	4.0	12.6
Gross of agricultural output	4.0	8.0
National income	3.8	9.8
GDP	4.0	10.0

Source: "Country Profile China and North Korea," (Hong Kong: Economist Intelligence Unit, 1986–87), p. 18.

The PRC government's officially announced priorities of economic development in the seventh five-year plan for 1987 to 1991 include (*China Market,* January 1987):

- importation of advanced technologies and equipment from abroad for the priority sectors of energy, telecommunications, and new materials
- importation of generating equipment for thermal, hydro-, and nuclear power
- enhancement of mining and mechanization
- solutions for transportation difficulties
- development of natural gas and oil reserves
- development of the chemical industry
- focus on metallurgy
- rise in the quality of basic elements and components in the machinery and equipment industry
- enhancement of the quality and variety of communications
- development of other industries to meet the needs of the people.

Trade and Aid   Although China has long favored a policy of "self-reliance" through the restriction and diversification of imports and foreign credits to avoid dependence, the current leadership recognizes the need for foreign trade and technology in China's modernization strategy. China currently trades with more than 150 countries. The regional breakdown of China's trade has taken a dramatic turn since 1960, when about 70 percent was with the Soviet bloc. Today, Eastern Europe and the Soviet Union have been replaced by non-Communist states that account for a large proportion of China's trade. Foreign trade has expanded rapidly since 1978 and in 1985 totaled almost US$45 billion.

The importation of plant, equipment, and technology has required access to foreign financing, and, as the world's largest less-developed country, China has obtained large lines of credit from foreign governments and international financial institutions. In addition, specific policies encourage incoming foreign capital and the simultaneous increase of China's export capabilities. These policies include joint ventures, trade compensation arrangements, and establishment of "special economic zones" for foreign investors interested in manufacturing for export to hard-currency countries.

China's trade practices are cautious and conservative. Nevertheless, China is moving rapidly toward greater economic interdependence with industrialized Western nations, and, to a lesser extent, with the Third World.

Agriculture and Industry   China's economy is dominated by agriculture, although only 11 percent of the land is suitable for cultivation. Virtually all arable land is used for crops, and China is the world's largest producer of rice, potatoes, millet, peanuts, tobacco, tea, and pork. Major industrial crops include cotton and other fibers, sugar, and various oilseeds. Although intensive cultivation techniques already secure high yields on many of its major crops, China hopes to increase agricultural production even further through improved plant stocks and technology. Agricultural exports furnish a large portion of China's foreign trade revenue.

An expanding but still inadequate manufacturing sector supplies China's capital and consumer goods. Major industries are iron and steel, coal, machine building, armaments, and textiles. Shortages exist in the manufacture of complex machinery and equipment. The lack of a comprehensive transportation system is a major hindrance to China's developing industry. A better rail system and other transport-related projects are part of an ongoing improvement program.

Energy and Mineral Resources   China possesses vast, largely untapped energy resources. Energy shortages resulting from past mismanagement will probably impede China's economic development for some time to come. Chinese policies encourage investment in energy exploration and development. Domestic energy needs are supplied by coal (70 percent), oil (24 percent), hydroelectric power (3 percent), and natural gas (3 percent).

Coal is by far China's most important source of energy. With 540 billion metric tons (MT) of identified and recoverable reserves, China's total coal resources are exceeded only by those of the United States and the Soviet Union. The Chinese anticipate coal exports of 10.8 to 14.4 billion MT per year in the mid-1980s, but they will need to improve transportation facilities to meet this goal. In 1982, China produced 606 million MT of coal.

China is the world's eighth largest oil producer. Although most is consumed domestically, China also exported 300,000 barrels of petroleum and petroleum products per day in 1982 and plans to maintain this level.

China produced almost 12 billion cubic meters of natural gas in 1982. However, Beijing has announced no plan to expand natural gas development.

China's electric power generation grew from 4.3 billion kilowatt hours (kWh) in 1949 to almost 328 billion kWh in 1982. Generation, transmission, and control techniques, however, are still ten to twenty years behind the West's, and local power shortages are frequent. Although China has the world's greatest hydroelectric potential, only 3 percent of its capacity is being tapped. The Chinese are undertaking an ambitious hydroelectric development program to exploit this potential and lessen power shortages.

China's metal and mineral resources, though believed to be substantial, are largely unexplored. China is a major producer and exporter of tin, antimony, tungsten, fluorspar, and talc. China also exports strategic metals such as molybdenum, titanium, tantalum, and vanadium. China is deficient in reserves and production of copper, chromite, nickel, and zinc.

Foreign Investment

A 1988 study of potential Canadian investment in the PRC suggests some specific issues of concern to investors.

Respondents appear to see the Chinese market as very attractive and as providing many potential opportunities. The attractiveness, however, is largely a function of the size of China's internal market. The market becomes less attractive when the Chinese government's encouragement of exports from the PRC is combined with a lack of hard currency available in the PRC. This means that both exports to and investment in must be viewed cautiously. Companies need to be sure they will be paid in an acceptable currency and that they will have access to the internal Chinese market. Companies should try to maximize the use of PRC currency for local expenses within the PRC wherever possible and be prepared to defer repatriation for several years if necessary.

Infrastructure is also a major concern, and interviewees comment that it is sometimes impossible to serve the Chinese market because of inadequate infrastructure. There is little likelihood that this issue will be solved in the immediate future because building an adequate infrastructure is a long-term proposition.

COUNTRY PROFILES

This means that companies may have to be innovative if they want to access desired markets. This lack of infrastructure may provide an opportunity for companies who have developed expertise in providing infrastructure services overseas.

Differences in economic systems and business practices are also a consideration. Interviewees stress the bureaucracy as a major obstacle to getting things done. The best solution appears to be to expect delays and factor them into timetables. At the same time, having local contacts to guide one through the lengthy steps involved in proposal approval and negotiations is very important.

Chinese culture is not considered important, yet interviewees say that living conditions in China are very hard for westerners to accept and that language can be a big problem.

By its establishment of special economic zones, the ongoing identification of its legal system and its efforts in such areas as bilateral double-taxation treaties, the Chinese government has signaled to both the outside world and its own people that the non-Chinese are welcome and are encouraged to trade with and to do business in China.

Government

State Structure   The Chinese government is subordinate to the Chinese Communist party (CCP); the government's role is to implement party policies. The primary instruments of state

Exhibit **C3.4**   Government Data

Type: People's republic; established: 1 October 1949

Constitution: 1982

Branches: Executive—State Council (cabinet); legistative—National People's Congress, 1986 (6th); party—Party Congress, 1982 (12th)

Political Parties: Chinese Communist party, about 40 million members, 8 minor parties

Administrative Subdivisions: 21 provinces, 5 autonomous regions, 3 special municipalities

Suffrage: Universal over age 18

Flag: In the upper left corner of a red field (representing Communism) sit 5 yellow stars: the 1 larger represents leadership in the Communist party and the 4 smaller represent the 4 kinds of workers

COUNTRY PROFILES

power are the State Council, an executive body corresponding to a cabinet, and the National People's Congress (NPC), a legislative body. Members of the State Council include a variable number of vice-premiers, the heads of ministries, and the heads of other commissions and special agencies attached to the State Council.

Under the Chinese constitution, the NPC is, theoretically, the state's leading government body. It meets annually for about two weeks to review and pass on major new policy directions, laws, the budget, and major personnel changes. These initiatives are advanced for consideration by the State Council after previous endorsement by the Central Committee. Although the NPC generally approves State Council policy and personnel recommendations, various NPC committees hold active debate in closed sessions, and changes may be made to accommodate alternate views.

In late 1982, the Sixth NPC adopted a reformist-oriented new constitution and enacted a new five-year plan keyed to Deng Xiaoping's economic modernization policies, moving China another step away from its Maoist past.

Chinese Communist Party The 40-million member CCP, authoritarian in structure and intent, dominates virtually all sectors of national society. Nevertheless, China's geographical vastness and social diversity frustrate any attempt to rule China's one billion people by fiat from Beijing. Instead, party leaders rule by building consensus for new policies among party members, influential nonparty persons, and the population at large.

In periods of relative democratization, such as has been under way since 1978, the influence of persons and organizations outside the formal party structure tends to increase. Nevertheless, in all important government, economic, and cultural institutions in China, party committees all work to guarantee that party and state policy guidance is followed and that nonparty persons do not mobilize to create autonomous organizations that could challenge CCP rule. Party control is tightest in government offices and in urban settings. It is considerably looser in the rural and national minority areas, where 80 percent of the people live and work.

Theoretically, the highest body of the CCP is the Party Congress, which is supposed to meet at least once every five years. In terms of day-to-day power, the hierarchy of the CCP includes, in descending order of importance:

1. the six-member Politburo Standing Committee
2. the Politburo, consisting of twenty-four full and three alternate members

COUNTRY PROFILES

3. the Party Secretariat, the principal administrative mechanism of the CCP, consisting of a party general secretary and eight secretaries
4. the Party Military Commission, consisting of one chairman and four vice-chairmen
5. the large Discipline Inspection Commission charged with rooting out corruption and malfeasance among party cadres
6. the Central Advisory Commission consisting of about 175 party elders.

All are elected directly by the Party Central Committee.

Legal System   China's leaders are determined to develop a legal system that will prevent the recurrence of the unchecked exercise of official authority and revolutionary excess of the Cultural Revolution. In November–December 1982, the fifth session of the Sixth National People's Congress adopted a new state constitution that emphasizes a rule by law under which even CCP members will be accountable. In keeping with the emphasis on predictability and the law, the NPC delegates also passed a number of new statutes. One effect of these will be to provide added assurances to foreigners transacting business with China that agreements and contracts will be honored and that arbitrary behavior will not be sanctioned.

In other legal developments, the first civil procedure law in the history of the People's Republic of China was promulgated for provisional use in 1982, filling a major gap in the legal system. The government announced that more than 300 laws and regulations, most of them economic, have been implemented since 1979, when the drive to establish a functioning legal system began. The use of mediation committees (groups of informed lay-people who resolve about 90 percent of China's civil disputes and some minor criminal cases) continued to expand in 1982. There are more than 800,000 such committees, in both rural and urban areas. However, the dearth of lawyers and trained legal aides in China complicates the delivery of legal services. This should change now that law schools, closed during the Cultural Revolution decade, have been reopened, and the Chinese government is committed to expanding legal training.

Foreign Relations   Since early 1982, China has placed increasing importance on building closer ties with the Third World but still emphasizes the need to oppose "hegemonism" and to safeguard world peace. These goals are designed to create a secure international strategic environment for China and to foster good relations with countries that can aid the nation's economic development. To this end, China looked to the West for assistance with its modernization drive and for help in countering Soviet expansionism, which it continued to characterize as the greatest threat to its national security and to world peace.

These efforts flow from China's roles as a historic great power in East Asia and as the world's largest developing country. China has maintained its consistent opposition to "superpower hegemonism," focusing on the expansionist actions of the Soviet Union and Soviet proxies such as Vietnam and Cuba, but it also has placed growing emphasis on a foreign policy independent of both superpowers. In keeping with its moderate repositioning toward the Third World, China closely follows economic and other positions of the Nonaligned Movement, although China is not a formal member.

Since its establishment, the People's Republic has sought to gain international recognition for its position that it is the sole legal government of China, including Taiwan. Since the early 1970s, Beijing has essentially achieved this goal. Beijing assumed the China seat in the United Nations in 1971 and became increasingly active in multilateral organizations. The number of countries that have transferred diplomatic relations from Taipei to Beijing has risen to 125, leaving only about 23 that still consider Taipei as the seat of China's government.

In the 1960s, after their falling out with the USSR, the Chinese competed with the Soviets for political influence among Communist parties and in the developing world generally. Following the 1968 Soviet invasion of Czechoslovakia and clashes in 1969 on the Sino-Soviet border, Chinese opposition to the Soviet Union increasingly reflected concern over China's own strategic position. In late 1978, the Chinese also became concerned over Vietnam's efforts to establish open control over Laos and Kampuchea (Cambodia) and to exert pressure on Thailand. In response to the Soviet-backed Vietnamese invasion of Kampuchea, China fought a brief border war with Vietnam (February–March 1979) with the stated purpose of "teaching Vietnam a lesson." The Chinese were and are concerned about expanding Soviet access to Vietnamese and other military facilities in Indochina. Chinese anxiety about Soviet strategic advances was heightened following the Soviet Union's December 1979 invasion of Afghanistan, which extended the Soviet encirclement of China and threatened the security of Pakistan, China's long-term ally. Sharp differences between China and the Soviet Union persist over Soviet support for Vietnam's continued occupation of Kampuchea, the Soviet invasaion of Afghanistan, and the Soviet military buildup along the Sino-

Soviet border, including Mongolia. Sino-Soviet talks on these and other issues began in October 1982. Subsequent rounds were held in March and October 1983. These talks have produced no apparent breakthrough on major differences, but bilateral trade and cultural exchanges have increased.

China has continued to make strong efforts to reduce other border tensions by strengthening relations with North Korea and maintaining close and cordial ties with Japan. It also has cultivated a more cooperative relationship with members of the Association of South East Asian Nations (Malaysia, Singapore, Thailand, Indonesia, and the Philippines), and has begun border talks and increased nonpolitical exchanges with India. Further afield, Premier Zhao Ziyang's month-long visit to Africa in 1982 through 1983 underscored the importance China attaches to this region and to strengthening Third World ties. Although it is a developing country, China has a modest program of foreign aid designed to bolster national pride and counter Soviet influence in the Third World. Asian and African developing countries have been the primary beneficiaries, receiving Chinese grants and credits amounting to more than US$5 billion between 1953 and 1981. Only about one-half of the amount extended has been drawn down. Chinese aid is interest-free, usually in the form of small, labor-intensive, light industrial projects, of which textile mills are the most popular. Terms require that any Chinese employed on the projects be paid at local wage scales.

Membership in International Organizations China is a member of the United Nations (UN) and its specialized agencies, INMARSAT, INTELSAT, International Committee of the Red Cross, and others.

Infrastructure　　　See Exhibit C3.5.

Life-Style and Travel Notes　　　China, before 1949, had undergone years of war and civil strife. The coming to power of the Chinese Communist party in 1949 resulted in administrative consolidation that brought increased employment and the eradication of great disparities of wealth and opportunity.

However, since 1949, China has moved between order and relative chaos. Such wide-reaching phenomena as the Great Leap Forward and the Cultural Revolution effected much social disorder and interrupted the country's efforts at improving the living standards of its people. Since 1979, the Chinese leadership has moved toward more pragmatic positions in almost all fields. The party encouraged artists, writers, and journalists to adopt more critical approaches, although open attacks on party authority have not been permitted. By late 1980, after a succes-

Exhibit **C3.5** National Transportation Systems

Year	Mileage open to traffic (thousand kilometers)	Volume passenger revenue (million persons)	Volume passenger revenue (thousand metric tons)
Railways			
1949	22	103	55,890
1957	29.2	313	274,210
1965	37.4	407	483,580
1975	48.4	517	867,460
1980	51.9	922	1,112,790
% increase in 1980 over 1949		895	1,919
% average annual increase in 1949−80		7.3	10.1
Highways			
1949	80.7	18	79,630
1957	54.6	238	375,050
1965	514.5	437	489,870
1975	783.6	1,012	724,990
1980	875.8	2,228	760,170
% increase in 1980 over 1949		12,378	955
% average annual increase in 1949−80		16.8	7.5

	Volume of passenger revenue (million persons)	Volume of freight revenue (thousand tons)
Inland Waterways		
1949	16	25,430
1957	89	154,380
1965	114	229,930
1975	210	349,870
1980	264	426,760
% increase in 1980 over 1949	1,650	1,676
% average annual increase in 1949−80	9.5	9.5

Note: 1 km = .62137 mi; 1 sq km = .3861 sq mi

Source: China—Facts and Figures: Communications and Transport (Beijing: Foreign Languages Press, May 1982), p. 5.

C O U N T R Y

P R O F I L E S

sion of earlier attacks on the Cultural Revolution, the period was officially proclaimed to have been a catastrophe.

At the 1982 Twelfth Party Congress, the importance of the earlier announced economic modernization drive was stressed by the adoption of the goal of quadrupling the nation's gross national product by the year 2000. Also, the National People's Congress in December 1982 adopted a new state constitution, the fourth since 1949. This new constitution replaced a much more leftist document promulgated in 1978 by the now disgraced Hua Guofeng; it provides a legal framework for the ongoing reforms in China's social and economic institutions and practices.

A developing country with a low per capita GNP, China's peoples are only now being allowed access (and being able to afford, on a limited scale, such access) to such modern conveniences as refrigerators and television sets. With approximately 80 percent of its population residing outside of the cities, and largely attached to agricultural communes, China faces major hurdles in information transmittal and in effecting changes in traditional values and approaches. Its family planning efforts have met persistent stumbling blocks (for example, infanticide is sometimes practiced in the case of firstborn female babies as a result of China's one-child policy: parents want a son to provide support in later retirement years).

Access to local Chinese society by foreign visitors is limited by a number of factors including: the lack of acceptable quality roadways, the practice of isolating non-Chinese in foreign residential compounds, language barriers (most Chinese do not speak non-Chinese languages, and Chinese languages pose serious adaptation hurdles to students from other lands), and living conditions of Chinese (for example, many buildings in China are not heated in the winter).

Prior to Mao's death, China had long held very xenophobic views. The official press was known for its vitriolic descriptions of foreigners and foreign ways. That approach has, however, given way to a recognition that China's desire for investment and technical assistance from the outside world is essential to its economic advancement.

The Chinese government receives tens of thousands of visa requests annually from U.S. citizens but cannot accommodate all of them because the number of hotels, interpreter-guides, and other facilities, although increasing, is still limited. According to U.S. Department of State estimates, more than 300,000 Americans have visited China since the beginning of 1982. Chinese travel to the United States has also been extensive. In 1982, 5,547 Chinese official business representatives or delegates traveled to the United States. This figure was almost matched during the first seven months of 1983.

Business visas are issued on the basis of an invitation from a Chinese foreign-trade organization. Those who intend to visit China for business should correspond directly with the appropriate organization in China (such as the China National Machinery Import–Export Corporation).

Until recently, tourist visas were difficult to obtain except for members of tour groups. Since November 1982, twenty-nine major Chinese urban and tourist centers have been opened to unrestricted travel. Since mid-1982, the official policy toward individual travel has also been relaxed, so that a well-planned private trip is now feasible. However, Chinese language capability is recommended except in the most traveled areas. Persons interested in tourist travel should inquire at travel agencies and airlines that offer tours in China. Visas for tour members are usually obtained by the organization arranging the tour. To qualify for a visa, the individual traveler must write first to obtain a "letter of confirmation" from China International Service or obtain an invitation from an individual or institution in China.

Tour members with special interests, such as visits to hospitals or universities, should notify the tour organizer to arrange for such visits. Persons traveling to China must have in their possession a valid Chinese visa, even if they do not leave the aircraft. Otherwise, a U.S. $1,000 fine can be levied against them.

Persons in Hong Kong may take short tours to Guangzhou (Canton) and other locations in China. Space on these tours is sometimes available on short notice. Written inquiries may be sent to any of the various private travel agencies in Hong Kong.

Profile **4** France

This report has been prepared from information provided by:

Department of State, Bureau of Public Affairs, *Background Notes—France* (Washington, D.C.: U.S. Government Printing Office, 1986).

"France" La documentation française, Paris, 1984.

Geography

Located at the western extreme of the European Continent, France is a compact and balanced land—often compared in shape to a hexagon—stretching some 590 mi (950 km) from east to west and also from north to south. It is the largest country in western Europe, with an area roughly equivalent to the combined areas of the Federal Republic of Germany, the United Kingdom, Belgium, and the Netherlands.

France lies between latitudes 42 and 51 north, a geographical situation affording a temperate climate. Her 3,000 km of coastline, on the Channel, the Atlantic and the Mediterranean, have naturally lent themselves to the development of shipping, fisheries, and other industries connected with the sea. France is bordered by Spain and Andorra in the south; Italy, Switzerland, the Federal Republic of Germany and Belgium to the east and northeast. The English Channel and the Atlantic Ocean border the northwest and west. The Mediterranean Sea lies along the southeast.

France is two-thirds flat plains or gently rolling hills and one-third mountainous. A broad plain covers most of northern and western France from the Belgian border in the northeast to Bayonne in the southwest, and rises to uplands in Normandy and Britanny in the east. The large plain is bounded on the south by the steeply rising ridges of the Pyrenees; on the southeast by the mountainous plateau of the Massif Central; and on the east by the rugged Alps, the low ridges of the Jura, and the rounded summits of the densely forested Vosges. The principal rivers are the Rhône in the south, the Loire and the Garonne in the west, the Seine in the north, and the Rhine—which forms part of France's border with the Federal Republic of Germany— in the east. Northern and western France generally have cool winters and mild summers. Southern France has a Mediterranean climate, with hot summers and mild winters.

Population Density   France ranks fourth in population among the EEC countries, after the Federal Republic of Germany, Italy, and the United Kingdom, and is the seventh most densely populated in Europe with an average of 250 inhabitants per sq mi (100 per km) in 1983. More than seven in ten French people are town dwellers. Broadly speaking, the high-density areas are to be found near the coasts and along the inland waterway systems, with a ring of towns acting as centers of attraction for development. The 1982 census revealed that the French have been leaving the regions in the north and east to move to those south of the Loire. The regions that have seen substantial net gains in population through migration are Provence–Cote d'Azur, Languedoc–Roussillon, Midi–Pyrenees, and Aquitaine.

Exhibit **C4.1** Map of France

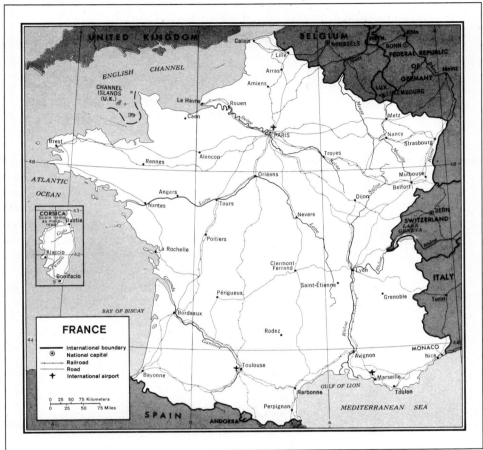

Exhibit **C4.2** Geographic Data

Area: 220,668 sq mi (551,670 sq km); largest West European country, about four-fifths the size of Texas

Terrain: Varied

Climate: Temperate; similar to that of eastern United States

C O U N T R Y   P R O F I L E S

Ethnic Groups Traditionally, France has had a high level of immigration. About 3 million people entered the country between the two world wars. Most resident aliens are South Europeans (52 percent of total) and North Africans (26 percent of total), the two principal nationalities being Portuguese and Algerian.

Religion About 90 percent of the people are baptized Roman Catholic, less than 2 percent are Protestant, and about 1 percent are Jewish. Over one million Muslims immigrated in the 1960s and early 1970s from North Africa, especially from Algeria.

Demography

Language The French language is descended from the vernacular Latin spoken by the Romans in Gaul. Although French includes many Celtic and Germanic words, its structure and most of its words derive from Latin. Since the early Middle Ages, French has been an international language and is spoken around the world today. French is a common second language and, like English, is an official language at the United Nations.

Education Education is free beginning at age three, and mandatory between ages six and sixteen. The public education system is highly centralized and has a budget amounting to about 4.4 percent of the GDP. Private education is primarily Roman Catholic. Higher education in France, which began with the founding of the University of Paris in 1150, enrolls about

Exhibit **C4.3** Demographic Data

Nationality: noun—Frenchman (men); adjective—French

Population (1985 est.): 55,041,000

Annual Growth Rate (1985 est.): 0.4%

Cities: Capital—Paris; other cities—Marseille, Lyon, Toulouse, Strasbourg, Nice, Bordeaux

Ethnic Groups: Celtic and Latin with Teutonic, Slavic, North African, Indochinese, and Basque minorities

Religion: 90% Roman Catholic

Language: French

Education: Years compulsory—10; adult literacy—99%

---

one million students in 69 universities in continental France and an additional 60,000 in special schools such as the Grandes Ecoles and technical colleges.

Economy

France is one of the world's foremost industrial and agricultural countries. It has substantial agricultural resources, a diversified modern industrial system, and a highly skilled labor force.

In late 1974, following the energy crisis, the economy experienced a steep downturn accompanied by accelerated inflation, rising unemployment, and large balance-of-payments deficits. Real growth since 1973 has averaged 2.4 percent. In 1981, the election of a socialist president and the ensuing parliamentary elections that returned a socialist majority led to changes in economic orientation. A number of large manufacturing firms were nationalized, along with much of the commercial banking sector. The initial socialist policies were stimulative, relying partly on income redistribution and partly on increased government spending with a view toward increasing growth and holding down unemployment. These policies were out of phase with those of France's trading partners, and the resulting increase in import demand was not offset by an increase in demand for French exports. By early 1983, the growing trade deficit and relatively high inflation rate put severe pressure on the currency. This pressure culminated in three devaluations. Inflation for 1985 was lower than previous years, averaging just over 5 percent, and reaching below 5 percent by year's end. Declining costs of imports and continued high

Exhibit **C4.4** Economic Data

GDP (1985): US$563.5 billion

Average Annual Growth Rate (1985): 1.2%

Per Capita Income (1985): US$10,260

Average Inflation Rate (1985): 5.3%

Natural Resources: Coal, iron ore, bauxite, fish, and forests

Agriculture: Beef, dairy products, cereals, sugar beets, potatoes, and wine grapes

Industry: Steel, machinery, textiles and clothing, chemicals, food processing, aircraft, and electronics

COUNTRY PROFILES

Exhibit **C4.5** Trade Statistics

Exports (1984): US $97.5 billion

Imports (1984): US $100.3 billion

Major Trading Partners: Federal Republic of Germany, Belgium, Luxembourg, Italy, United States, United Kingdom, Netherlands, and Japan

Exchange Rate (avg. 1985): 8.98 French francs = US $1

---

unemployment was expected to continue downward pressure on prices; however, continued low inflation will depend in large part on a lower dollar, falling world oil prices, and wage negotiations with French workers. The manufacturing sector has been handicapped by high labor costs and overstaffing; this is particularly severe in the steel, coal, shipbuilding, and automobile sectors.

Government

The Constitution of the Fifth Republic was approved by public referendum on 28 September 1958. It greatly strengthened the authority of the executive in relation to Parliament. Under the constitution, the president is elected directly for a seven-year term. Presidential arbitration assures regular functioning of the public powers and the continuity of the state. The president names the prime minister, presides over the Cabinet, commands the armed forces, and concludes treaties. The president may submit questions to a national referendum and can dissolve the National Assembly. In certain emergency situations, the president may assume all powers. The president is thus the dominant element in the constitutional system.

The most distinctive feature of the French judicial system is that it is divided into two categories: a regular court system and a court system that deals specifically with legal problems of the French administration and its relation to the French citizen. The Court of Cassation is the supreme court of appeals in the regular court system; at the top of the administrative courts is the powerful Council of State.

Traditionally, decision making in France has been highly centralized, with each of France's departments headed by a prefect appointed by the central government. In 1982, the national government passed legislation to decentralize authority by giving a wide range of administrative and fiscal powers

C
O
U
N
T
R
Y

P
R
O
F
I
L
E
S

Exhibit **C4.6** Government Data

Type: Republic

Constitution: 28 September 1958

Branches: Executive—president (chief of state); prime
minister (head of government); legislative—
bicameral Parliament (577-member National
Assembly, 315-member Senate); judicial—Court of
Cassation (civil and criminal law), Council of State
(administrative court), Constitutional Council
(constitutional law)

Political Parties: Socialist Party (PS), Rally for the Republic
(RPR—Gaullists/Conservatives), Union for
French Democracy (UDF—Center-Right),
Communist Party (PCF), National Front
(FN), various minor parties

Suffrage: Universal over 18

Subdivisions: 22 administrative regions containing 95
departments (continental France); 5 overseas
departments (Guadeloupe, Martinique, French
Guiana, Reunon, and Saint-Pierre, and
Miquelon); 5 overseas territories (New
Caledonia, French Polynesia, Wallis and Futuna
Islands, and French Southern and Antarctic
Territories); and 1 special-status territory
(Mayotte)

Defense (1985): 18.7% of central government budget

Flag: 3 vertical stripes of blue, white, and red

to locally elected officials. These laws are still in the process
of being implemented.

Stimulation of foreign trade has become a cornerstone of
government policy. The state has provided support for exports
with particular emphasis on promoting the signature of major
capital development contracts (with Algeria, Iraq, the USSR, the
developing countries, and so on); these efforts are backed by
an insurance scheme administered by the Compagnie française
d'assurance du commerce exterieur, subsidized credit facilities
and acquisitions of shareholdings in exporting companies. In
1982, total aid to export amounted to FFr19.7 billion.

Foreign Relations

A charter member of the United Nations, France holds one of the permanent seats in the Security Council and is a member of most of its specialized and related agencies, including the UN Educational, Scientific, and Cultural Organization (UNESCO), the International Labor Organization (ILO), and the World Health Organization (WHO). France is also a member of several other organizations—for example, the North Atlantic Treaty Organization (NATO), the Organization for Economic Cooperation and Development (OECD), the Western European Union, the European Economic Community, and INTELSAT.

Europe   France is a leader in Western Europe because of its size, location, strong economy, membership in European organizations, strong military posture, and energetic diplomacy. France has worked to strengthen Europe's economy in general, within the framework of the EEC.

Middle East   France supports the Israeli–Egyptian peace treaty and Israel's right to exist within secure boundaries. It also believes in the necessity for a comprehensive Middle East peace settlement that would include Israel's withdrawal from all occupied territories and the establishment of a Palestinian homeland. France continues its active role in efforts to bring stability to the Middle East, including a participation in the Sinai Multinational Force and Observers.

Africa   France plays a significant role in Africa, especially in its former colonies, through extensive aid programs, commercial activities, military agreements, and cultural leadership. Key advisory positions are staffed by French nationals in many African countries and in former colonies where French presence remains important. France contributes to political, military, and social stability.

Asia   France has extensive commercial relations with Asian countries, including Japan, Korea, Indonesia, and China; however, Japanese competition in automobiles, electronics, and machine tools has been a major concern for French business. France is making a large contribution to resettling Indochinese refugees and is seeking to broaden its influence with Vietnam and Laos.

Latin America   French economic interests in the region are growing but remain only a small portion of France's worldwide economic activities.

C
O
U
N
T
R
Y

P
R
O
F
I
L
E
S

Business

France's highly developed and diversified industrial enterprises generate about one-third of the GDP and employ about one-third of the work force. This distribution is similar to that of other highly industrialized nations. The government is a significant factor in the industrial sector, both in its planning and regulatory activities and in its ownership and operation of important industrial facilities. Government involvement traditionally has been strong in France and was increased by the 1981 nationalizations. Government-owned firms are concentrated in the large, capital-intensive industries. These companies are under the general supervision of the government, their majority shareholder, but function independently in terms of ongoing operations.

The most important areas of industrial production include steel and related products, aluminum, chemicals, and mechanical and electrical goods. France has been notably successful in developing dynamic telecommunications, aerospace, and weapons sectors. France has virtually no domestic oil production and has banked heavily on development of nuclear power, which now produces about 40 percent of the country's electrical energy.

Compared to the EEC's average of 43 percent, only 20 percent of the French work force is unionized. There are several competing union confederations. The largest, oldest, and most powerful union is the Communist-dominated General Labor Confederation (CGT), followed by the Workers' Force (FO), and the French Democratic Confederation of Labor (CFDT). Following is a summary of France's major industries.

Metals   Between 1974 and 1983, French output of crude steel fell by over 30 percent from 27 million to about 17 million tn. Over the same period 58,000 jobs were lost in the steel industry, leaving only 97,200. The state has taken over the two leading steel groups, Usinor and Sacilor, to restructure the industry around them; however, the reorganization and revival of the steel industry necessarily entails further job losses. A steel plan was adopted in August 1982, but the forecasts that it contained had to be revised downward by March 1984; steel production had to be reduced to 18 million tn a year. The work force is to be cut by between 20,000 and 25,000 employees over four years, with accompanying social measures to help those affected. Despite these difficulties, France was still the seventh largest steel-producing country in the world in 1982. The abundance of France's bauxite deposits and the quality of French technology has resulted in a leading position (sixth in the world) in aluminum production. France has only scarce

C
O
U
N
T
R
Y

P
R
O
F
I
L
E
S

natural resources for other nonferrous metals, however, and the accent in its long-term strategy is accordingly placed on securing reliable sources of supply abroad and building up substantial strategic stocks.

Automotive Industry   The automotive industry plays a key role in the national economy. With almost 10 percent of the industrial work force (400,000 employees) and a trade surplus of FFr26 billion. In 1983, the industry exported 54 percent of its output and France stood third in the list of exporting countries, after Japan and the Federal Republic of Germany. Two French groups, Renault and Peugeot-Talbot-Citroën, are among the top seven manufacturers in the world. France's motor manufacturers are redefining their industrial strategies and stepping up investment on the development of new models to match changing patterns of demand.

Mechanical and Electrical Capital Goods   The total value of mechanical and electrical capital goods produced in France in 1980 was in excess of FFr100 billion, with a surplus on foreign trade of FFr16 billion (11 billion on mechanical and 5 billion on electrical goods). France is relatively well placed in the market for large installations and major complexes, where it is among the world leaders in certain fields (electricity generation and transmission equipment, offshore operations, sugar refineries, cement works). The worldwide decline in capital development projects, however, has heightened the need for French industry to concentrate its efforts on equipment and components incorporating a large value-added element.

Light Engineering, Metal-Working, Electrical, and Domestic Appliances   Although these branches are relatively less important to France's economy, they provide employment for more than half a million people, and the pace of technological change in this type of industry has been very rapid in recent years.

Machine Tools and Robotics   The outlook for these industries is one of dramatic expansion, given that the automation of production processes has become a necessity for the industrialized countries in a context of strong international competition and rapid technological and social change. Renault is becoming one of the world's leading manufacturers of industrial robots, but it is not alone in this field, which has seen the emergence of several companies during the 1980s: Carel-Fouche, Languepin, Aro, Sciaka SA, La Calhene, and Compagnie de signaux et d'entreprises electriques.

C
O
U
N
T
R
Y

P
R
O
F
I
L
E
S

Chemicals The agrochemical group of industries employs a work force of about 2 million, and in 1983 its export–import cover rate was 129 percent.

Here are some notable facts about France's chemical industry: France is Europe's leading manufacturer of fertilizers; Saint-Gobain is one of the outstanding glass manufacturers in the world; Michelin is the forefront of rubber and tire markets worldwide; Lafarge-Coppee has had notable success in exporting its technology in building materials throughout the world. The situation in the heavy chemical engineering industry has recently been more difficult. A contraction of the market, associated with economic difficulties, higher oil prices, and a displacement of production facilities toward countries with the raw materials has left Europe with surplus capacity. This has made for fierce competition, uneconomic prices, and heavy losses for less competitive manufacturers. Growth in demand is shifting downward, in favor of fine chemicals; the fine chemicals sector accounts for a quarter of the chemical industry's business in France and employs a work force of 50,000. It is characterized by an expanding range of products, the speed of its innovation cycle, a correspondingly high rate of investment in research and development (between 5 percent and 10 percent of revenue), complex manufacturing processes, a high value-added element, and a high degree of interdependence between products in the various lines. This is an advanced sector of vital importance to many other branches of industry, from electronics and health, to energy and aerospace.

Consumer Goods The industries producing consumer goods in France employ almost a million people. They are a heterogeneous group, with products ranging from jewelry to hosiery, from light fittings to footwear, from spectacles to sports goods. Their current fortunes vary correspondingly, from decline to major expansion.

Textiles The textiles and clothing sector remains a vital part of the French economy with sales of some FFr100 billion; it employs a work force somewhat in excess of 510,000 people; almost two-thirds of them are in small- and medium-sized businesses. It accounts for a significant proportion of employment in the manufacturing industry in some parts of the country, such as the North, the East, and the Rhône–Alpes region. Although the French textile industry is still the third largest in the world, for the past ten years it has suffered the effects of stagnant demand in the domestic market and progressively worsening foreign trade conditions. Nevertheless, this industry

has a certain advantage because of its ability to adapt to fluctuations in demand, high standards, development of finishing
processes, and the world-renowned quality of French haute
couture.

Construction   The building industry, made up of some 330,000
businesses employs a work force of about 1.4 million and is a
key component of the French economy and prime mover of
growth. This industry is going through a process of concentration brought about by takeovers and mergers, and includes large
groups specializing in both building and civil engineering
(Bouygues is a dynamic example). The scale of state aid to
housing construction is substantial, and mortgage finance is
arranged under a variety of schemes for at least a quarter of a
million dwellings a year.

Craft Industry   The revenues of France's 800,000 craft businesses, which employ 2.4 million people, is FFr400 billion; its
revenues are substantially greater than those of the farming
industry, twice as much as those of the automotive industry,
and six times those of the steel industry. The number of craft
businesses has been rising by about 3.3 percent per annum,
and the number of people they employ at the slightly slower
rate of 3 percent per annum. The government is pursuing an
active policy in support of businesses in distributive trades and
crafts industry.

The French work force in 1984 was 23.8 million and the
unemployment rate in 1983, 10.3 percent. Since 1970, there
has been a fall in working hours, and this reduction has been
regarded by the government as a means of achieving social
progress and combatting unemployment. On 1 February 1982,
the statutory work week was reduced to thirty-nine hours. In
its ordinance of 16 February 1982, the government extended
the right to five weeks' vacation to all employees. Since 1950,
all workers have been entitled to a minimum wage; it was
originally linked to the price index, but since 1970, when it
became known as the "salaire minimum interprofessionel de
croissance" (SMIC), it has been linked to the overall wage
index. The minimum wage serves as the reference for reviews
of the lowest levels of pay, and as such is a useful instrument
for reducing inequality. Wage policy has been aimed at achieving a higher rate of increase in low wage levels. In 1982, the
government introduced a series of laws and ordinances that
strengthen the arrangements for representation of employees
and sanction their bargaining rights.

Infrastructure

Banking and the Financial System The Banque de France, founded in 1800 and nationalized in 1945, is the sole bank of issue in France. Acting on behalf of the state, it administers the nation's foreign exchange reserves, regulates the franc's relationship to other currencies, and oversees the activities of the banks. The 1982 Nationalization Act, while restoring ownership of the majority of French banks to the nation, contained no provisions detracting from their independence in the distribution of credit.

Since the early 1970s, there has been a rapid increase in lending by the various credit institutions and in the volume of securities issued, in parallel with the general expansion of the economy. Diversification has been the cornerstone of the development of banking business. The differences between the activities of deposit banks, merchant banks, and medium- and long-term lending banks are becoming less clear-cut. There are about 310 banks in France. In addition, there are over 420 financial institutions, which generally transact the same types of business as the banks but do not take deposits from customers; they finance their activities out of shareholders' equity and loans raised on the money market. The savings banks (of which there are 483, with 13 regional associations) are officially recognized as nonprofit-making bodies of public utility.

Transportation The French transport system is internationally renowned; it has adjusted successfully to the age of mass transport and the associated industries represent one of the strengths of the French economy, with substantial foreign currency earnings from exports of technology and equipment. The French spend about 12.5 percent of their annual budgets on transport. Each year the transport system in France realizes tens of billions of francs in revenue and investment, carries about 1.7 billion tn of freight, and makes a considerable contribution to export earnings. About 34,00 businesses are involved in transport, including a small number of large public corporations; these provide direct employment in the industry for between 700,000 and 800,000 people.

Rail and Road Transport The railways have entered a new era of transportation with the development and rapid extension of a comprehensive network of express lines. In 1982, the railway carried 714 million passengers (56.9 billion passenger-km) and 184 million tn of freight. Rail has retained a relatively large share of the domestic transport market. France has one of the finest networks of roads and motorways in the world; it is well maintained and provides comprehensive coverage of

COUNTRY PROFILES

the country as a whole. Of the total freight market in 1982 (136 billion tn km), road haulage captured 47.3 percent of the transport market compared with the railways' 41.8 percent, and the inland waterways' 7.5 percent.

Air Transport   France is a focal point of international air traffic. The three national airlines, Air France, UTA, and Air Inter, ranked fifth in the world in 1982 in terms of passenger-kilometers. International traffic far outweighs domestic traffic. The basic statistics for the French airlines' traffic in 1982 are as follows: 21.8 million passengers; 37.69 billion passenger-km; and 2,200 million tn km of freight. Paris airport handles more passengers than any other in Europe with the exception of London.

Inland Waterway Transport   The volume of goods carried by the inland waterways amounted to over 10 billion tn km in 1982, representing about 8 percent of total freight traffic.

Medical Facilities   By 1990, France is expected to have 160,000 doctors, one for every 332 inhabitants. Altogether, 750,000 medical and nonmedical staff are employed in 1,080 hospitals in the public sector and 2,726 in private clinics, which together offer 610,000 beds; more than 200,000 self-employed professionals practice in the health field, including 23,418 nurses and 22,308 physiotherapists.

Schools   The school and university population (13,866,234 in 1982–1983) makes up a quarter of the total population of France. Education in the state primary and secondary schools is free of charge, while registration fees for higher and further education are modest. Schoolbooks and materials are supplied free in the primary schools and colleges, and paid for by the parents in the lycée. Primary education is compulsory, lasts for five years, and concentrates on the basic skills of reading, writing, and arithmetic, as well as the acquisition of learning skills.

The Media   The French people spend over thirty-two hours a week, on average, listening to and watching the media. The public sector in this field comprises three television channels (TF1, Antenne 2, and France-Regions FR3), one national radio broadcasting corporation (Radio-France), and radio and TV service to the French Overseas Departments and Territories (RFO). The operational structure is completed by national production companies, a marketing company, and a public corporation responsible for transmission, maintenance of the network, and engineering. The Institut national de la communication audiovisuelle (INA) performs the roles of carrying out research, keeping archives, and organizing courses for foreign as well as French trainees. French public broadcasting is financed by a license fee payable by everyone who has a television set, and up to a limit of 25 percent by fees for commercials screened between programs. The three TV channels put out over 9,200 hours of broadcasts a year. News programs are most frequent, followed by drama, then variety and games; special programs are made for the young. The decentralization of radio and television has paved the way for the gradual establishment of local radio stations (in 1984, there were thirteen, under the aegis of Radio-France or regional radio companies) and the planning and broadcasting of programs by twelve regional television companies. In 1984, the government authorized the creation of a fourth channel (Canal Plus); this is a private channel, financed by subscriptions, providing televised services, and showing recent films.

The press has a large readership in France; one person in two reads a newspaper every day and 43 percent regularly read magazines. Ownership of the press has become more highly concentrated in recent years, but is still less than in the Federal Republic of Germany or Great Britain. The press earns 60 percent of its revenue from advertising. It receives substantial support on an impartial basis from the state in the form of direct aid, tax exemptions, and concessionary postal and rail-freight charges. Freedom of the press is enshrined in the constitution.

Life-Style

The standard of living is the twelfth highest in the world. The gross domestic product per capita was US$12,130 in 1981, the eighth highest among the member countries of the Organization for Economic Cooperation and Development—higher than the overall average for these countries but lower than in Scandinavian countries, Switzerland, and the Federal Republic of Germany.

According to the January 1983 statistics on consumer durables, 96.2 percent of households had a refrigerator; 91.6 percent had a television; 82.4 percent had a washing machine; 72.3 percent had a car; 31.6 percent had a freezer; 20.6 percent had a dishwasher; and 80 percent had a telephone. In addition, leisure spending continues to rise sharply.

State support for the arts is aimed at making culture accessible to all. The government's activities in the arts are aimed at three main objectives: to conserve and protect the national heritage, to bring the arts to a wider public, and to encourage artistic creation.

Profile **5** India

This report has been prepared from information provided by:

> Department of State. Bureau of Public Affairs, *Background Notes — India* (Washington, D.C.: U.S. Government Printing Office, May 1985).

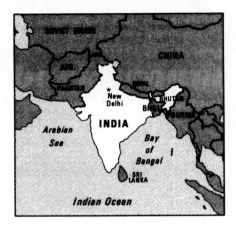

Geography

Area   India is made up of 1,268,884 sq mi (2,287,263 sq km) of land area (2.4 percent of the world's land area). India dominates the South Asian subcontinent geographically. It has common borders with Bangladesh, Burma, Pakistan, China, Nepal, and Bhutan, and Sri Lanka lies beyond a narrow strait off India's southern tip.

India has three main topographical areas:

1. the sparsely populated Himalayan Mountains, extending along much of the northern border (includes Nanda Dein — at 25,645 ft, India's highest mountain)

2. the heavily populated Gangetic Plain, a well-watered and fertile area in the north

3. the peninsula, including the Deccan Plateau, which is generally of moderate elevation.

The climate varies from tropical in the south to temperate in the north, with three well-defined seasons throughout most of the country: a cool season from November to March; a dry, hot season from March to June; and a hot, rainy season during the remainder of the year. Much of southeastern India is subject to a second rainy season during the cool season. Precipitation ranges from more than 400 in. (1,000 cm) annually in the northeast Assam Hills to fewer than 5 in. (12 cm) in the northwest Rajasthan Desert. About 80 percent of the population live in over 550,000 villages; the remainder live in more than 200 towns and cities.

C
O
U
N
T
R
Y

P
R
O
F
I
L
E
S

Exhibit **C5.1** Map of India

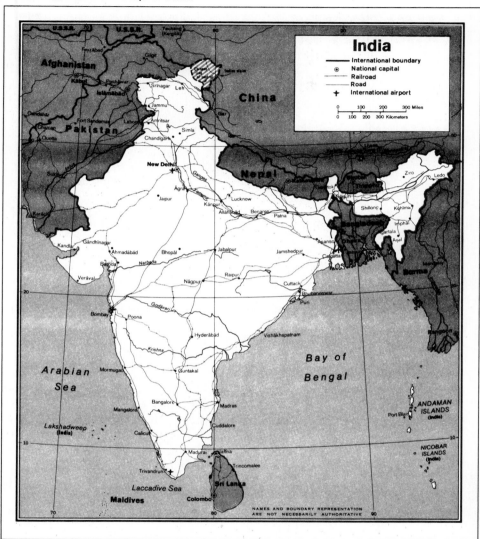

Demography

India's population amounts to nearly 15 percent of the total world population (only China's is larger). A large percentage of India's population is in its teens, and 40 percent of Indians are younger than fifteen years of age. Two major ethnic strains predominate in India: the Aryan in the north and the Dravidian in the south. An aboriginal tribal population lives largely in the central forests and mountains, and some Mongoloid people live in the far northern mountain regions.

Exhibit **C5.2**   Demographic Data

Nationality: Noun and adjective—Indian

Population (1983 est.): 746 million

Annual Growth Rate: 2.24%

Density: 588/sq mi (227/sq km)

Ethnic Groups: 72% Indo-Aryan, 25% Dravidian, 2% Mongoloid, 1% others

Religions: 83% Hindu, 11% Muslim, 2.6% Christian, Jewish, Sikh, Jain, Buddhist, Parsi

Languages: Hindi, English, and 14 other official local languages

Education: Years compulsory—9 (to age 14); adult literacy (1984 est.), 40%

Health: Infant mortality rate (1984 est.)—116/1,000

Life Expectancy: 54.9

C
O
U
N
T
R
Y

P
R
O
F
I
L
E
S

Although 83 percent of the people are Hindu, India is also home to 80 million Muslims, giving it one of the world's largest Muslim populations. The caste system, comprising the "classes" of Indian society, historically has been based on employment-related categories ranked in a theoretically defined hierarchy. Traditionally, four classes were identified, plus a class of outcasts or untouchables. Despite economic development and modernization and the laws countering discrimination against the lower end of the class structure, the caste system remains an important factor in Indian society.

Economy

Domestically, India has made considerable economic progress since independence in 1947. A relatively sophisticated industrial base and a large pool of skilled labor have been created; agriculture, however, remains the crucial sector, supporting 70 percent of the people, and contributing approximately 40 percent of gross national product.

Modest gains in per capita GNP have been achieved. The Indian economy, one of the largest in the world, has been growing relatively slowly; an average of 3 to 4 percent annually.

Exhibit **C5.3** Economic Data (1984–1985 estimates US$)

GNP: $182 billion

Real Growth Rate: 4.0%

Per Capita GNP: $246

Real per Capita GNP Growth Rate: 2.0%

Annual Inflation Rate: 7.2%

Natural Resources: Coal, iron ore, manganese, mica, bauxite, chromite, limestone, and barite

Agriculture (40% of GNP): Textile crops, jute, and crops for processed food

Other Major GNP Components: Steel, machinery, transport, equipment, cement, aluminum, and fertilizers

Trade: Exports ($9.5 billion)—crude oil, engineering goods, precious stones, cotton apparel and fabrics, handicrafts, and tea; imports—($14.7 billion)—crude oil, machinery and transport equipment, edible oils, and fertilizer; major partners—USA, USSR, Japan, UK, Iraq, Iran

Economic Aid Received (1951–1984): Total—$45 billion from multinational lending agencies, OECD, Communist, and OPEC countries (U.S. aid, $12 billion)

The population has been increasing in recent years by more than 2 percent per year.

Agricultural production has increased at an average annual rate of about 3 percent. There was a surge in production in the late 1960s and early 1970s partly due to the "green revolution," which made India virtually self-sufficient in grain production through improved use of hybird seed, irrigation, and fertilizer. A record food grain harvest of 133 million metric tn occurred in the 1981 to 1982 season. This was followed by a drop in production, resulting from the absence of the 1982 summer monsoon, but improved rainfall during 1983 increased grain production to a new high of 151.54 million metric tn.

Cotton and jute textile production continues to be India's most important industry, but public sector firms in steel, heavy

C
O
U
N
T
R
Y

P
R
O
F
I
L
E
S

industry, and chemicals have become important since 1960, and India manufactures various finished products for domestic use and export. Substantial mineral resources have been only partially exploited. Unemployment, low productivity, and high costs remain major problems.

India's foreign trade in 1983 to 1984 totaled US $24.0 billion, accounting for a relatively small share (about 13 percent) of the GNP. Increased domestic crude oil production has enabled India to reduce its trade deficit from a record US $7.4 billion in 1980 to 1981 to an estimated US $5.2 billion in 1983 to 1984.

Although India's exports have increased at a slow pace in recent years, there have been certain growth areas (precious stones, including gems, and particularly jewelry, have been important exports). Crude oil is the leading export, but this is expected to decline with the installation of refining equipment to process this crude domestically. The United States is India's largest trading partner. In 1984, bilateral trade was US $4.1 billion, almost unchanged from US $4 billion in 1983. Prospects for further growth are very good.

India's foreign reserves improved in the early 1980s. This was attributable to the International Monetary Fund's (IMF) US $5.7 billion loan, approved in November 1981, as well as remittances from Indians abroad, and the preference of nonresident Indians, particularly in the Persian Gulf region, to save in Indian commercial banks in the form of term deposits. Gross foreign exchange reserves, excluding gold, in 1983 to 1984 totaled US $6.2 billion — the equivalent of about five months' imports.

Business

India's Industrial Policy Resolution (1956) set the stage for India's large public enterprises, operating in a mixed economy. Government, through its ministries and state companies, took direct and encompassing responsibility for industrial development and regulation in the national interest. Focus was placed on initiating and encouraging large industrial enterprises. Toward the end of the 1970s, a new industrial policy was initiated with a significant, though limited, shift in emphasis from large-scale industry to entrepreneurial cottage and small enterprises.

The Indian government welcomes foreign direct investment, but within strict and somewhat detailed guidelines. Generally, foreigners can hold majority control of a business enterprise only where Indian technical skills are deficient, or where specific export capabilities are possible.

Freedom of repatriation of capital and of remittances of profits and dividends exists for approved enterprises — within the

C
O
U
N
T
R
Y

P
R
O
F
I
L
E
S

government's Reserve (Central) Bank regulations. The government of India has reserved certain areas of industrial operation for its state-owned enterprises.

Exhibits C5.4 through C5.8 provide statistics for production in a number of sectors in the early 1980s.

Exhibit **C5.4** Agricultural Statistics, Principal Crops ('000 metric tons year ending 30 June)

Crop	1980–1981	1981–1982	1982–1983
Rice (milled)	53,631	53,248	46,481
Sorghum (Jowar)	10,431	12,062	10,676
Cat-tail millet (Bajra)	5,343	5,537	5,130
Maize	6,957	6,897	6,274
Finger millet (Ragi)	2,420	2,960	2,611
Small millets	1,574	1,638	1,245
Wheat	36,313	37,452	42,502
Barley	2,293	1,993	1,862
Total cereals	118,962	121,787	116,781
Chick peas (Gram)	4,328	4,642	5,092
Pigeon peas (Tur)	1,957	2,236	1,919
Dry beans, dry peas, lentils and other pulses	4,342	4,629	4,558
Total food grains	129,589	133,294	128,350
Ground nuts (in shell)	5,005	7,223	5,553
Sesame seed	446	590	502
Rapeseed and mustard	2,002	2,382	2,472
Linseed	423	482	476
Castor beans	204	310	345
Total oil seeds	8,080	10,987	9,348
Cotton lint*	7,010	7,884	7,714
Jute**	6,508	6,817	na
Kenaf (Mesta)**	1,652	1,583	na
Tea (made)	572	561	na
Sugar cane:			
production gur	15,770	18,727	na
production cane	154,248	186,358	189,129
Tobacco (leaves)	481	525	na
Potatoes	9,668	10,075	na
Chilies (dry)	509	515	528

Note: *Production in '000 bales of 170 kg each
**Production in '000 bales of 180 kg each

C
O
U
N
T
R
Y

P
R
O
F
I
L
E
S

Exhibit C5.5
Mining Statistics (all figures in metric tons except gold, diamonds, and natural gas)

	1980	1981	1982
Coal	109,102	123,048	128,304
Lignite	4,549	5,966	6,675
Iron ore	41,940	41,354	6,675
Manganese ore	1,692	1,526	1,448
Bauxite	1,788	1,923	1,860
Chalk (fireclay)	756	833	732
Kaolin (china clay)	452	509	531
Dolomite	2,028	2,028	2,133
Limestone	948	948	948
Crude petroleum	29,184	31,848	33,528
Sea salt	9,397	14,925	19,729
Chromium ore	321	336	336
Phosporite	528	551	542
Kyanite	49	39	34
Magnetite	385	463	407
Steatite	348	341	288
Copper ore	26,819	na	na
Lead concentrates	16,764	20,017	21,747
Zinc concentrates	46,488	52,876	52,839
Mica (crude)	8,400	8,400	8,400
Gold (kg)	2,452	2,495	2,238
Diamonds (carats)	14,436	14,542	12,792
Natural gas (million cu m)	1,464	1,992	2,568

Government

According to its constitution, India is a sovereign, socialist, secular, democratic republic. The central government has great power in relation to that of its states, and government is patterned after the British parliamentary system. The government exercises its broad administrative powers in the name of the president, whose duties are largely ceremonial.

Real national executive power is centered in the Council of Ministers, led by the prime minister. The president appoints the prime minister, who is designated by the legislators of the political party, or coalition of parties, commanding a parliamentary majority. The president then appoints subordinate ministers on the advice of the prime minister.

India's independent judicial system's concepts and procedures resemble those of Anglo-Saxon countries. The Supreme Court consists of a chief justice and twenty-five other justices, all appointed by the president on the advice of the prime minister.

C
O
U
N
T
R
Y

P
R
O
F
I
L
E
S

Exhibit **C5.6** Industrial Statistics, Selected Products

	1980	1981	1982
Refined sugar ('000 m tons)	3,864	5,148	8,436
Cotton cloth (million m)	8,314	8,119	na
Jute manufactures	1,382	1,367	1,253
Paper and paper board	1,066	1,205	1,243
Sulfuric acid	2,260	2,134	na
Soda ash	505	612	612
Fertilizers	3,024	4,092	4,344
Petroleum products	23,601	27,576	30,000
Cement	17,796	20,772	22,476
Pig iron	8,480	9,464	9,612
Finished Steel	5,537	6,758	6,701
Aluminum	184,512	212,832	216,476
Diesel engines (stationary)	154,524	174,696	166,596
Sewing machines	345,600	333,600	333,600
Radio receivers	1,920,000	2,668,000	1,728,000
Electric fans	4,104,000	4,176,000	4,044,000
Passenger cars and jeeps	47,436	61,669	63,983
Motor cycles and scooters	310,572	311,802	379,951
Bicycles	3,892,000	4,728,000	4,840,000

Source: The Far East and Australia, 1984–85, 16th ed. (London: Europa Publications Limited, 1984), p. 367

Exhibit **C5.7** Tourism Statistics

Foreign visitors from:	1980	1981	1982
Australia	22,630	20,940	23,395
Canada	23,783	25,358	25,991
France	58,682	57,272	59,267
Germany, Federal Republic	54,736	54,311	49,610
Italy	29,002	28,503	29,791
Japan	30,575	29,032	29,103
Malaysia	26,405	26,458	26,552
Saudi Arabia	23,525	26,024	27,846
Switzerland	13,287	14,111	14,609
United Kingdom	104,483	116,684	120,772
United States	78,608	82,052	86,806
Total (incl. others)	800,150	853,148	860,178

COUNTRY PROFILES

Exhibit **C5.8**   Economically Active Population, 1971 Census

Industry	Number of people employed
Agriculture, hunting, forestry, and fishing	130,058,097
Mining and quarrying	922,821
Manufacturing (incl. repair services)	17,068,958
Electricity, gas, and water supply	534,704
Construction	2,219,101
Trade, restaurants, and hotels	8,831,449
Transport, storage, and communications	4,402,979
Finance, insurance, property, and business services	1,209,182
Community, social, and personal services (excl. repair services)	15,237,715
Total	180,485,066

At the state level, some of the legislatures are bicameral, patterned after the two houses of the national Parliament. The states' chief ministers are responsible to the legislatures in the same way the prime minister is responsible to Parliament. Each state also has a governor, appointed by the president, who has ceremonial powers in normal times but who assumes certain broad powers during any period of breakdown of state parliamentary government. The central government exerts greater control over the union territories than over the states. Some states are implementing a policy of revitalizing the traditional village councils and introducing "grassroots democracy" at the village level, where 80 percent of the people live.

The Congress (I) party has ruled India since independence, with the exception of the 1977 to 1979 period of Janata party rule. The prime minister, Rajiv Gandhi, succeeded to office following the assassination in October 1984, of the then Prime Minister Indira Gandhi, his mother. Toward the end of 1984, Mr. Gandhi's party won 401 of the 508 parliamentary seats contested in national elections. Communal violence and demands by states for more authority have featured prominently during Mr. Gandhi's tenure; the Sikh independence movement in the state of Punjab has continued to attract national and international attention. Following on Mrs. Gandhi's assassination by Sikh gunmen, anti-Sikh violence erupted throughout India.

India has strained relationships with Pakistan, common-border problems with Bangladesh, and is attempting to improve its relationship with China (since its 1962 border war with that country). India enjoys a good relationship with the United States

Exhibit **C5.9** Government Data

Type: Federal Republic

Independence: 15 August 1947

Constitution: 26 January 1950

Branches: Executive—president (chief of state), prime minister (head of government), Council of Ministers (Cabinet); legislative—bicamerial Parliament (Rajya Sabha or Council of States and Lok Sabha or House of the People); judicial—Supreme Court

Political Parties: Congress (I)—ruling party; Congress (S); Lok Dal; Bharatiya Janata party; Janata party; communist parties (CPI and CPM); and numerous regional and small national parties

Suffrage: Universal over 21

Political Subdivisions: 22 states, 9 union territories

Central Government Budget (1985–86 est.): $41.0 billion

Defense (1985–86 est.): 3.3% of GNP.

Membership in International Organizations: UN, Non-Aligned Movement, Commonwealth, Colombo Plan, Asian Development Bank (ADB), International Atomic Energy Agency (IAEA), International Monetary Fund (IMF), World Bank, and INTELSAT.

Flag: 3 horizontal stripes of orange (Islam), white, and green (Hinduism); a blue "Wheel of Law" is centered on the white stripe

and strong ties with the USSR (a 1971 twenty-year treaty touched on peace, friendship, and cooperation).

Infrastructure   See Exhibits C5.10 and C5.11.

History and Life-Style   The people of India have had a continuous civilization since about 2500 B.C., when the inhabitants of the Indus River Valley developed an urban culture based on commerce, trade, and, to a lesser degree, agriculture. This civilization declined about 1500 B.C., and Aryan tribes originating in central Asia absorbed

COUNTRY PROFILES

Exhibit **C5.10**   Transportation Statistics (year ending as of 31 March)

	1979–80	1980–81	1981–82
Railways (in millions)			
Passengers	3,505.4	3,612.6	3,704.4
Passenger-km	198,656.7	208,558.0	220,787.4
Freight (metric tn)	217.8	220.0	245.8
Freight (metric tn-km)	155,995.2	158,473.9	174,201.8
Road traffic (motor vehicles in use)	(1979)	(1980)	(1981)
Private cars			897,975
Jeeps	995,835	1,054,404	118,715
Taxis			99,936
Buses and coaches	113,163	140,346	153,383
Goods and vehicles	443,632	472,093	526,765
Motorcycles and scooters	1,887,618	2,115,254	2,527,736
Total	4,058,969	4,513,986	5,171,998
International seaborne shipping			
Vessels ('000 net reg. tn)			
Entered	25,379	25,204	25,913
Cleared	21,274	23,025	24,709
Freight ('000 metric tn)			
Loaded	30,611	na	na
Unloaded	33,942	na	na
Civil aviation ('000)	(1980)	(1981)	(1982)
Kilometers flown	83,911	88,067	91,161
Passenger-km	10,680,422	12,038,726	13,263,882
Freight tn-km	378,372	427,719	432,363
Mail tn-km	35,371	37,332	36,811
Communications media	(1980)	(1981)	(1982)
Radio receivers	na	10,178,555	na
Television receivers	1,547,871	1,672,628	2,196,000
Telephones	na	2,212,000	2,384,000
Daily newspapers	1,173	1,264	1,334
Nondaily newspapers and other periodicals	16,967	17,880	18,603

Source: The Far East and Australia, 1984–1985, (London: Europa Publications, Limited, 1984), p. 372

parts of its culture as they spread out over the South Asian subcontinent.

During the next few centuries, India flourished under several successive empires. The Arabs expanded into western India in

Exhibit **C5.11** Banking System

> Reserve Bank
>   India's Central Bank:
>
> - banker to government
> - sole authority to issue bank notes
> - administer exchange control regulations
> - government mechanism for national monetary policy
>
> Commercial Banks
>   Four categories:
>
> 1. State Bank of India (biggest commercial bank; public sector bank) and its subsidiaries
> 2. nationalized banks
> 3. foreign banks
> 4. nonnationalized Indian-scheduled banks
>
> Other Countrywide Financial Institutions
>   Main source of institutional finance:
>
> - Industrial Development Bank of India
> - Industrial Credit and Investment Corporation of India
> - Industrial Financial Corporation of India
> - Industrial Reconstruction Corporation of India
> - Life Insurance Corporation of India
> - Unit Trust of India

the seventh and eighth centuries A.D., bringing with them the Islamic faith and beginning a period during which the two cultures, the prevailing Hindu and the Muslim, mingled, leaving lasting influences on each other. Before the British arrived, the Mogul Empire, a Muslim dynasty, controlled much of the subcontinent.

The first British outpost in South Asia was established in 1619 at Surat, on the northwestern coast of India. Later in the century, permanent trading stations were opened by the East India Company at Madras, Bombay, and Calcutta, each under the protection of native rulers. The British gradually expanded their influence from these footholds, until, by the 1850s they controlled almost the entire area of present day India, Pakistan, and Bangladesh. A widespread mutiny in 1857 led the British government to remove the last vestiges of political power from the East India Company. From then until independence in 1947, the U.K. administered most of India directly and controlled the rest through treaties with local rulers.

COUNTRY PROFILES

Beginning in 1920, Indian leader Mahatma Gandhi transformed the Indian National Congress into a mass movement
and used it to mount a popular campaign against British colonial
rule. The Congress used both parliamentary and extraparlia-
mentary means, nonviolent resistance and noncooperation, to
seek its goal.

Independence was attained on 15 August 1947, and India
became a dominion within the Commonwealth of Nations with
Jawaharlal Nehru as prime minister. Longstanding frictions
between the Hindus and Muslims led the British to create two
countries out of British India—India and Pakistan—with Pakistan as the homeland for the Muslims. India's constitution was
promulgated on 26 January 1950, when the country became a
republic within the Commonwealth.

Prime Minister Nehru governed the nation until his death
in May 1964. He was succeeded by Lal Bahadur Shastri, a veteran of the Congress movement. When Shastri died in January
1966, power passed to Jawaharlal Nehru's daughter, Indira Gandhi, who was prime minister from 1966 to 1977. In that year,
Prime Minister Gandhi was replaced by Moraji Desai, a veteran
political leader who headed the Janata party, an amalgam of
five opposition parties that had united against Mrs. Gandhi and
the Congress party. In 1979, dissension within the Janata government led to Desai's loss of a majority in the Parliament. He
was succeeded as prime minister by Charan Singh, whose interim
government set the stage for new elections, which returned
Mrs. Gandhi to office in January 1980. Rajiv Gandhi succeeded
his mother following her assassination on 31 October 1984.

Western visitors find India exotic and full of contrasts, from
the holy river, the Ganges, to the ceremony and display of
military forces of its annual Republic Day parades, to the
squalor and abject poverty of its city slums. India is also a
nation of engineers and scientists endeavoring to make the
nation an industrial power. Its majority Hindu population and
large Muslim sector, combined with a cosmopolitan ambience,
often perplexes foreigners. In addition, Hinduism's fatalistic
approach to life exists side-by-side with rational and scientific
approaches.

Finally, India is a land of widespread poverty, with major
inequalities in income and wealth distribution. By national and
international standards, it has been estimated that approximately 50 percent of India's population falls below the poverty
line.

Climate and Clothing   Summer clothing is suitable year round
in the south. In the north, lightweight woolens are necessary
from mid-December to mid-March.

Customs and Currency   U.S. citizens must have a valid visa good for six months for a length of stay of ninety days in India. Foreign currency (including travelers checks) must be declared to customs on arrival if it totals more than US $1,000, but is not otherwise restricted. Import and export of Indian currency are prohibited.

Health   Tap water is unsafe throughout India. In hotels and restaurants, drink only bottled or carbonated water and avoid ice cubes. Typhoid, tetanus, hepatitis, and diphtheria shots are recommended. Health requirements change; check the latest information.

Transportation   Many international carriers provide service to New Delhi, Bombay, Calcutta, and Madras. Indian Airlines has flights to many Indian cities. The railway system provides service throughout the country. The 900 mi (1,450 km) trip from New Delhi to Calcutta or Bombay takes from sixteen to twenty-four hours. The 1,535 mi (2,470 km) trip from Delhi to Madras takes about forty hours. It is possible to travel almost everywhere by road during the dry season; however, outside urban areas the roads are narrow and often impassable during the monsoon. Local transportation includes buses, taxis, three-wheeled scooters, cycle rickshaws, and horse-drawn tongas. Buses are overcrowded and service is irregular. Taxis are plentiful in the larger cities.

Profile 6   Jamaica

This report has been prepared from information provided by:

Department of State, Bureau of Public Affairs, *Background Notes—Jamaica* (Washington, D.C.: U.S. Government Printing Office, 1987).

COUNTRY PROFILES

Geography   Jamaica, the third largest island in the Caribbean, is located approximately 600 mi south of Miami and 700 mi southwest of Puerto Rico. Jamaica is largely (80 percent) mountainous. Blue Mountain, at 7,402 ft (2,221 m), is the island's highest point. Jamaica is largely limestone with east-west mountains and volcanic rises.

The island has a humid, tropical climate, with the coolest months being the November to March period (70° F to 80° F). Northern regions are cooler than the rest of the island and receive up to 200 in. (506 cm) of rainfall annually; the southern and southwestern plains are essentially dry with annual average rainfall of 77 in. (196 cm). Jamaica lies within the hurricane belt and hurricanes have, on occasion, caused extensive damage and flooding.

Demography

See Exhibit C6.2. Historically, emigration by Jamaicans has been significant. Most permanent departures since the late 1960s have been to the United States (approximately 15,000 per annum) and to Canada (3,000 per annum). There are large numbers of expatriate Jamaicans in New York, Miami, Chicago, Toronto, and the UK.

Availability and Types of Labor

The total labor pool is arrayed approximately as follows:

- 1% mining and quarrying
- 5% construction and installation
- 11% public administration
- 12% commerce

Exhibit **C6.1** Map of Jamaica

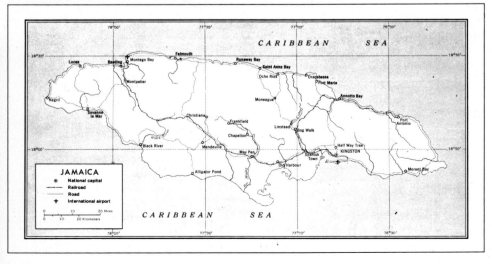

12% manufacturing

25% agriculture

34% other

Economy

Jamaica has many natural resources, primarily bauxite, and an ideal climate conducive to intensive agriculture and tourism. The Jamaican economy traditionally was based on plantation agriculture, primarily sugar and bananas. Although agriculture remained basic to Jamaican life, the discovery of bauxite in the 1950s and the subsequent establishment of the bauxite–alumina industries became the dominant factors in the island's economic growth. During the 1960s, the expansion of tourism and the establishment of local manufacturing industries were emphasized. Substantial foreign investment in the bauxite–alumina industries and construction of large-scale tourist facilities also provided domestic venture capital, which in turn, stimulated an economic expansion from 1965 to 1971.

In 1972, the prime minister, Mr. Michael Manley, launched policies to improve social conditions and restructure the

Exhibit **C6.2** Demographic Data

Nationality: Noun and adjective—Jamaican(s)

Population: 2.3 million

Annual Growth Rate (1975–1985): 1.1%

Ethnic Groups: 76.3% African, 15.1% Afro-European, 1.2% Chinese and Afro-Chinese, 3.4% East Indian and Afro-East Indian, 3.2% Europeans, 0.9% other

Religions: Anglican, Baptist, Protestant, Roman Catholic, and other

Languages: English, Creole

Education: Compulsory to age 14 in most schools; literacy (age 15 and over) 73.1%

Health: Infant mortality rate—28.0/1,000

Life Expectancy: Approximately 71 years

COUNTRY PROFILES

Exhibit **C6.3**   Economic Data

GDP (1985 est.): J$11,023

Real Growth Rate (1985): 3.7%

Per Capita Income (1985): J$4,770

Average Inflation Rate (1985): 23.1%

Natural Resources: Bauxite, gypsum, and limestone

Agriculture: Sugar, bananas, citrus fruits, coffee, pimento, allspice, and coconuts

Industry: Mining, garments, processed foods, sugar, rum, molasses, cement, metal, paper, chemical products, and tourism

Trade (1985 Preliminary): Exports—US$568.5 million in alumina, bauxite, sugar, bananas, citrus fruits and products, rum, and cocoa; imports—US$1.1 billion in machinery, transportation and electrical equipment, food, fuels, and fertilizer

Distribution of Exports by Volume: Major markets—USA 33%, UK 17%, Canada 16%, CARICOM 7%, USSR 5%; major suppliers—USA 44%, Venezuela 13%, Netherlands Antilles 9%, UK 5%, Canada 4%, CARICOM 4%

Official Exchange Rate: The exchange rate is adjusted twice weekly by the Bank of Jamaica (the country's central bank), based on supply–demand indicators; as of the end of 1986 (and since November 1985), the exchange rate is stabilized at J$5.50 = US$1

Economic Aid Received (1985, US$): USA—$171 million; IMF—$81 million; multilateral organizations—$41 million; bilateral countries—$164 million

economy to ensure a more equitable allocation of income and resources. The extent of public ownership of the economy increased, and idle land was redistributed to landless farmers and to the unemployed. The government introduced a minimum wage law, free secondary school education, paid maternity leave, and other benefits. A stiff bauxite levy, linked to the world market price of aluminum, was adopted in 1974 to capture for the government more of the earnings from bauxite.

Jamaica's economy deteriorated during the 1970s. Negative growth occurred each year from 1973 and 1980, and production of traditional export crops, bauxite–alumina, and manufactured goods fell. Jamaica's balance of payments performance worsened, and net international reserves declined in 1980. During the late 1970s, Jamaica entered into two successive agreements with the IMF, which lapsed when performance criteria were not met. The Manley government finally decided to break negotiations with the IMF in 1980.

Both external and internal factors contributed to the economic decline. The impact of the middecade recession in the industrialized countries on sugar and aluminum demand, the increase in interest rates in international capital markets, and in particular, the large increases in oil prices all adversely affected Jamaica. The government's social welfare and land redistribution programs led to an overextended public sector and a growing budget deficit. Government policies, such as the bauxite levy, also were responsible for a decline in production in the export sector. The government's increasingly socialist-style rhetoric and growing friendship with Cuba discouraged tourists and foreign investors and influenced local capital and skilled manpower to emigrate.

On assuming office in 1980, the Seaga government attempted to revitalize the economy using a private sector and export-oriented strategy. It entered into a three-year extended fund facility agreement with the IMF in April 1981 and obtained additional official and commercial financing for raw material and capital goods imports. The government launched initiatives to attract foreign investment and to diversify the production of nontraditional agricultural crops.

The economy grew by 3 percent in 1981, the first year of positive growth since 1972; inflation was reduced from 25 to 5 percent. But the momentum was not maintained: growth was marginally positive during 1982 and 1983, and inflation rose. In 1984, the economy declined by 0.4 percent while the Jamaican dollar depreciated by 50 percent; restrictive fiscal and monetary measures were implemented within the framework of the

IMF standby agreement; and unfavorable external market conditions and underlying structural problems continued. In 1985, domestic production contracted by 3.7 percent due to a short fall in bauxite–alumina exports, a decline in real investment, and continued tight monetary and fiscal measures designed to secure an improvement in the balance of payments. Consumer prices rose by 23 percent, down from 31.2 percent in 1984. The central government deficit was reduced from 6 percent of GDP in 1984 to 85 to about 5.2 percent in 1985 to 86. However, the deficits of both the Bank of Jamaica and publicly owned enterprises rose, largely because of interest on foreign debt. New economic measures were taken during 1985 and early 1986; the Jamaican dollar stabilized in late 1985; and a tax reform package was enacted in January 1986.

Although Jamaica faces a difficult short-term economic situation, the long-term economic outlook is more promising. Increased tourism, a revival in the bauxite industry, trade benefits under the U.S. Caribbean Basin Initiative, the impact of the 1986 Canadian CARIBCAN agreement, and access to the EEC under the Lome Convention are all seen as positive.

Business

Jamaica welcomes foreign investment, particularly in areas that earn or save foreign exchange, generate employment, and use local raw materials. The government provides a wide range of incentives to investors, including remittance facilities, tax holidays, and duty-free access to machinery and raw materials imported for approved enterprises. To facilitate the investment process, the prime minister has established a joint-investment committee that sets time frames for execution by official entities of specific responsibilities in the investment process.

Garment manufacturing, light manufacturing, and data entry are some of the activities being undertaken by Jamaican and foreign-owned firms in the country's free zones. Over 120 U.S. firms have operations in Jamaica, and total private U.S. investment, including bauxite and alumina, has been established at over US$1 billion (as at the end of 1986).

The Jamaican government's Jamaica National Investment Promotion, Limited, (JNIP) is the country's investment promotion agency. JNIP provides a number of services to foreign investors, Jamaican investors, or both with the intent of expanding and diversifying the country's productive base. JNIP's services extend from the inquiry stage through project implementation and beyond. Such services include:

- the compilation and provision of general, economic data on Jamaica

Exhibit **C6.4**   Principal Trading Partners (J$'000)

	1982	1983
Imports		
Canada	107,885	121,268
Japan	99,130	109,373
Netherlands	29,055	18,324
Netherlands Antilles	324,187	307,994
Trinidad and Tobago	103,535	63,721
United Kingdom	191,842	190,484
United States	868,860	1,111,374
Venezuela	353,345	313,769
Total (incl. others)	2,460,309	2,840,991
*Exports**		
Barbados	19,319	27,551
Canada	159,139	166,475
Ghana	51,584	13,843
Germany, Federal Republic	6,649	7,195
Norway	108,489	113,345
Trinidad and Tobago	96,320	127,001
United Kindgom	250,536	272,503
United States	441,720	455,518
Venezuela	18,743	11,188
Total (incl. others)	1,328,108	1,363,671

Note: *Excluding reexports.

Source: "Jamaica Statistical Survey," *The Europa Yearbook 1985—A World Survey,* vol. II *(London: Europa Publications, Limited, 1985).*

- acting on behalf of potential investors in obtaining such government permits and approvals as work permits, import licenses, and investment incentives
- matching of foreign and local investors in joint-venture partnerships
- feasibility studies and business counseling
- providing access to local and international sources of financing.

JNIP has assisted with a wide variety of projects. The following figures summarize export orientation and capital investment by sector of this assistance:

Export orientation

Indirect exporters	14%
Direct exporters	34%
Potential exporters	51%

Capital investment by sector

Manufacturing	23%
Tourism	34%
Agribusiness	44%

Corporate income tax rates are:

- agricultural companies not engaged in prescribed agricultural activities—25 percent
- nonagricultural companies—35 percent *plus* all nonexempt companies are subject to additional profits tax of 10 percent
- corporate dividends on distribution—37.5 percent.

Exempt from corporate income tax are:

- companies accorded "approved status" under laws designed to promote investment in Jamaica, for periods ranging from five to ten years
- income from prescribed agricultural activities (which include horticulture, fruit growing, livestock keeping, and fishing or fish farming)
- manufacturing operations carried out under the Jamaica Export Free Zone Act and producing exclusively for export, in perpetuity.

Various incentive laws exist under which individual applications are examined on a case-by-case basis regarding maximum concessions possible from Jamaican government import duties, corporate income tax rates, and other general statutory provisions. Jamaica is a member of the International Monetary Fund (IMF). Jamaica guarantees repatriation of profits, dividends, and capital, after approval, based in part on evidence of the payment of any applicable withholding tax.

Infrastructure   **Transportation**   Railways in 1977 serviced 1.2 million passengers, 83 million net passenger-km, and 186 million net freight tn-km. Roads in 1973 to 1974 carried 151,591 licensed vehicles (including cars, trucks, tractors, buses, motorcycles, and trailers). In shipping in 1976, freight unloaded totaled 2,587,000 tn, and freight loaded 7,505,000 tn. Twenty-seven shipping companies connect Jamaica with foreign ports. In civil aviation in 1980, passengers carried totaled 676,000, and freight carried

C
O
U
N
T
R
Y

P
R
O
F
I
L
E
S

115 million tn-km. Ten regularly scheduled air carriers operate in and out of Jamaica.

Communications   There were 856,960 radio receivers in use in 1983; 119,000 telephones in use in 1980; and 3 daily newspapers (estimated combined daily circulation 128,000) in 1979.

Access   Major sea ports include Kingston, Montego Bay, and Port Antonio. International airports are located in Kingston and Montego Bay (runways between 2,700 and 4,000 yards).

Banking   The Bank of Jamaica is the central banking authority and has direct control over the country's monetary policy. (The Bank of Jamaica's function and authority is similar to that of the U.S. Federal Reserve System.) There are some thirteen commercial or merchant banks operating in Jamaica.

Education   Jamaica's Mona Campus of the University of the West Indies offers well-respected bachelor- and graduate-level courses in a number of disciplines, including medicine and the social sciences.

Government

The Constitution   The constitution came into force at the independence of Jamaica on 6 August 1962.

Head of State   The head of state is the British monarch, who is locally represented by a governor-general chosen on the advice of the prime minister and the leader of the Opposition.

The Legislature   The Senate or Upper House consists of twenty-one senators, 13 of whom will be appointed by the governor-general on the advice of the prime minister, and eight by the governor-general on the advice of the leader of the Opposition. The House of Representatives consists of sixty elected members of Parliament.

The Privy Council   The Privy Council consists of six members appointed by the governor-general after consultation with the prime minister, at least two of whom are persons who hold or have held public office. The functions of the Council are to advise the governor-general on the exercise of the Royal Prerogative of Mercy and on appeals on disciplinary matters.

The Executive   The prime minister is appointed from the House of Representatives by the governor-general as the person who, in the governor-general's judgment, is best able to command the support of the majority of the members of that House. The leader of the Opposition is appointed by the governor-general as the member of the House of Representatives, who, in the governor-general's judgment, is best able to command the support of the majority of those members of the House who do not support the government. The Cabinet consists of the prime minister and not fewer than eleven other ministers appointed by the governor-general on the advice of the prime minister.

The Judicature   The judicature consists of a Supreme Court, a Court of Appeal, and minor courts. Judicial matters, notably advice to the governor-general on appointments, are considered by a Judicial Service Commission.

Membership in International Organizations   Jamaica is a member of the UN and some of its specialized and related agencies, including the World Bank, General Agreement on Tariffs and Trade, and Inter-American Development Bank (IDB). In addition, Jamaica belongs to the Organization of American States, Group of 77, Non-Aligned Movement, Commonwealth, Caribbean Development Bank (CDB), Caribbean Community and Common Market (CARICOM), International Bauxite Association (IBA), and INTELSAT, and has access to the European Economic Community under the Lome convention.

Life-Style and Travel Notes

Jamaica has a rich cultural history. There is a thriving indigenous artistic community producing internationally acclaimed crafts; short stories, poetry, and other literary works; and music. The local Rastafarian movement has found adherents both locally and throughout the Caribbean islands; beyond its original religious orientation, many of the region's youth have adopted its particular approach to life.

A multiracial society, Jamaica has a vibrant artistic milieu, with much emphasis culturally on tracing ethnic origins, especially African. Reggae music, born out of these roots, has become internationally known and adopted by many popular non-Jamaican musicians.

A friendly people, Jamaicans are fiercely proud of their nation, and are known for their strongly held political affiliations. As is true in much of the English-speaking Caribbean, Jamaicans (by comparison to the cultural mores of North America) are a relatively easygoing people: the foreign investor would be well advised to allow a longer period to see projects negotiated and effected. Jamaica is an open society, welcoming foreigners into their midst. For the foreign investor, the island's striking natural beauty and pleasant climatic conditions offer much that is attractive. International-level hotel and residence accommodations are readily available, although, particularly in the Kings-

C
O
U
N
T
R
Y

P
R
O
F
I
L
E
S

ton area, foreigners are advised to take precautions toward personal and property security.

Climate and Clothing Summer clothes are suitable year round. The evenings can be chilly, especially from November through March, and light wraps or sweaters are recommended.

Customs For U.S. citizens, a passport or other proof of U.S. birth or citizenship is required for entry. Visas are not required except of official and diplomatic travelers. No inoculations are required.

Health Municipal water supplies are potable. Fruits and vegetables are safe. Doctors are available twenty-four hours in Kingston and in the principal resort areas.

Telecommunications International telephone and telegraph services are good. Jamaica is in the eastern standard time zone.

Transportation Local buses are overcrowded but provide fairly regular service. Taxis are available. Almost all main roads are paved; but as Jamaica is mountainous, they are often narrow and winding, with uneven surfaces. Jamaica has a thriving rental car business. Traffic moves on the left.

Tourist Attractions

Kingston

National Gallery of Jamaica	New Castle
Jamaica Conference Center	Devon House
Hope Botanical Gardens	Zoo
University of West Indies	Pine Grove
Castleton Gardens	Port Royal
Fort Clarence and Hellshire Beach	Lime Cay
Caymanus Park	Caymanus Club

Port Antonio

Reach Falls	San San Beach
River Rafting-Rio Grande	Boston Bay
Frenchman's Cove Beach	Mitchell's Folly

Ocho Rios

Strawberry Fields	Harmony Hall
Mammee Bay Beach	Shaw Park Gardens
Fern Gully	Dunns River Falls

C O U N T R Y

P R O F I L E S

Montego Bay

Greenwood Great House

Rose Hall Great House

Rockland Feeding Station (bird sanctuary)

Profile 7 Japan

This report has been prepared from information provided by:

Department of State, Bureau of Public Affairs, *Background Notes—Japan* (Washington, D.C.: U.S. Government Printing Office, February 1987).

"The Japan of Today," Ministry of Foreign Affairs, Japan.

Japan: A Pocket Guide, 1986 ed., Foreign Press Center, Japan

Geography

Area Japan consists of four main islands—Hokkaido, Honshu, Shikoku, and Kyushu—in addition to a number of island chains and thousands of smaller islands and islets. The archipelago, lying off the eastern coast of the Asian continent, stretches in an arc, 2,360 mi (3,800 km) long. It covers an area of 145,834 sq mi (377,708 sq km).

Climate The islands of Japan lie in the temperate zone and at the northeastern end of the monsoon area; the climate is generally mild, although it varies considerably from place to place. The four seasons are clearly distinct. Summer, which is warm and humid, begins around the middle of July following a rainy season that lasts about a month. Except in northern Japan, winter is mild. Spring and autumn are balmy with bright sunshine, although in September typhoons may strike with torrential rains and violent winds. Rainfall is abundant and snow is heavy in the northern parts of the country and in the interior mountainous regions in winter, providing good sites for winter sports. Tokyo, the capital city, enjoys a relatively mild winter with low humidity and only an occasional snowfall. The combination of plentiful rainfall and a temperate climate produces rich forests and luxurious vegetation that cover the entire countryside.

C
O
U
N
T
R
Y

P
R
O
F
I
L
E
S

Exhibit **C7.1** Map of Japan

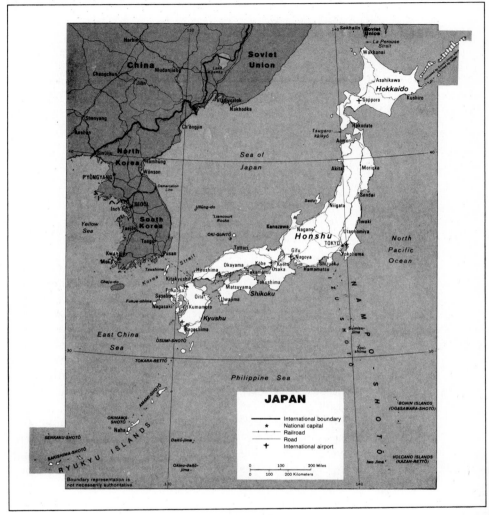

Topography Japan has a complex topography with a long and rocky coastline, many small but excellent harbors, and a large number of mountainous areas with many valleys, swift-flowing rivers, and lakes; mountains account for about 72 percent of Japan's total land area.

Demography Freedom of religion is guaranteed to all under the constitution of 1946. Buddhism is the major religion and had a following of 83,504,000 as of the end of 1979. Buddhism is important to Japan's culture and has exerted a profound influence on the

Exhibit **C7.2**   Demographic Data

Nationality: Noun and adjective—Japanese

Population (1985 est.): 121 million

Population Density: 822.8 persons per sq mi (317.7 per sq m)

Urban–Rural Dispersion: 76% urban

Ethnic Groups: Japanese; 0.6% Korean

Religions: Shintoism and Buddhism; 0.8% Christian

Language: Japanese

Education: 100% adult literacy

fine arts, social institutions, and thought. Most Japanese consider themselves members of one of the major Buddhist sects. Shintoism is an indigenous religion founded on myths, legends, and ritual practices of the early Japanese. Neither Buddhism nor Shintoism is an exclusive religion; most Japanese observe both Buddhist and Shinto rituals, the former for funerals and the latter for births, marriages, and other occasions. Confucianism, more an ethical system than a religion, continues to have a basic and pervasive influence on Japanese thought. About 1.5 million people in Japan are Christians; of these, approximately 60 percent are Protestant and 40 percent Roman Catholic.

Japan provides free public schooling for all children through six years of elementary school and three years of junior high school. Most students go on to three-year senior high schools, and those able to pass the difficult entrance examinations enter four-year universities or two-year junior colleges. Students may attend either public or private high schools, colleges, and universities, but they must pay tuition in any case. Japan enjoys one of the world's highest literacy rates, and nearly 90 percent of Japanese students complete high school.

Economy   Japan is a small island country, poorly endowed with natural resources and supporting a large population of 120 million. Nevertheless, the economy is a thriving complex of industry, commerce, finance, agriculture, and other elements of an industrialized structure, served by a massive flow of information and highly developed transportation networks. Manufacturing and service make a major contribution to the country's net domestic

C O U N T R Y   P R O F I L E S

product, while primary industries such as agriculture and fisheries have a minor share.

International trade is important to Japan's economy. In 1986, the ratio of manufactured imports to total imports reached a record of 41.8 percent. This can be attributed to an increase in the value of the yen and crude-oil price declines. The yen exchange rate against the U.S. dollar appreciated by 41.5 percent during 1986; this brought import prices down and at the same time lower crude-oil prices and stagnant primary-product prices caused the value of raw material and fuel imports to decrease, resulting in a higher manufactured import ratio.

In 1986, exports amounted to US$126.4 billion, down 2.4 percent from 1985, but manufactured imports hit an all-time high of US$52.8 billion, a 31 percent increase over the previous year.

Japan's surpluses in trade with the United States and the EEC have been growing, reaching US$39.5 billion with the United States and US$11.1 billion with the EEC in 1985; these surpluses have led to increasingly serious friction with these countries. Japan has responded by implementing a series of market-opening measures since 1981. These measures have included tariff-rate cuts that have brought Japan's rates down to a level lower than that of both the United States and the EEC. Recently, therefore, the thrust of U.S. and EEC demands has shifted toward the removal of the nontariff barriers presented by Japan's standards and certification systems and by its business practices; it has also shifted things in favor of the opening up of the service sector, including financial markets and lawyers' services. In July 1985, the Japanese government announced an "action pro-

Exhibit **C7.3** Economic Data

GNP (1985): US$1,322 trillion

Real Growth Rate: 4.5% in 1985; 4.3% in 1975–85

Per Capita GNP (1985): US$10,922

Natural Resources: Negligible mineral resources, and fish

Agriculture: Rice, vegetables, fruits, milk, meat, and silk

Industry: Machinery, equipment, metals and metal products, textiles, automobiles, chemicals, electrical, and electronic equipment.

Exhibit **C7.4** Trade Statistics

Exports (1985): US$175.6 billion

Major Markets: USA, 37.1%; EEC, 11.4%; Southeast Asia, 18.9%; communist countries, 9.2%

Imports (1985): US$129.5 billion

Major Suppliers: USA 19.9%; EEC, 6.9%; Middle East, 23.1%; Southeast Asia, 23.4%; Communist countries, 6.5%

Fiscal Year: 1 April–31 March

Exchange Rate (Sept. 1986): ¥155 = US$1

---

gram" comprising a wide-ranging package of measures to improve access to the Japanese market. The package goes far beyond all earlier steps Japan has taken in this area both quantitatively and qualitatively. The major planks of the program are (1) the reduction or elimination of tariffs on 1,865 items, (2) a complete overhaul of standards and certification systems, (3) a great simplification of government procurement formalities, and (4) a further liberalization of financial markets. The government has promised implementation of all the proposed measures within three years.

Government

The constitution upholds ideals of peace and democratic order, including the following provisions:

- The emperor is the symbol of the state and of the unity of the people. Sovereign power now rests with the people.
- Japan renounces war as a sovereign right. It also renounces the threat or use of force as a means of settling disputes with other nations.
- Fundamental human rights are guaranteed as eternal and inviolable.

Members of the House of Councillors and the House of Representatives are elected as representatives of all the people. The House of Representatives has preeminence over the House of Councillors. Executive power is vested in the Cabinet, which is collectively responsible to the Diet. Local self-government is established on an extensive scale. The emperor has no powers related to government. He performs only those acts stipulated in the constitution; thus, he appoints the prime minister and

COUNTRY PROFILES

Exhibit **C7.5** Government Data

> *Type:* Parliamentary democracy
>
> *Constitution:* 3 May 1947
>
> *Branches:* Executive—prime minister (head of government); legislative—bicameral Diet (House of Representatives and House of Councillors); judicial—civil law system with Anglo-American influence
>
> *Political Parties:* Liberal Democratic party (LDP), Japan Socialist party (JSP), Democratic Socialist party (DSP), Komeito (Clean Government party), Japan Communist party (JCP)
>
> *Suffrage:* Universal over 20
>
> *Political Subdivisions:* 47 prefectures
>
> *Flag:* Red sun on white field

the chief justice of the Supreme Court. The prime minister, however, is first designated by the Diet and the chief justice by the Cabinet.

Executive power is vested in the Cabinet, which consists of the prime minister and not more than twenty ministers of state and is collectively responsible to the Diet. The prime minister is designated by the Diet and must himself be a member of the Diet. He has the power to appoint and dismiss the ministers of state, all of whom must be civilians and a majority of whom must be members of the Diet.

Foreign Relations The basic objective of Japanese foreign policy is to contribute to world peace and stability and to the harmonious progress of the entire international community by further promoting cooperation and dialogue among the nations of the world. Japan has been ruled for more than thirty-five years by moderate and conservative political interests and is one of the most politically stable of all postwar democracies. A generally close cooperation among politicians, as well as an efficient and dedicated bureaucracy, have given cohesion to national policy making.

The conduct of Japan's monetary policy is entrusted to the nation's central bank, the Bank of Japan. The policy tools that the bank uses are the official discount rate, open-market operations, and reserve requirements. In the past, when virtually all interest rates were controlled, changing the discount rate was the most powerful means for the bank to implement its policies. Recently, in response to the deregulation and internationalization of Japan's financial markets, open-market operations have become more important, though the discount rate remains an important indicator of official policy. The Bank of Japan also regards the growth rate of the broad money supply (M2 + certificates of deposit), as an important monetary policy guideline. The annual rate of increase of this broad money supply has been fairly stable at around 8 percent in recent years.

Membership in International Organizations   Japan is a member of the UN and several of its specialized and related agencies, including the International Monetary Fund (IMF), International Court of Justice (ICJ), General Agreement on Tariffs and Trade, International Labor Organization, International Energy Agency (IEA), Organization for Economic Cooperation and Development (OECD), and INTELSAT.

Relationship with the United States   The two countries enjoy close and mutually beneficial economic relations, with two-way Japan–U.S. trade having exceeded US$63.9 billion in 1981. The two nations also share a commitment to democratic values and institutions, and the two governments are dedicated to a cooperative multilateral effort to strengthen world peace and promote world stability and economic social development.

Relationship with the Soviet Union   Japan and the Soviet Union have signed a joint declaration terminating the state of war between the two countries and reestablishing diplomatic relations. Relations have developed gradually but steadily in various fields, such as trade, aviation, and cultural interchange, and these relations are expanding year after year.

Relationship with China   Relations between Japan and China were normalized in September 1972 when the prime minister visited Peking to meet the Chinese leaders. Since then, ambassadors have been exchanged and the four agreements provided for in the Japan–China Joint Communique of September 1972—trade, aviation, shipping, and fishery—have been concluded. Thus, on the basis of this framework, relations with China are steadily developing. After a series of negotiations, the Treaty of Peace and Friendship was signed between the two countries in August 1978.

Relations with Other Asian Countries   It is Japan's basic policy to promote mutual understanding and friendly and coop-

C
O
U
N
T
R
Y

P
R
O
F
I
L
E
S

erative relationships with the nations of Asia and to contribute to the peace and prosperity of this region. The maintenance and furtherance of friendly and cooperative relations with the Republic of Korea (South Korea)—Japan's closest neighbor— is part of the basis of Japanese foreign policy. Positive cooperation with the Association of Southeast Asian nations (ASEAN) and Burma in their own efforts for peace and prosperity is stressed; and Japan has maintained diplomatic relations with the Socialist Republic of Vietnam since 1976, when North and South Vietnam were reunified. In 1976, diplomatic relations with Democratic Kampuchea were established, while the ties with Laos were preserved after the foundation of the Lao People's Democratic Republic in 1975.

Business

Smaller business establishments—defined as wholesale businesses with fewer than 100 employees, those in service-sector businesses with fewer than 50 employees, and those in all other businesses with fewer than 300 employees—account for 99 percent of all Japanese companies. They command about 50 percent of all shipments by manufacturing industries, about 60 percent of wholesale business, and about 80 percent of retail business. Many of these businesses have organized cooperative systems of one form or another for varied purposes such as common management and sharing of plant and sales facilities. The government encourages such moves through financial assistance and tax incentives.

The Japanese economy, though basically made up of private business firms, also includes a number of public business and financial corporations, such as the *kosha,* essentially a nationalized industry, and the *kodan,* a business organization wholly capitalized by the government.

Japan's labor force consists of more than 59 million workers, 40 percent of whom are women. Members of labor unions number about 12.5 million, or about 28.9 percent of the nonagricultural labor force. In December 1985, the unemployment rate was 2.6 percent.

"Lifetime employment," where workers who enter a company directly after finishing their education remain there until reaching retirement age, is more common than in the West. Wage increases are granted according to the length of service and employees receive semiannual bonuses or special cash earnings in addition to wages, overtime payments, and allowances (in 1981, the average total bonus payment for all industries amounted to the equivalent of 4.3 months of the regular wages).

Japanese wage levels have been going up rapidly since 1960, a rise made possible by the even faster rate of productivity gains. According to a Labor Ministry survey of business estab-

C
O
U
N
T
R
Y

P
R
O
F
I
L
E
S

lishments with 30 or more employees, average monthly wages per person were ¥310,463 in 1984. Income of regular workers is 50 percent higher at companies employing more than 5,000 workers than at those with fewer than 100 workers. Apart from the legally mandated social security expenses, Japanese companies spend substantial amounts on nonmandatory fringe benefits for workers.

Japan's labor–management system underwent a reorganization after World War II with the enactment of new labor legislation, which includes detailed provisions concerning labor–management relations, as well as employment practices. The Labor Standards Law stipulates working hours, paid holidays, safety and hygiene conditions, protection of women and young workers, and other minimum standards, which generally are similar to those of other countries. The following industries play an important role in the Japanese economy.

Metals   Production of metals, especially iron and steel, has expanded remarkably since World War II. Japan now ranks as the world's second largest steel producer after the Soviet Union. Japan's iron and steel industry depends heavily on imports of raw materials such as iron ore, coking coal, and scrap iron. The key to the development of Japan's steel production has been the modernization of facilities and the application of new technologies developed both in Japan and overseas.

Manufacturing   Even before World War II, Japan was not only self-sufficient in shipbuilding, rolling stock, and textile machinery but was exporting these items in considerable volume. Since the war, the machinery industry has set the pace for Japan's economic growth. Evidence of the growth, diversification and high technical standards of the Japanese machinery industry can be seen in almost every corner of the world. Ships made in Japanese yards sail the seven seas. Japanese cameras, transistor radios, and watches, television sets, tape recorders, and electronic calculators have a reputation for quality and are in wide demand in world markets. Japanese cars, buses, and trucks are helping to meet transportation needs on six continents. Electrical generators and other heavy electrical machinery made in Japan are helping supply light and power for homes and industries. Japanese spinning and weaving machinery is being used in the textile industries in many countries of Asia and other parts of the world. Machinery exports in 1984 amounted to US$119.8 billion, or 70.4 percent of total exports.

Electrical machinery represents a significant sector of Japanese industry. Exports of electric and electronic products amounted to US$44.6 billion, or 26.1 percent of total exports, in 1984.

Shipbuilding   In the early 1970s, Japan commanded more than 50 percent of the world market; the Japanese shipbuilding industry introduced new techniques, expanded and rationalized equipment, and developed economy-type bottoms, supplying high-grade and high-performance large bottoms to not only Japanese ship owners but also the world shipping industry. The oil crisis of late 1973 changed the course of the world economy from expansion to contraction, and brought about a sharp worldwide decline in transport of oil and other ocean cargoes. This led to a decline in the demand for new vessels; consequently, the Japanese shipbuilding industry, which until then had continued to develop along with the high growth of the Japanese economy, suffered a sharp decrease in orders, especially for supertankers. In 1979, this trend was reversed; orders received by Japanese shipbuilders were more than twice the figure of the previous year. In 1984, Japan's share of world shipbuilding was 53.1 percent and about 9.4 million ton were launched.

Motor Vehicles   The Japanese automobile industry has enjoyed steady growth parallel to the rapid development of motorized transport throughout the nation. In 1984, Japan's automobile industry was the largest in the world, producing about 11.5 million four-wheeled motor vehicles. Japan's motor vehicle exports totaled 6.4 million units in 1984, and motor vehicles were the largest export item in value, accounting for 17.5 percent of Japan's total export value that year. Exports of knock-down cars for overseas assembly and the manufacturing of car parts abroad has been growing; overseas assembly plants were first established in countries in Asia, Latin America, and Africa, and later in Oceania, the Middle East, Europe, and the United States. Japan is also the world leader in both the production and the export of motorcycles; in 1984, Japan produced 4.0 million motorcycles of which 2.1 million, or 52.6 percent, were exported.

Rolling Stock   Japan's highly developed network of public and private railways has ensured a steady demand for rolling stock. Production has been at a high level for the past decade because of extensive development of the Japanese National Railways (JNR) system and private lines. The technical standards of Japan's rolling stock industry are rated highly throughout the world.

Precision Machinery   The high technical standard and the rapid technological advance achieved by Japanese industries are reflected in the field of precision machinery. Outstanding examples are to be found in the optical goods industry, including cameras, binoculars, and electron microscopes, and in the growing production of timepieces, including watches, clocks, and precision timers.

Chemicals   The chemical industry represents one of the most important fields of industrial activity in Japan today. Japan now ranks among the world's major producers of various basic chemical raw materials. The extremely rapid growth of the industry has been achieved despite the fact that such essential materials as petroleum, salt, potassium salt, phosphate ore, and oils and fats have to be imported. The industry has undergone a significant structural change in recent years involving a shift in production from chemical fertilizers and industrial soda chemicals to synthetic organic chemicals such as synthetic resin and plastics.

Textiles   The textile industry is assuming a proportionately declining role in the economy, as emphasis has shifted from light to heavy industries. Before the war, textiles accounted for more than half of Japan's total exports. By 1981, they had declined to 5 percent.

Infrastructure

Banks   The Bank of Japan was established in 1882 as the central bank and is the sole issuer of bank notes. It plays the focal part in determining and carrying out monetary policies formulated by the Policy Board, which includes representatives of government agencies, banks, and industrial circles.

Private banks, which supply more than half of the nation's industrial funds, constitute the heart of Japan's financial institutions. Private financial institutions at the end of 1985 included city banks (of which there were 13), regional banks (64), foreign banks (77), long-term credit banks (3), trust banks (7), mutual savings and loan banks (69), credit associations (468), and credit cooperatives (448). There are also various government financial institutions, including the postal savings system.

The trust banking business has been the exclusive domain of the seven trust banks and Daiwa Bank, the only city bank authorized to conduct trust activities in the past. But, in response to pressure from foreign institutions attracted by the potential of Japan's private pension funds, it was decided in June 1985 to allow nine foreign banks to enter the domestic trust business.

Foreign exchange activities are conducted by credit associations, as well as by institutions ranging in size and scope from city banks to mutual savings and loan banks, with the result that external transactions can be settled easily anywhere in the country.

Bank of Japan statistics show that the financial resources managed by all of Japan's financial institutions in the form of deposits and savings (including pension and insurance reserves) totaled ¥580 trillion as of the end of March 1985—31 percent was held by city banks, 16 percent by the postal savings system, 15 percent by regional banks, and 8 percent by credit associations.

As a part of the move to make Japan's financial system more open, a process of interest-rate liberalization was instituted with money market certificates (minimum denomination ¥50 million) made available in March 1985, and interest rates on deposits of ¥1 billion or over were deregulated in October of the same year. The minimum maturity and denomination of certificates of deposit have also been lowered step-by-step.

Insurance Companies Insurance companies operating in Japan include 20 domestic life insurance companies, 18 foreign-affiliated life insurance companies, 21 nonlife insurance companies, 2 nonlife reinsurance companies, and some 42 foreign-affiliated nonlife insurance companies. As of March 1985, the volume of life insurance in force was 807.7 trillion, or 2.7 times the gross national product. The volume is second only to that of the United States.

Total savings by individuals, including insurance and securities, stood at ¥460 trillion at the end of March 1985. The propensity of the Japanese to save is very high by international standards, and a 1984 survey of wage earners' households revealed average savings of ¥6,489,000, an amount exceeding the average annual household earnings figure of ¥5,453,000.

Transportation The rapid growth of the Japanese economy has resulted in a heavy demand on transportation facilities, and Japan's transport industry has responded by introducing faster, safer, and more economical means of transportation. In fiscal 1984 (April 1984 to March 1985), Japan's domestic transport volume comprised 832.3 billion passenger-km of passenger traffic (up 1.3 percent over the previous year) and 434.6 billion tn-km of freight traffic (up 2.9 percent). Both passenger and freight traffic increased over 1983 thanks to improved economic conditions in Japan and abroad.

The greatest proportion of passenger traffic in fiscal 1984 was transported by passenger cars and buses (56.4 percent of all domestic passenger-km transported), followed by railways (38.9 percent), airplanes (4.0 percent), and ships (0.7 percent). The proportion of domestic freight traffic carried by ships in fiscal 1984 was 48.3 percent, followed by trucks (46.2 percent). The national railway system saw its share of the freight business drop from 6.4 percent in fiscal 1983 to 5.2 percent in 1984. Private railways carried 0.1 percent.

The Japanese National Railways, a public corporation, is the largest single railway enterprise in Japan. As of March 1985, the JNR was operating 13,105 mi (21,091 km) of railways and accounted for 59.9 percent of total railway passenger traffic (in passenger-km) and 97.8 percent of total railway freight traffic (in tn-km). The JNR operates trains faster than any but France's "Trains à grande vitesse," on the Shinkansen (literally, "new trunk lines"). At present, these trains run at a maximum speed of 240 km per hr. The JNR is, however, in trouble—burdened with a huge and growing debt; in fiscal 1984 alone, the JNR suffered net losses of ¥1,650 billion; as of the end of March 1985, its cumulative deficits totaled ¥12,275 billion, and its long-term debt outstanding came to ¥21,827 billion. In July 1985, the Japanese National Railways Reform Commission called for the JNR to be split up and privatized.

Japan has the world's second largest merchant fleet, after Liberia, with 40.4 million gross tn of shipping capacity in 1984, including both oceangoing and coastal vessels. There are problems, however, and in August 1985, Sanko Steamship, a major tanker operator, was forced into bankruptcy.

The number of passengers entering and exiting Japan on international air carriers stood at 16.1 million in fiscal 1984, 2.6 times the level of 10 years before. At the end of January 1986, there were 36 foreign carriers operating regularly scheduled flights in and out of Japan; among the Japanese carriers, Japan Air Lines enjoyed a virtual monopoly on scheduled international service. Regular flights link Japan with 77 foreign cities in 39 countries and Hong Kong. The volume of air freight to and from Japan in fiscal 1984 was 794,000 tn, 3.4 times the level of 10 years earlier.

As of June 1981, Japan had 1,789 mi (2,879 km) of expressways. The government has carried out, since 1954, plans for a national network of arterial expressways whereby eventually 32 routes will be built totaling approximately 5,154 mi (8,294 km). Subway lines are in service in eight large cities—Tokyo, Osaka, Nagoya, Kobe, Yokohama, Sapporo, Kyoto, and Fukuoka. Tokyo's ten lines covered a total distance of 116.1 mi (186.7 km) as of June 1981 and Tokyo now ranks fourth after New York, London, and Paris in total length of subway lines.

Medical Facilities   The government stresses the importance of preventive medicine and had established 855 health centers throughout the country by April 1982, as a means of improving environmental sanitation and preventing the spread of communicable diseases in their early stages. The number of doctors and dentists per 100,000 population was 156.2 and 53.6, respectively, at the end of 1980, indicating that Japan's stan-

C
O
U
N
T
R
Y

P
R
O
F
I
L
E
S

dards are now on a level more or less similar to Western nations that are advanced in public welfare. However, ratios vary by locality; they are high in urban districts, while insufficient in the remote inland areas or distant islands.

Schools As of May 1984, approximately 27.8 million people were receiving education at schools and universities throughout Japan. The school attendance rate for the nine years of compulsory education is 99.99 percent. The rate of advancement from compulsory education to upper secondary schools stood at 94.1 percent in 1984. The rate of advancement to universities and junior colleges was 35.6 percent.

Education from elementary through upper secondary school is conducted in accordance with teaching guidelines determined by the national government. Textbooks compiled by private firms in conformity with these guidelines must obtain the authorization of the Ministry of Education. Each locality chooses its textbooks from those that have received the ministry's approval. Textbooks for elementary and lower secondary schools are distributed to children free.

As of May 1981, a total of 7,179 foreign students were enrolled in Japanese universities. The majority of these students, or 5,578, were from Asia (including 776 from the Republic of Korea and 2,986 from Taiwan). There were 633 from North America, 337 from Europe, 297 from Latin America, 130 from the Middle East, 83 from Oceania, and 117 from Africa. In addition, many young people from Asia and other countries come to Japan for technical training at scientific and technological institutes or at various industrial plants and factories.

Mass Media The constitution guarantees freedom of speech, including freedom of the press, as a fundamental human right. Accordingly, there is no media censorship. In the case of television and radio broadcasting stations, which must operate within the limited range of the wavelengths available, the Wireless Telegraphy Law and the Broadcast Law of 1950 lay down the basic framework for operation. Although a license to set up a broadcasting station must be obtained from the government and renewed every three years, the Broadcast Law clearly leaves programming and program content to the discretion of the broadcasters themselves. There is virtually no government interference in broadcasting.

In October 1985, the nation's 125 daily newspapers had a combined circulation of 68.3 million; the diffusion rate was as high as 569 newspapers per 1,000 persons. Of the nation's total 1984 advertising expenditure, 28.7 percent, or ¥855.0 billion, went to newspapers. The total 1985 magazine circulation was estimated at 3.9 billion, weeklies accounting for 2.3 billion and monthlies for 1.6 billion. In 1985, the annual gross revenue from magazines was reported to be ¥1,013 billion.

The broadcasting system in Japan is divided into the public sector, represented solely by Nippon Hoso Kyokai (NHK, or the Japan Broadcasting Corporation), and the commercial sector. The viewing fees collected from households that have reception contracts with NHK (which are mandatory for owners of TV sets) are the corporation's only source of revenue. NHK operates a nationwide network with two medium-wave radio channels and two TV channels (each medium has separate channels for general and educational programs), one FM radio channel, and a shortwave overseas radio broadcasting service known as Radio Japan. Commercial broadcasting companies now in operation number 136; of these, 36 offer both radio and television services, 67 provide television services only, and 33 offer radio services only. All private broadcasting companies depend on advertising for revenue. In 1985, television companies captured 35 percent (¥1,054 billion) of the national advertising market. Radio took ¥156 billion, or 5.2 percent of the market. Almost every household has both radio and TV sets, and nearly all TV programs are broadcast in color.

Life-Style

Profound changes have occurred since the end of the war and are continuing to occur in Japanese family life. Postwar democratization has affected many aspects of family life, and a series of measures to democratize the nation's family system were carried out shortly after the war. For example, the Civil Code was revised in 1947 to give women equal legal status with men in all phases of life. Both husband and wife enjoy equality under the law, with equal rights in contracting marriage, in inheriting and owning property, and in suing for divorce. The recent rapid growth of Japan's economy has also had a major impact on daily living patterns. The changes in the cultural and living environment due to advanced urbanization and technological progress have served to strengthen the general tendency toward smaller family units, consisting basically of the immediate parents and children, as opposed to the large family unit of prewar years. In recent years, however, a reappraisal of the larger family unit has apparently been taking place as evidenced by an increase in the number of households in which parents live with their married children. Family solidarity still remains relatively strong in Japan, contributing in large measure to the stability of the people's lives.

The mode of living has also changed under the influence of widespread use of modern household appliances, together with the mass production of instant foods, an expanding supply of

COUNTRY PROFILES

frozen foods, ready-made clothes and other apparel, and various sorts of daily necessities. This has made possible additional time for relaxation, as well as educational and cultural pursuits for the entire family.

Profile 8 Malaysia

This report has been prepared from information provided by:

Department of State, Bureau of Public Affairs, *Background Notes—Malaysia* (Washington, D.C.: U.S. Government Printing Office, February 1986).

The Far East and Australia, 1984–1985, 16th ed. (London-Europa Publications, Limited, 1984).

Malaysia—Your Profit Center in Asia (Kuala Lumpur: Malaysian Industrial Development Agency, August 1986).

Geography

Malaysia occupies the southern half of the Malay Peninsula and the northern quarter of the neighboring island of Borneo West. They are separated by about 400 mi (650 km) by the South China Sea.

East Malaysia shares the island of Borneo with Brunei and the Indonesian territory of Kalimantan. It consists of the states of Sarawak and Sabah. Sarawak (the capital at Kuching) is about 500 mi (800 km) long and a maximum of 150 mi (240 km) wide; a broad, frequently swampy coastal plain, drained by wide rivers, merges into jungle-covered hills and mountains in the interior. Sabah has a narrow coastal plain and a mountainous, jungle-covered interior culminating in Mount Kinabalu, the highest peak in Southeast Asia at 13,455 ft (4,100 m). The capital of Sabah is the seaside city of Kofa Kinabalu.

A range of forested mountains runs north and south along the center of Peninsular Malaysia, flanked on the east and west by coastal plains. Peninsular Malaysia borders Thailand in the north and is separated from Singapore in the south by the narrow Johore Strait. About 50 percent of the area is covered by tropical jungle, the rest by extensive rubber or palm oil estates and other agricultural holdings. The coastline in the west is largely mangrove and mud flats, with occasional bays and other indentations. The east coast is a continuous stretch

Exhibit **C8.1** Map of Malaysia

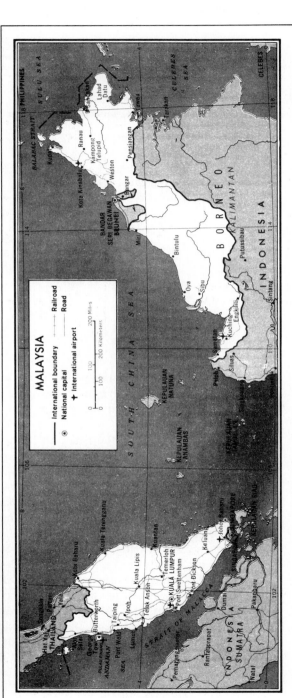

of sand and surf bordered by tropical vegetation. The total coastline is more than 1,200 mi (1,930 km).

The mean monthly temperature throughout most of Malaysia is 27° C, or 80° F. Malaysia experiences annual southwest and northwest monsoons; annual rainfall averages 100 in (254 cm).

Demography

The population of Malaysia is distributed as follows:

1986 Forecast in millions	
Peninsular	13,382
Sarawak	1,485
Sabah	1,228
Total	16,095

Malaysia's population comprises many ethnic groups. The largest, the Malays, make up 50 percent of the population. The politically dominant Malays are indigenous and, by constitutional definition, Muslim. They remain largely rural and economically lag behind the large Chinese and Indian minorities. Ethnic groups are distributed in Peninsular Malaysia as follows:

1986 Forecast in millions	
Malays	7.57
Chinese	4.38
Indians	1.347
Other	0.08

Nearly one-third of Malaysians are Chinese. Most of the Chinese are descended from families that immigrated during the nineteenth and early twentieth centuries. The Chinese are mainly urban and, by virtue of their important role in trade, business, and finance, possess considerable economic power. They speak various Chinese dialects including Mandarin. The majority are Confucianists, Buddhists, and Christians.

Malaysians of Indian descent make up nearly 10 percent of the population. Their ancestors cam from India, Pakistan, and Ceylon (now Sri Lanka), primarily as laborers on rubber plantations, around the turn of the twentieth century. Hindus, Buddhists, and Muslims continue to speak various Indian languages. Malaysian Indians are well represented in the professions, as well as in agriculture and the service trades.

Non-Malay indigenous groups make up more than 50 percent of Sarawak's population and about two-thirds of Sabah's, primarily Ibans among the former and Kadazan and Murut among

Exhibit **C8.2**   Demographic Data

Nationality: Noun and adjective—Malaysian

Population Distribution: 42% urban

Annual Growth Rate (1984 est.): 2.2%

Religions: Muslim, Hindu, Buddhist, Confucian, Christian
(Malaysians enjoy freedom of religious expression,
within a framework of state Islamic faith)

Languages: Malay, Chinese dialects, English, Tamil

Education: Years compulsory—9; attendance—96.5%
(primary), 48% (secondary); adult literacy 80% in
Peninsular Malaysia, 60% in Sabah and Sarawak

Health: Infant mortality rate—25/1,000

Life Expectancy: 66 years

the latter. The non-Malays are divided into dozens of distinct ethnic groups, but they share some general patterns of living and culture. Until quite recently most practiced traditional religions, but many have now become Christians or Muslims.

About 85 percent of Malaysia's population speaks Malay, the "national language," but with considerable variation in facility; English is used widely in government and business. Some of the indigenous people of East Malaysia and the aboriginal people of Peninsular Malaysia have adopted elements of the Malay culture and the Islamic religion; otherwise, cultural assimilation among the various ethnic groups has been limited. The Chinese, Malays, and Indians, while all considering themselves Malaysians, tend to maintain their own cultural identities.

Economy

During the past two decades, Malaysia has had one of the most successful economic records in Asia. The economy experienced impressive real growth, averaging 8 percent between 1971 and 1981. Inflation during the 1970s was low by world standards, averaging 5 to 6 percent. Malaysia's traditional exports (tin, rubber, palm oil, and timber) grew in volume and value during the late 1970s, while the petroleum sector expanded rapidly and Malaysia became an oil exporter. New foreign and domestic investment in manufacturing, much of it from the United States, led to increasing exports of electronic compo-

Exhibit **C8.3** Economic Data

> *Natural Resources:* Petroleum, liquefied natural gas (LNG), tin, and minerals.
>
> *Agriculture:* Rubber, palm oil, timber, cocoa, rice, pepper, pineapples, and forestry
>
> *Industry:* Electronics, electrical products, rubber products, automobile assembly, and textiles.

nents, textile products, and other manufactured goods. Manufacturing grew from 13.4 percent of the GDP in 1970 to 18 percent in 1984.

Malaysia felt the effects of the 1981 to 1982 worldwide recession. Depressed demand for Malaysia's traditional commodity exports pushed prices to record lows in real terms. Malaysia's financial position remains strong, however, and the country has had little difficulty in arranging overseas loans on favorable terms. Foreign reserves at the end of 1984 were about US$4 billion, sufficient to finance 3.6 months of merchandise imports.

Malaysia's prospects for continuing growth and prosperity are good. When demand in the industrialized countries picks up, Malaysia's export earnings should recover and grow quickly. Petroleum and gas production is expected to grow steadily as new fields reach full production.

Agriculture is still the largest sector of the Malaysian economy, although its relative importance has declined. In 1984, it accounted for about 21 percent of the GDP, provided employment for about 36 percent of the labor force, and accounted for 36 percent of Malaysia's export earnings.

Natural rubber continues to be an important part of the economy; although crude oil and palm oil now exceed rubber in export earnings, Malaysia participates in the International Natural Rubber Organization, which seeks to stabilize rubber prices. In recent years, palm oil has overshadowed rubber as the "golden" crop. Palm oil is a vegetable oil used for a variety of purposes such as cooking oil, soap, and as an ingredient in margarine. Malaysia is the world's number-one palm oil producer, and production is expected to increase as new acreage is developed and trees mature.

Timber is also important as a foreign exchange earner, and Malaysia is one of the world's largest exporters of tropical hardwood. All of the timber exported from Malaysia comes from virgin forest in East Malaysia. Malaysia exports large quantities of pepper (from Sarawak), cocoa, and coconut products, as well. Government price supports and production subsidies have helped to increase the production of rice to about 75 percent of domestic consumption. Malaysia produces most of its domestically consumed rice, pork, and chicken, but relies on imports of beef, dairy, vegetable, wheat, and some fruit products.

Malaysia's economy has become increasingly reliant on the petroleum sector. Oil production in 1984 reached 440,000 barrels per day, and oil and gas exports accounted for about 27 percent of 1984 export earnings. All of Malaysia's liquefied natural gas (LNG) exports are shipped to Japan from East Malaysia. Oil production is roughly equally divided between fields offshore of East Malaysia and Peninsular Malaysia. Gas reserves offshore of West Malaysia are currently being developed to supply Peninsular Malaysia and Singapore. All petroleum and LNG is produced under production-sharing agreements between the national oil company, PETRONAS, and foreign oil companies.

Malaysia remains the world's largest exporter of tin, although weakening demand for tin and export restrictions have reduced production by one-third since 1980. Malaysia is a party to the Sixth International Tin Agreement (1982), which seeks to stabilize prices through a buffer stock and export controls.

Before independence in 1957, only a few local industries were developed, and engineering industries were limited to repair work and the manufacture of spare parts. Since 1957, the government has promoted industrialization to provide employment for the rapidly expanding labor force and to buffer the economy against excessive dependence on exports of primary commodities. Manufacturing has been a rapidly growing sector. Major products are motor vehicles, electrical products, and textiles. Malaysia is the world's leading exporter of integrated circuits.

Business

The Malaysian government has recently given greater emphasis to the role of the private sector in development of the economy. The government has also taken steps to privatize a number of government-owned corporations and government agencies including the national airline and telecommunications. Historically, the Malaysian government has pursued a policy of caution and prudence in economic development and has taken steps to reduce government expenditures and foreign borrowing. The economy is relatively open, although there are high tariffs on some individual products.

The Malaysian government encourages foreign investment. Total foreign investment including petroleum is conservatively estimated at US$10 billion. The Malaysian Industrial Development Authority and state economic development agencies assist foreign investors in investing in Malaysia, and the Investment Incentives Act of 1972 provides substantial incentives to foreign investors. U.S. investment alone is approximately US$3 billion, most of which is invested in petroleum development and integrated circuit production. Japan and Singapore also have substantial investments.

The twenty-year New Economy Policy (NEP), adopted in 1971, aims to eradicate poverty and eliminate the identification of race with economic function. This program has been implemented by expanding equity, employment, and educational opportunities for the economically disadvantaged *bumiputra* (ethnic Malays and other indigenous groups). The program does not seek to transfer wealth from one group to another but, rather, to channel a greater portion of incremental growth toward the *bumiputra* with a minimum of dislocation to the private sector. A goal of the policy is that, by 1990, *bumiputra* will control 30 percent of the corporate equity of limited companies in Malaysia; other Malaysians will control 40 percent and foreign interests will control no more than 30 percent (this contrasts with 4 percent, 34 percent and 62 percent, respectively, in 1971).

Considerable progress toward attainment of NEP goals has been achieved through the purchase of stock in limited companies at market prices by government agencies on behalf of *bumiputra* and as a result of generalized economic progress. By 1983, *bumiputra* ownership had risen to 18.7 percent, and that of other Malaysians to 47.7 percent. Another goal is for the employment structure to reflect the national ethnic composition, particularly in managerial and technical positions.

Malaysia recognizes the role played by foreign investors in achieving the economic growth on which the NEP is based. The government has been flexible in implementing the NEP guidelines. Generally, foreign firms have accepted the NEP in doing business in Malaysia, and they recognize that the achievement of its goals is important to maintaining a favorable environment for their activities in Malaysia. Exhibit C8.4 summarizes applications for projects received by the Malaysian Industrial Development Authority in 1985 and 1986.

Malaysia's principal investment incentives for the manufacturing, agricultural, and tourist sectors are contained in the Promotion of Investments Act of 1986, and the Income Tax Act of 1967. Exemptions are possible from:

- income tax (40 percent rate)
- development tax (5 percent)
- excess profits tax (3 percent).

COUNTRY PROFILES

Exhibit **C8.4**   MIDA Applications Received for the Establishment of Industrial Projects, 1985 and 1986

	New projects		Expansion/ diversification		Total	
	1985	1986	1985	1986	1985	1986
Number	544	242	230	130	774	372
Potential employment	40,675	27,710	17,926	10,227	58,601	37,937
Proposed called-up capital (US$ Million)	1,689.1	1,224.3	173.4	83.2	1,862.5	1,307.5
Malaysian equity:						
bumiputra	861.4	412.8	62.6	17.8	924.0	430.6
non-bumiputra	359.1	416.5	67.0	25.5	426.1	442.0
Foreign equity	468.6	395.0	43.8	39.9	512.4	434.9
Loan (US$ million)	4,069.6	2,830.1	392.7	145.7	4,462.3	2,975.8
Total proposed capital investmment (US$ million)	5,758.7	4,054.4	566.1	228.9	6,324.8	4,283.3

Some specific provisions are as follows:

1. Manufacturing sector incentives include:

   - pioneer status—five-year relief from tax
   - investment tax allowance (alternative to pioneer status)—up to 100 percent of qualifying capital expenditures in first five years
   - accelerated depreciation allowance
   - reinvestment allowance
   - industrial building allowance.

2. Export-oriented incentives include:

   - export credit refinancing scheme—preferential interest rate financing concerning exports
   - double deductions on export credit insurance premiums and on promotion of export expenses.

3. Research and development (R and D) incentives include:

   - double deductions for approved R and D.

4. Agricultural sector incentives include:

   - pioneer status (as above)
   - investment tax allowance (as above)
   - agricultural allowance—certain capital expenditures are given preferential deduction rates

- export allowance—5 percent of free on board (f.o.b.) value of exports.

5. Tourist sector incentives include:

- pioneer status (as above)
- investment tax allowance (as above)
- industrial building allowance
- incentives for tour operators—relief from income tax on profits realized on foreign tourist tours.

Salaries and wages vary according to industry and profession. Exhibits C8.5 and C8.6 show some figures for 1984.

Government

Malaysia is a constitutional monarchy, nominally headed by the *Yang di-Pertuan Agong,* or paramount ruler. The ruler is elected for a five-year term from among the nine sultans of the Peninsular Malaysian states, who meet regularly to consider matters of importance to the royalty. The ruler is also the leader of the Islamic faith in Malaysia, as are the sultans in their own states.

Exhibit **C8.5** Salaries—Management Personnel (currency in Malaysian Ringgit, M$)

Occupations	Salary per month—M$
Chemist	900–1,200
Engineer	1,200–1,300
Accountant	1,100–1,200
Assistant accountant	750– 850
Personnel officer	900–1,200
Executive officer	900–1,100
Technical assistant	700– 900
Economist	900–1,200
Public relations officer	800–1,200

Most companies supplement salaries with benefits such as:

- free medical treatment
- insurance coverage (life and accident)
- transportation subsidies
- entertainment allowances
- 2- to 3-week vacations annually
- annual bonuses
- retirement provisions

Source: Malaysian Industrial Development Authority, *Malaysia—Manpower for Industry,* Kuala Lumpur, August 1985.

COUNTRY PROFILES

Exhibit **C8.6** Average Monthly Wage Rates for Selected Occupations and Industries (M$)

Occupation	Industrial Machinery & Parts	Plywood	Chemicals	Electronics	Textiles
Office clerk					
Male	300–760	300–475	350–800	330–670	280–640
Female	250–570	250–440	350–750	300–700	280–550
Bookkeeping clerk					
Male	350–700	380–600	350–800		
Female	350–760	295–650	650–1000		
Typist					
Female	250–500	295–650	300–550	290–750	280–500
Plant maintenance mechanic					
Male	280–950	480–800		390–1200	230–550
Female				310–920	
Production Supervisor					
Male	530–1700	490–1300	620–1600	690–2000	450–1110
Female		380–490	350–1000	640–1500	350–610
Moulder (floor foundry)					
Male	340–820				
Moulder (pit foundry)					
Male	430–880				
Machine setter operator					
Male	380–740				
Lathe setter operator					
Male	320–820				

Occupation				
Metal products, fitter assembler				
Male	320–820			
Welder				
Male	390–920			
Boiler-Maker				
Male	380–1000			
Laboratory technician				
Male		750–1000	800–1000	450–650
Rubber Millman				
Male		450–850		
Female		450–800		
Rubber Compounder				
Male		250–560		
Rubber extruding machine operator				
Male		270–560		
Female		200–370		
Rubber molding press operator				
Male		500–870		
Female		250–370		
Rubber goods assembler				
Male		250–550		
Female		250–500		
Packer				
Male		200–450	320–900	
Female		200–600	250–760	
Mixing machine operator				
Male		380–620		
Female		250–350		

continued

Exhibit **C8.6** continued

Occupation	Industrial Machinery & Parts	Plywood	Chemicals	Electronics	Textiles
Cooker, chemical & related processors					
Male			380–1000		
Reactor-convertor					
Male			420–1000		
Quality control inspector					
Male				290–710	
Female				260–570	
Material handler					
Male				250–500	
Female				250–660	
Carpenter					
Male					280–600
Textile bleacher					
Male					200–470
Female					190–360
Garment cutter					
Female					160–510
Spinner					
Female					160–280
Sewer					
Female					160–480

Source: Malaysian Industrial Development Authority, *Malaysian Industrial—Manpower for Industry,* Kuala Lumpur, August, 1985, p. 8.

Exhibit **C8.7** Government Data

Type: Federal parliamentary democracy on the Westminster model with a constitutional monarch.

Independence: 31 August 1957 *Constitution:* 1957

Branches: Executive—*Yang di-Pertuan Agong* (head of state, with ceremonial duties), prime minister (head of government), Cabinet; legislative—bicameral Parliament, comprising 58-member Senate (26 elected by the 13 state assemblies, 32 appointed by the king) and 154-member House of Representatives (elected from single-member constituencies); judicial—Federal Court, high courts

Political Parties: National Front (Borisan Nasional), a broad coalition comprising the United Malays National Organization (UMNO) and 10 other parties, most of which are ethnically based; Democratic Action party; Islamic party (PAS); Saboh United party; including the foregoing, there are over 30 registered political parties, 3 of which have representatives in the federal partliament.

Suffrage: Universal adult, over age 21

Subdivisions: 13 states and the federal territory (capital— Kuala Lumpur); each state has an assembly and government headed by a chief minister; 9 of these states have hereditary rulers, generally titled "sultan," while the remaining 4 have appointed governors in counterpart positions.

Membership in International Organizations: UN (including the World Bank, IMF, GATT, UNESCO, and International Atomic Energy Agency); Association of South East Asian Nations; Asian Development Bank; Five-Power Defense Arrangement; Commonwealth; Non-Aligned Movement; Organization of the Islamic Conference; INTELSAT

Flag: A yellow cresent (representing Islam) and star lie on a blue field in the upper left corner; the star's 14 points and the flag's 14 red and white stripes represent the original states of Malaysia

Executive power is vested in the Cabinet and led by the prime minister—the leader of the political party that wins the most seats in a parliamentary election. The Cabinet is chosen from among members of Parliament and is responsible to that body.

In the 1982 federal elections, the United Malays National Organization (UMNO)—led by the National Front—won 140 of the 154 seats in the lower house of Parliament. In simultaneous state assembly elections in Peninsular Malaysia, the National Front won 282 of 312 seats and retained control of all 11 peninsular state governments. An opposition party won control of the East Malaysian state of Sabah in 1985.

In world affairs, Malaysia maintains a nonaligned posture. Support for regional cooperation is viewed as the cornerstone of Malaysia's foreign policy, and Malaysia has participated in the Association of South East Asian Nations since the organization's inception in 1967.

The government has emphasized enhanced relations with Islamic countries and Asian neighbors. In its "look east" policy, the government has urged Malaysians to view Japan and South Korea as models for Malaysia's economic development.

Infrastructure   See Exhibit C8.8.

Exhibit **C8.8**   Transportation Information

	1980	1981	1982
Railways			
(Peninsular Malaysia)			
Freight ('000 m tn)	3,668	3,429	3,316
Freight (tn-km '000)	1,198,933	1,128,208	1,112,805
Passenger journeys ('000)	8,130	8,032	7,792
Passenger-km ('000)	1,631,008	1,663,769	2,041,427
Road traffic			
(registered vehicles in use)			
Private motor cycles	1,459,727	1,634,184	1,831,001
Private motor cars	847,089	942,649	1,050,617
Buses	15,287	15,608	17,099
Trucks and vans	190,081	207,800	227,283
Taxis	18,912	21,188	23,002
Other	101,692	112,998	108,554

Exhibit **C8.8** continued

	1980	1981	1982
Shipping (vessels over 75 net registered tons)			
Entered:			
No. of vessels	5,611	5,961	6,534
'000 net registered tn	34,132	36,362	41,654
Cleared:			
No. of vessels	5,558	5,959	6,499
'000 net registered tn	34,072	36,102	39,886
Coastal trade (Peninsular Malaysia)			
Entered:			
No. of vessels	6,210	7,736	5,889
'000 net registered tn	3,456,833	4,025,503	3,239,437
Cleared:			
No. of vessels	6,172	7,740	5,868
'000 net registered tn	3,424,286	4,024,196	3,258,686
Civil aviation			
No. of aircraft			
Landings	91,969	99,377	97,902
Take offs	121,383	132,399	140,609
No. of passengers			
Embarked	3,576,761	4,589,536	4,597,188
Disembarked	3,570,003	4,441,907	4,700,284
Total freight handled ('000) kg.			
Landed	31,468	33,430	36,976
Dispatched	26,604	28,399	29,973
Total mail handled ('000 kg)			
Landed	4,456	5,511	5,929
Dispatched	3,564	5,234	6,289
Communications media			
Television receivers licensed	1,118,527	1,226,056	1,303,985
Radio receivers licensed	276,981	291,905	259,250
Telephone subscribers	395,640	488,675	585,387

Life-Style and Travel Notes

History The early Buddhist Malay kingdom of Sriwijaya, based at what is now Palembang, Sumatra, dominated much of the Malay Peninsula from the ninth to the thirteenth centuries A.D. The powerful Hindu kingdom of Majapahit, based on Java, gained control of the Malay Peninsula in the fourteenth century. Con-

COUNTRY PROFILES

version of the Malays to Islam, beginning in the early fourteenth century, accelerated with the rise of the State of Malacca under the rule of a Muslim prince.

Malacca was a major regional entrepot, where Chinese, Arab, Malay, and Indian merchants traded precious goods. Drawn by this rich trade, a Portuguese fleet conquered Malacca in 1511, marking the beginning of European expansion into Southeast Asia. The Dutch ousted the Portuguese from Malacca in 1641, and in 1795 were replaced by the British, who had occupied Penang in 1786.

Full European control over the sultanates of the Malay peninsula, Sabah, and Sarawak was not achieved until the latter half of the nineteenth century. In 1826, the British settlements of Malacca, Penang, and Singapore were combined to form the Colony of the Straits Settlements. From these strong points in the nineteenth and early twentieth centuries, the British established protectorates over the Malay sultanates on the peninsula. Four of these states were consolidated in 1895 as the Federated Malay States.

During British control, a well-ordered system of public administration was established, public services were extended, and large-scale rubber and tin production was developed. To provide manpower for the rapidly expanding economy, the British colonial government encouraged immigration from China and India until the 1930s.

The Federation of Malaysia was established in 1948 from the British territories of Peninsula Malaysia, and independence from the United Kingdom was negotiated under the leadership of Tunku Abdul Rahman, who became prime minister. The British colonies of Singapore, Sarawak, and Sabah (North Borneo) joined the Federation of Malaya to form Malaysia on 16 September 1963. Singapore withdrew, however, on 9 August 1965, and became an independent republic. Neighboring Indonesia objected to the formation of Malaysia and pursued a program of economic, political–diplomatic, and military "confrontation" against the new country. This confrontation policy ended after the fall of Indonesia's President Sukarno in 1966, soon after which cordial Malaysian-Indonesian relations were established.

After World War II, local Communists, almost all Chinese, expanded their influence and planned for an armed struggle. A state of emergency was declared in June 1948, and a long, bitter guerrilla war ensued. The emergency ended in 1960; however, remnants of the Communists regrouped in southern Thailand, where they still clung to bases in the rugged border area. In recent years, small bands of Communist guerrillas have occasionally been encountered in northern Peninsula Malaysia. A small-scale Communist insurgency, which began in the mid-1960s in Sarawak, has been nearly extinguished.

Malaysia welcomes foreign investment, as evidenced by its incentives geared toward attracting non-Malaysian capital and technical expertise. The government, however, has set guidelines for foreign investment infusions with special reference to its *bumiputra*-related goals.

For the foreigner residing in Malaysia, the country's cosmopolitan air and rich cultural heritage offer much that is attractive. Foreign-geared schools exist for the education of children of expatriates, as do international-level resort shopping, housing, and recreational facilities.

Customs   Visas are not required of U.S. citizens arriving as tourists or for business for less than fifteen days. Business travelers who will be residing in Malaysia, and visitors for purposes other than business or tourism should arrange for visas with a Malaysian embassy in advance. Vaccination certificates for cholera and yellow fever are required only of visitors arriving from infected areas.

Climate and Clothing   Lightweight clothing is generally suitable for the tropical climate, except in the highland resort areas where somewhat warmer clothing is needed.

Telecommunications   Telephone service to the United States is available twenty-four hours daily, and except during the Christmas season, requires no advance booking. Direct dialing for international phone calls is available from some Kuala Lumpur exchanges. Telegraph service is also available. Kuala Lumpur is thirteen hours ahead of eastern standard time.

Transportation   The modern Subang International Airport is 12 mi (19 km) from Kuala Lumpur. Many daily flights connect the capital with most major cities in the region, Europe, the Middle East, and North America. Daily train service connects Kuala Lumpur with Penang, Singapore, and Bangkok. Bus transportation is available. Taxis are metered, and fares are reasonable. Traffic moves on the left.

Tourist Attractions   Malaysia has a well-developed tourist industry with excellent hotels and a great variety of restaurants in the capital. Besides the capital's sights, such as the National Mosque, Parliament, and the National Museum, a stay in Kuala Lumpur offers the traveler the opportunity to visit nearby rubber estates and tin mines. The hill resorts to the north offer a refreshing change from Malaysia's tropical climate. Penang (Pulau

Pinang) on the west coast is an island with many first-class beach resort hotels. Penang's capital, Georgetown, is a charming combination of Chinese shop-houses, stately residences, and tree-lined streets. Visitors there may also see Southeast Asia's tallest office building, and its largest bridge—linking Penang Island with the mainland. The east coast of Malaysia offers the visitor expanses of unspoiled beaches. Malay sultans, Chinese traders, and Portuguese, Dutch and British conquerors all left their mark on the culture and architecture of the city of Malacca, which is an easy drive from Kuala Lumpur. Visitors with more time may visit the states of Sabah and Sarawak on the island of Borneo, where many cultural traditions predate the arrival of Islam.

Profile 9   Saudi Arabia

This report has been prepared from information provided by:

"Saudi Arabia—Energy and Mineral Resources," "Saudi Arabia—Agriculture and Water Resources," "Saudi Arabia—Education and Human Resources," "Saudi Arabia—Facts and Figures, 1985," "Saudi Arabia—Transportation and Communication," "Saudi Arabia—Health and Social Services," "Saudi Arabia—Islam, 1985" (Washington, D.C.: The Royal Embassy of Saudi Arabia, 1986).

Department of State, Bureau of Public Affairs, *Background Notes—Saudi Arabia* (Washington, D.C.: U.S. Government Printing Office, December 1986).

Institutional Investor, *Saudi Arabia—Continued Growth and Investment Potential,* Ministry of Finance and National Economy of Saudi Arabia, 1983.

Nation's Business, "Saudi Arabia (A Decade of Development)," March 1985.

Geography   See Exhibits C9.1 and C9.2.

Demography   See Exhibit C9.3.

Economy   Saudi Arabia, with 1986's proven oil reserves at around 169 billion barrels, possesses more than 25 percent of the non-Communist world's oil reserves.

Saudi Arabia is a founding and principal member of the Organization of Petroleum Exporting Countries (OPEC), and has

C
O
U
N
T
R
Y

P
R
O
F
I
L
E
S

Exhibit **C9.1** Map of Saudi Arabia

been instrumental in formulating and guiding the actions of that organization. Up until 1985, Saudi Arabia acted as OPEC's "swing producer," adjusting its oil production in response to the fluctuations in the world oil market. In this role of absorbing reductions of OPEC's overall production and supporting the organization's production increases by changing its own production levels, Saudi Arabia's stated intent had been to contribute to the stability of the world economy through moderating oil prices and ensuring adequate supplies. By the summer of 1985, however, the Saudi government had abandoned this "swing producer" role; world oil prices fell within the next several months to approximately US $15 per barrel—half their pre-1986

Exhibit **C9.2** Geographic Data

Area: 830,000 sq mi (2,331,000 sq km); about one-third the size of the continental United States

Highest Elevation: Jebal Sawda, 10,279 ft above sea level

Location: Southwest Asia (Middle East); bounded on the north by Jordan, Iraq, and Kuwait; on the east by the Persian Gulf, Qatar, and the United Arab Emirates and linked to Bahrain by a man-made causeway; on the southeast by Oman; on the south by the People's Democratic Republic of Yemen, and Yemen; and on the west by the Red Sea; boundaries are not fully defined in the south and southeast

Terrain: From mountain ranges in the southwest (near the Red Sea), the land slopes gently eastward toward the Persian Gulf (called the Arabian Gulf in Saudi Arabia); the topography is mainly desert, including the Rub Al-Khali (Empty Quarter), a vast 250,000 sq mi uninhabited expanse of sand

Regions:

- the Asir, a mountainous region along the southern Red Sea coast
- Nejd, the heartland of the country and the site of Riyadh, the capital city and new diplomatic center
- the Eastern Province (al-Hasa), bordering the Persian Gulf and containing the largest concentration of proven oil reserves in the world
- the Northern Region, which has the largest percentage of Bedouin inhabitants (nomads)

Climate: Rainfall is erratic, averaging 2–4 in. (5–10 cm) annually except in the Asir, which averages 12–30 in. (30–75 cm) in the summer; during the summer, the heat is intense over much of the country, frequently exceeding 120°F (48° C) in the shade, with high humidity along the coasts; in winter, temperatures sometimes drop below freezing in the central and northern areas, but snow and ice are uncommon; the country experiences sandstorms called *giblis,* which can last for several days at a time.

Exhibit **C9.3** Demographic Information

Nationality: Noun—Saudi(s); Adjective—Saudi Arabian or Saudi.

Population (1985 est.): 9.6 million, 50% resident foreigners—many Arabs from nearby countries are employed in the kindgom; also, there are significant numbers of expatriate workers from North America, South Asia, Europe, and the Far East; over 40% of the population is 15 years of age or younger

Population Density: 11.6 per sq mi (4.1 per sq km); some cities and oases have densities of 2,000 per sq mi (770 per sq km); until the 1960s, most of the population was nomadic or seminomadic, but under the impact of rapid economic growth, urbanization has advanced rapidly, and about 95% are now settled

Growth Rate (1985 est.): 2.8% annually

Ethnic Groups: Arab (90% of native population); Afro-Asian

Religion: Islam (the fundamentalist Wahabi sect of Sunnite Islam is the state religion)

Education (1985 est.): Attendance—80% in primary school; free schooling from kindergarten through university level; during the 1985–86 academic year, almost 1,300 new schools were opened, admitting 339,000 additional students, and by the end of 1985, there were some 15,000 Saudis studying at foreign universities; literacy—men 50%, women 25%

Training: At the primary and secondary level, technical education and vocational training are available as part of the general education program; at the advanced level, there are training facilities throughout the country, including the Royal

Exhibit **C9.3** continued

> Technical Institute in Riyadh; the government, as part of its incentive package geared toward companies, will pay the wages of any trainees during training programs, with additional subsidies applicable to the posttraining employment period (up to 50% of the wages)

level. Prices, by mid-1987, had rebounded to approximately US$20 per barrel.

The Kingdom's massive spending since the early 1970s has been made possible by revenue increases as a result of world oil prices going from less than US$3 per barrel in 1973, to US$34 per barrel by 1980. (After adjusting for the effects of inflation, the real rise was approximately half the nominal increase). The country's oil revenues increased by 1100 percent to US$120 billion over the eight years following OPEC's 1973 price increases.

Since the sharp rise in petroleum revenues began in the early 1970s, Saudi Arabia has been one of the economically fastest-growing nations in the world. Until only recently, it enjoyed a substantial surplus in its overall trade with other countries. Imports had increased rapidly, spurred by government and consumer spending. Ample government revenues and foreign exchange resources were available for defense, development, and aid to other Arab and Islamic countries. Saudi Arabian foreign assets had increased by 2900 percent by 1982, from their 1973 level of under US$5 billion. The management and productive investment of these surpluses, in the domestic economy and abroad, was a formidable task for Saudi government executives and planners.

The world oil glut in 1982, however, introduced an element of planning uncertainty for the first time in a decade. Saudi Arabian oil production, which had increased from fewer than 3 million barrels per day (b/d) in 1969 to almost 10 million b/d during 1980 to 81, dropped to a twenty-year low of around 2 million b/d in August 1985. In fiscal year 1982 to 83, the government began experiencing budgetary deficits of 10 to 20 percent of its total expenditures and had to draw down its foreign assets. Since then, these assets (to 1986) have fallen by at least US$40 billion.

Within the context of five-year development plans, the government has sought to allocate its petroleum income to transform its relatively underdeveloped oil-based economy into that of a modern industrial state, while maintaining the kingdom's traditional Islamic values and customs. Although economic planners have not achieved all of their goals, the economy has progressed rapidly, and the standard of living of most Saudis has improved significantly. Dependence on petroleum revenue continues, but industry and agriculture now account for a larger share of total economic activity. A shortage of skilled Saudi workers at all levels remains the principal obstacle to rapid development. Consequently, more than 3 million non-Saudis are employed in the economy.

Saudi Arabia's first two five-year development plans, covering the 1970s, emphasized infrastructure—telecommunications, roads, ports, electricity, and water. The results were impressive: the total length of paved highways tripled; power generation increased twenty-eight times; and the capacity of the seaports grew tenfold.

For the third plan, covering 1980 to 1985, the emphasis changed. Although the share of infrastructure in development spending remained higher than planned, it declined substantially. Spending on education, health, and social sciences rose markedly. The share allocated to expanding and diversifying the productive sectors of the economy (primarily industry) did not rise as planned, ostensibly because private sector funds were not available. Nevertheless, Jubail and Yanbu—two new industrial cities built around the use of indigenous oil and gas feedstock to produce steel, petrochemicals, fertilizer, and refined oil products—absorbed a large share of expenditures.

The fourth plan, covering the 1985 to 1990 period, continues these emphases, taking the position that the country's basic infrastructure is complete and that education and training to reduce the country's heavy dependence on foreign labor is the major area of concern. Private enterprise is encouraged and foreign investment, especially joint ventures with the Saudi government and private capital, is welcomed. The private sector has become an increasingly important element in the economy; its share of non-oil GDP had expanded to about 60 percent by 1984 to 1985. Its main activity is still trade and commerce, but in recent years private investment in industry, agriculture, banks, and construction companies has grown. To a large extent, the investments have resulted from the generous incentives, facilities, and policy support provided by the government. The government intends that all sectors of the economy, except petroleum extraction, will eventually be owned by Saudi individuals or corporations.

The changing make-up of Saudi Arabia's GDP can be seen in the following comparison of economic activities in the 1973-to-74 period versus the 1982-to-83 period:

COUNTRY PROFILES

Economic activities as a % of GDP		
Activity	1973–74	1982–83
Oil	65%	30%
Non-oil private sector	25%	48%
Government	10%	22%

Foreign Trade   See Exhibits C9.5 and C9.6.

National Budget   Saudi Arabia's 1984 to 1985 budget projected expenditures totaling US$76.5 billion (as broken down
in the table immediately below), and revenues of approximately
US$63 billion. The estimated US$13.5 billion deficit was to be
financed by drawing down on the country's general reserves.
(By 1982 those reserves totaled almost US$150 billion). In the
1984 to 1985 national budget, expenditures were allocated as
follows:

Infrastructure	3.7%
Domestic subsidies	3.9%
Specialized lending institutions	6.1%
Municipal services	6.6%
Economic resources	6.6%
Health & social development	6.9%
Transportation & communication	9.1%
Manpower development	10.3%
Education	11.6%
Public administration & other	34.5%

For the 1985 to 1986 period, the central government's budget had decreased to US$55 billion, with defense allocations
absorbing 33 percent of the budget.

Government   The modern Saudi government was founded by the late King
Abd al-Aziz Al-Saud. Recapturing the Saud dynasty's ancestral
capital (Riyadh) in 1902, Abd al-Aziz consolidated his hold by
making further territorial gains. In 1932, these territories were
unified as the kingdom of Saudi Arabia (the only nation named
after its ruling family). The King's descendants have retained
control to the present time.

The central institution of the Saudi Arabian government is
the monarchy. The authority of the monarchy is based on Islamic
law (Shariah). Though the King's powers are not defined, in

Exhibit **C9.4** Economic Data

	Fiscal years	
	1983–1984	*1985–1986*
Gross domestic product (GDP)	US$121 billion	US$98.1 billion
Per capita GDP	US$14,600	US$9,800
Average inflation rate	5%	−3.7%
Annual growth rate		
Overall	na	−8%
Nonoil share	na	−13%

1985–1986

Natural resources:	Hydrocarbons, iron, gold, and copper
Agriculture:	Grain, dates, and livestock; cultivated land: 0.3%
Industry:	Petroleum production, petrochemicals, cement, fertilizer, light industry (oil 40% of GDP)

practice they are limited because he must retain a consensus of the Saudi royal family, religious leaders (*ulema*), and other important elements in Saudi society.

The Kingdom's fourteen provinces are governed by princes or close relatives of the royal family. Despite rapid economic progress, Saudi society remains strongly conservative and religious, with a tribal orientation. The King's policy is to encourage modernization without undermining the country's stability and Islamic heritage. The Saudi Arabian approach can be described as "modernization without westernization." During the years of his reign, the current King (Fahd) has had to manage the adjustment of the Saudi economy to sharply lower oil revenues resulting from declining oil demand and prices, and to assure Saudi security against the risks of escalation of the Iran–Iraq war, including the threat it poses to freedom of navigation.

Saudi Arabia has no diplomatic relations with any Communist state (except the neighboring People's Democratic Republic of Yemen). It is a charter member of the Arab League and supports the Arab insistence that Israel withdraw from all formerly Arab territories occupied in June 1967, including East Jerusalem (Jerusalem is the third most revered city for Muslims). Saudi Arabia supports a peaceful resolution of the Arab–Israeli conflict.

COUNTRY PROFILES

Exhibit **C9.5**   Saudi Arabia's Leading Trade Partners

	1983		1982		1981	
	$ Million Imports	*Market Share*	*$ Million Imports*	*Market Share*	*$ Million Imports*	*Market Share*
Leading suppliers						
United States	7,454	19.7%	8,140	21%	7,141	21.4%
Japan	7,352	19.5%	7,430	19%	6,096	18.3%
West Germany	3,756	9.9%	4,269	11%	3,183	9.6%
Italy	2,851	7.6%	2,360	6%	2,237	6.7%
United Kingdom	2,335	6.2%	2,556	7%	2,068	6.2%
Leading buyers						
Japan	14,300	31.1%	17,966	23.8%	19,425	17.2%
United States	3,570	7.6%	5,891	7.8%	14,927	13.2%
France	3,060	6.6%	6,781	9.0%	10,793	9.5%
Italy	2,600	5.6%	3,740	5.0%	8,027	7.1%
West Germany	1,500	3.3%	3,274	4.3%	4,745	4.2%

Source: Saudi Arabian Monetary Agency

Exhibit **C9.6** 1985 Estimates of:
Exports − Imports + Net Deficit

Exports: US$30.2 billion

Imports: US$24.0 billion

Net Deficit on Trade in Service: US$20 billion

Official Exchange Rate: 3.75 Saudi riyals (SR) = US$1

Note: There are no foreign exchange currency restrictions on outflow from Saudi Arabia

Source: Nation's Business, *Saudi Arabia,* March 1985.

As the world's leading exporter of petroleum, Saudi Arabia has a special interest in preserving a stable and long-term market for its vast oil resources and a healthy Western economy, necessary for protecting the value of Saudi financial assets. It has generally acted to stabilize the world oil market and tried to moderate sharp price movements.

Exhibit **C9.7** Government Data

Political System: Monarchy with Council of Ministries

Unification: 23 September 1932

Constitution: None; governed according to Islamic Law (Shariah)

Branches: Executive—king (chief of state and head of government); legislative—none; judicial—Islamic Courts of First Instance and Appeals

Political Parties: none

Suffrage: none

Administrative Subdivisions: 14 provinces

Flag: Green and white; bears the Muslim creed in Arabic script: "There is no God but God; Muhammad is the Messenger of God." Under the script is a white horizontal sword.

C O U N T R Y   P R O F I L E S

Business

Oil   More than 95 percent of all Saudi oil is produced on behalf of the Saudi government by the Arabian American Oil Company (ARAMCO), which was originally owned by four major U.S. oil companies. ARAMCO's former assets are now owned by the Saudi government, with the economy receiving a per-barrel revenue based on production and the success of exploration programs.

The Japanese-owned Arabian Oil Company and U.S.-based Getty Oil operate in the former Saudi Arabia–Kuwait neutral zone and provide the rest of Saudi oil production.

Agriculture   Next to oil, agriculture is now the most important industry in Saudi Arabia: the kingdom has made impressive gains in various agricultural sectors:

- Overall agricultural output rose by 25 percent in 1983.
- Between 1975 and 1983, egg production increased dramatically, and Saudi Arabia now exports its excess.
- Self-sufficiency in dairy products was achieved in 1983.
- Local poultry production rose by almost 60 percent in 1983, to about 145,000 tn.
- Between 1970 and 1983, citrus production grew from 13,000 tn to 46,000 tn.
- Vegetables and legumes rose by 3.7 million tn in 1983.
- Saudi Arabia has 11 million date palms (10 percent of the world's supply); 1983 production exceeded 382,000 tn.
- Perhaps the most impressive of Saudi Arabia's agricultural gains has been in the production of cereal grains, particularly wheat. 1977's wheat production totaled 856,000 tn (90 percent of the country's consumption) and the 1984 harvest stood at 1.3 million tn—an almost 1000 percent increase in production in just over five years.

The government has provided free land and interest-free loans for farming projects approved by its agencies. Under the 1980 to 85 development plan, agricultural loan allocations totaled US$1.52 billion, with agricultural subsidies allocated a further approximate total of US$758 million. Saudi Arabia has built over one hundred dams, partly for consumption and agricultural use. It is also engaged in overland irrigation projects, and the development of significant desalination systems. Also, the government projects that within the next several years treated urban waste water will provide up to 15 percent of total water demand.

Foreign Investor Incentives   Initiated in 1974, the Joint Economic Commission was established to assist in the development of Saudi Arabia through cooperative programs in many fields including industrialization, trade, manpower training, agriculture, and science and technology. The commission is cochaired by the Saudi minister of Finance and National Economy and the U.S. secretary of the Treasury. The private sector has contributed much to the technology transfer involved in Joint Commission projects. Since 1975, about US $800 million in contracts has gone to the U.S. and Saudi Arabian private sectors. Some projects are carried out entirely by the private sector through direct contracts with U.S. government agencies, while others use private firms for aspects of an entire project.

The Saudi Arabian–United States Private Sector Dialogue was established in 1980 to provide a forum for contracts between the private sectors of both countries. It meets in conjunction with the annual Joint Commission meeting to discuss common concerns such as joint-venture regulations. By 1983, there were some 1,650 Saudi–foreign-investor joint ventures operating in Saudi Arabia. The incentives offered to foreign investors under two particular government agencies provide an illustration of the attractiveness of the governmental loans, relatively low in-country commercial loan rates, and tax holidays available.

The Public Investment Fund (PIF), is geared to large Saudi government–foreign-investor projects—those in the order of hundreds of millions or billions of dollars. Financing is available from the PIF for up to 60 percent of the total initial cost of a project, for up to fifteen years.

The Saudi Industrial Development Fund (SIDF) is targeted at smaller Saudi citizen–foreign-investor projects. SIDF will provide up to 50 percent of the total project cost, including the working capital for up to three months of operating expenses. (The proportion of the total costs is tied to the equity stake held by Saudis.) Repayment may extend for up to fifteen years, depending on the cash flow. As the charging of interest is disallowed under Islamic law, SIDF assesses an "evaluation" or "front-end" fee of between 2 and 3 percent at the start of the loan period with annual "follow-up" fees of less than 1 percent as the only subsequent charges.

At Saudi commercial banks, normal banking criteria are followed in assessing the viability of a project and in setting charges (that is, depending on the competition for funds, and the cost to the banks of those funds). However, with rates in the royal money market tending to be 1 to 2 percent lower than Euro-dollar rates, charges on bank loans usually fall between West German bank loan rates and the U.S. prime rate.

If a minimum of 25 percent of the total equity of a project is Saudi, industrial ventures can get a 10 percent exemption from corporate income taxes. Foreign-owned parts of companies are otherwise subject to corporate income taxes of 45 percent of all profits in excess of approximately US$150,000.

Infrastructure

Transportation In 1951, the country's first paved road was built. By October 1984, 19,500 mi of paved roads and 25,200 mi of unpaved roads had been constructed. Railroads in Saudi Arabia carried 400,000 passengers and 2 million tn of goods in 1986. In 1980, intercity and intracity bus ridership totaled 64 million passengers; in1983 to 1984, approximately 109 million passengers. Saudi Arabia has one national airline, Saudi Airlines, with a fleet that has grown from 3 planes in 1945 to 80 planes in 1984.

The National Shipping Company of Saudi Arabia took delivery of four of the world's largest ships in 1982; fleet expansion has continued.

Access Saudi Arabia has several domestic and international airports; the largest are at Riyadh, Jeddah, and Dhahran. In 1984, 21 seaports offered a total of 120 berths. There are four major ports: Dammam, Jeddah, Jizan, and Yanbu (whose 1984 tonnage totaled 45 million tn; the country's total annual capacity was then 47 million tn).

Communications In 1984, Saudi Arabia had 600 post offices and 8,500 postal employees; 1983 deliveries included 643 million postal articles. In 1985, 1,000,000 telephone lines, 450 microwave stations, and 30,000 telex lines (from 10,000 lines in 1981) served the country. Saudi Arabia is the twenty-first largest user of telex services in the world.

Health Care The Ministry of Health's 1980–1985 budget was nearly US$10 billion. In 1985, there were 30,000 hospital beds, 5.9 doctors per 1,000 residents, and 10.6 nurses per 1,000 residents. In 1984, total medical personnel numbered approximately 21,000.

Housing From 1980 to 1985, 7,000 government-built units were completed. From 1983 to 1984, the government lent 29,400 interest-free loans totaling US$2.3 billion for 37,000 private housing units. Also, 165 investment loans totaling over US$110 million were extended for housing and commercial unit construction.

C O U N T R Y   P R O F I L E S

Life-Style and Travel Notes

An understanding of the culture and institutions of Saudi Arabia involves an understanding of its unique geophysical characteristics, its history, and perhaps most significantly the Islamic religion.

The country's geographical and climatic make-up has influenced both the predominant and traditional way of life, and the location of its major urban centers. With its harsh climate of extremes of temperature and its defining desert landscape, its people have been either nomadic—always moving in search of grazing—or settled at oases or at the coastal regions, engaged in trade, agriculture, or fishing.

Historically, the Arab peoples have given the world much that formed the basis for the modern scientific process: fundamentals of mathematics and early medical insights, for instance. The nation's people have a tribal orientation, with strict moral and ethical codes; justice in Saudi Arabia is administered according to the Shariah (Islamic law), and is swift. Saudi Arabia prides itself on having one of the lowest, if not the lowest, crime rates in the world.

A proud and conservative people, the Saudis have welcomed technology (if at times hesitantly—the introduction of television followed much debate as to its religious and social implications) but are determined to do so within their own socioreligious customs. Saudi Arabia takes seriously its role as guardian of Islam's two holiest cities, Makkah and Medina. The annual Hajj or pilgrimage to Makkah, draws some two million Muslims from all over the world. The Saudi government takes specific measures to ensure the orderly and safe passage of these faithful.

Foreigners at work in Saudi Arabia are welcomed for their technical skills and investment input; they are, nevertheless, expected to respect and abide by the country's clearly defined laws and customs. Alcohol is banned, as is pornography. Again, Saudi justice is swift and, by the relatively liberal standards of the West, harsh. Social interaction with foreigners is not encouraged, so as to minimize the influence of differing mores, and the cities of Makkah and Medina are off-limits to non-Muslims.

Climate and Clothing Lightweight clothing is essential for the hot climate. Riyadh is dry, while Jeddah and Dhahran are humid most of the year. Conservative dress is required for women.

Entry and Residence Requirements Cholera shots are required for entry for travelers arriving from areas where cholera is endemic. U.S. citizens traveling to Saudi Arabia must have

COUNTRY PROFILES

valid Saudi visas. Saudi regulations have no provision for tourist visas. All applicants must have a letter of invitation from an employer or Saudi sponsor.

Health   Foreigners should eat and drink cautiously outside major hotels and restaurants. Hospital and emergency care and services in major cities approach U.S. standards.

Telecommunications   Telephone and telegraph service is expanding rapidly, and direct domestic and overseas dialing is available at many locations within the country. Riyadh is eight time zones ahead of eastern standard time.

Transportation   Many domestic and international flights are scheduled daily; taxis and rental cars are available in all major cities. Women are forbidden to drive, and women traveling alone are normally unable to rent hotel rooms.

Profile **10**   United Kingdom

This report has been prepared from information provided by:

"Britain in Brief," Central Office of Information, December 1986.

Department of State, Bureau of Public Affairs, *Background Notes — United Kingdom (Washington, D.C.: U.S. Government Printing Office, January 1987).*

Geography

The United Kingdom lies off the northwest coast of the European continent, separated from it by the English Channel, the Strait of Dover, and the North Sea. The United Kingdom (U.K.) is comprised of England, Scotland, Wales, and Northern Ireland. England, at the closest point, is 22 miles (35 km) from France; its capital and largest city is London (population 6.7 million). Scotland is in the north; its lowlands, about 60 mi (97 km) wide, divide the farming region of the southern uplands from the granite highlands of the north. Edinburgh (population 445,000) is Scotland's capital. Glasgow (population 761,000),

C
O
U
N
T
R
Y

P
R
O
F
I
L
E
S

Exhibit **C10.1** Map of United Kingdom

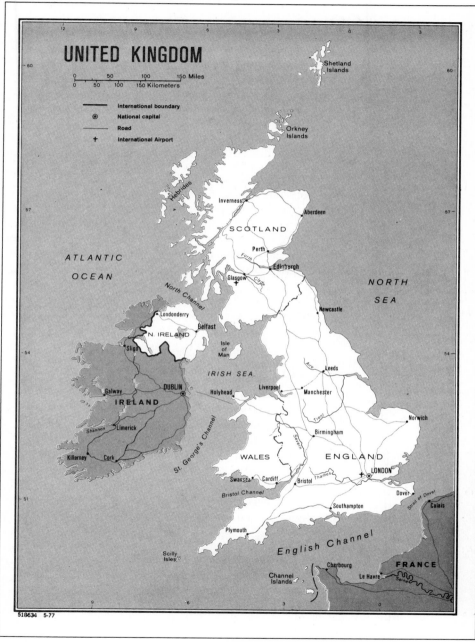

C O U N T R Y   P R O F I L E S

Exhibit **C10.2**   Geographic Information

> *Area:* 94,251 sq mi (244,111 sq km); slightly smaller than Oregon
>
> *Terrain:* 30% arable, 50% meadow and pasture, 12% waste or urban, 7% forested, 1% inland water
>
> *Climate:* Generally mild and temperate; weather is subject to frequent changes but to few extremes of temperature

one of the United Kingdom's great industrial centers, is Scotland's largest city. Wales borders England to the west and is almost entirely hilly and mountainous. Its largest city is Cardiff (population 280,000). Northern Ireland occupies the northeast corner of Ireland across the North Channel from Scotland. Its capital and largest city, Belfast, has an estimated population of 325,000.

The climate of the United Kingdom is temperate and equable, temperatures range from a mean of about 40° F (5° C) in winter to about 60° F (16° C) in summer. Average annual rainfall is 35 to 40 in. (60 to 102 cm), distributed relatively evenly throughout the year.

Demography

The population of the United Kingdom was estimated at 56.4 million in 1986, about 3.9 million more than 1961. Its population is the fourth largest in Europe (after the USSR, the Federal Republic of Germany, and Italy), and its population density is one of the highest in the world. Almost one-third of the population lives in England's prosperous and fertile southeast, with population declining in the more rugged areas to the north and west. The population is predominantly urban and suburban.

Although the Celtic languages persist to a small degree in Northern Ireland, Wales, and Scotland, the predominant language has long been English, a blend of Anglo-Saxon and Norman-French. The high literacy rate in the United Kingdom (99 percent) is attributable to the introduction of public primary education in 1870 and secondary in 1900. In 1981, over 11 million students attended Britain's 38,500 schools, most of which are publicly financed in whole or in part. Education is mandatory from ages five through sixteen.

The Church of England is the largest church, but virtually every religion and sect found in the world is represented in the United Kingdom.

Exhibit **C10.3** Demographic Data

> *Nationality:* Noun—Briton; adjective—British
>
> *Population (1986):* 56.4 million
>
> *Annual Growth Rate:* Negligible
>
> *Ethnic Groups:* British, West Indian, South Asian
>
> *Religions:* Church of England, Roman Catholic, Presbyterian
>
> *Languages:* English, Welsh, Gaelic
>
> *Education:* Years compulsory—12; attendance—nearly 100%; total literacy—99%

Economy

Britain has an open economy, in which international trade plays an important role; about one-third of its gross domestic product comes from the export of goods and services (one of the highest shares among the major economies).

Britain is the fourth largest trading nation in the world. Two-thirds of exports are manufactured goods, and machinery accounts for about 23 percent of the total. The importance of North Sea oil exports is shown by the 21 percent share of total

Exhibit **C10.4** Economic Data

> *GDP (1985):* US$453 billion
>
> *Annual Growth Rate (1985):* 3.0%
>
> *Per Capita GDP (1985):* US$8,032
>
> *Average Inflation Rate:* 1985—6.1%; 1986—3.1%
>
> *Natural Resources:* Coal, oil, and gas (North Sea)
>
> *Agriculture:* (2.1% of GDP)—cereals, livestock, livestock products, and fish
>
> *Industry:* (24.4% of GDP)—steel, heavy engineering and metal manufacturing, textiles, motor vehicles and aircraft, construction, electronics, and chemicals

COUNTRY PROFILES

Exhibit **C10.5** Trade Statistics

Exports (1985): US$100.8 billion

Major Markets: EEC, USA, Sweden, Saudi Arabia, Nigeria, Switzerland

Imports (1985): US$103.3 billion

Major Suppliers: EEC, USA, Japan, Norway, Sweden, Switzerland

Fiscal Year: 1 April–31 March

Exchange Rate (May 1986): 1 UK pound (£) = US$1.50

---

exports taken by fuels. Finished manufactures comprise some 44 percent of imports, and semimanufactures 25 percent; food represents a relatively small percentage of imports (9 percent), partly because of the recent success of British agriculture in meeting its demand for food. Britain, nevertheless, imports close to 50 percent of its food for home consumption. About 60 percent of Britain's trade is with Western Europe; six out of the top ten British export markets are members of the EEC. Japan accounts for 5 percent of imports, double the proportion of ten years ago. Britain remains committed to open trading and to the further liberalization of world trade. In accordance with its international obligations under the General Agreement on Tariffs and Trade and to the EEC, it has progressively abolished almost all quantitative import restrictions imposed on economic grounds. Although Britain applies the EEC's common customs tariff to those countries neither belonging to nor having any special arrangement with the EEC, about 80 percent of imports are admitted duty free; only 7 percent of visible imports are subject to any kind of nontariff restraint. A narrow range of goods is subject to export control.

Exchange controls were abolished in 1979. Inward and outward investment is welcomed—the latter because it helps develop markets for British exports and provides earnings, the former because it creates more jobs in Britain.

The economy is primarily based on private enterprise, which accounts for three-quarters of the GDP and a similar proportion of total employment. Since 1980, the annual rate of inflation has fallen from about 21 percent to just over 3 percent. In 1986, Britain was the world's fifth largest oil producer with its North Sea reserves. Since the early 1980s the economy has

C
O
U
N
T
R
Y

P
R
O
F
I
L
E
S

been growing by some 3 percent a year. Between 1980 and 1985, output per head increased by 14 percent in the economy as a whole and by 27 percent in manufacturing. This increased efficiency was due partly to a reduction of surplus labor.

Government

Britain is a parliamentary democracy with a constitutional monarch who is an impartial head of state acting on the advice of ministers. Democratic government has developed since the establishment of Parliament over 700 years ago. Parliament comprises the House of Commons, the House of Lords, and the king or queen acting in the constitutional role. The Commons consists of elected members of Parliament (MPs), each representing a local constituency area. The Lords is made up of hereditary and life peers and peeresses, and the two archbishops, and twenty-four most senior bishops of the established Church of England. The center of parliamentary power is the elected House of Commons. General elections to choose MPs must be held at least every five years. The government is formed by the party with majority support in the Commons, and the monarch appoints its leader as prime minister. As head of the government, the prime minister appoints a team of ministers, including about twenty in the Cabinet.

The Conservative Party was elected in 1979, and has remained in power through 1987. It has shifted resources from the public to the private sector, practiced fiscal and monetary restraint, and supported Britain's role in the North Atlantic Treaty Organization. The Conservatives' goal is to reduce the role of the government in the economy, moderate the growth of the money supply, and remove structural rigidities. The government has privatized a number of large state-owned companies, such as British Telecom, and has plans to privatize several more.

The exposure of more of the economy to market forces is a key element of the government's economic strategy. Direct controls on pay, prices, foreign exchange transactions, dividend payments, and commercial credit have been eliminated and a substantial program for transferring activities from the public to the private sector is under way. In addition, regulatory burdens on business are being reduced. Planning restrictions on industrial investment have been eased, while industrial subsidies have been made more selective and closely related to job creation. Particular efforts have been made to improve the flow of investment funds to small firms and to assist innovation in industry.

Britain has diplomatic relations with over 130 countries; its main foreign policy objectives are the peaceful resolution of disputes, disarmament and arms control, economic development of countries in the Third World, protection of human

COUNTRY PROFILES

Exhibit **C10.6** Government Data

Type: Constitutional monarchy

Constitution: Unwritten, partly statutes, partly common law
and practice

Branches: Executive—monarch (chief of state), prime
minister (head of government), Cabinet;
legislative—bicameral Parliament (House of
Commons, House of Lords); judicial—Magistrates'
courts, county courts, high courts, appellate courts,
House of Lords

Political Parties: Conservative, Labor, Liberal, Social
Democratic, and small Scottish, Welsh, and
Northern Irish parties

Suffrage: British subjects and citizens of the Irish republic
resident in the UK, 18 years or older

Political Subdivisions: Municipalities, counties, parliamentary
constituencies, province of Northern
Ireland, and Scottish regions

Government Expenditures (1985): 5.1% of GDP

Flag: The red, white, and blue Union Jack combines crosses
of the patron saints of England (St. George), Scotland
(St. Andrew), and Ireland (St. Patrick)

rights, and promotion of the rule of law. It is a member of many
international organizations including the United Nations, the
EEC, NATO, and the Commonwealth. Britain is one of the five
permanent members of the United Nations Security Council.

In 1973, Britain became a member of the EEC, which was
founded to ensure closer economic cooperation among member
nations; one of the EEC's main objectives is the creation
of a common market in which goods, services, people, and
capital can move without restriction. The EEC has abolished
internal tariffs and established an external customs tariff, a common
agricultural policy, and other policies, including the creation
of regional development and social funds; Britain is
supporting moves to extend this common market to include
financial and other services, transport, and freedom of establishment
for professional people. The twelve member states,
with a population of 320 million, account for a fifth of world
trade.

Since 1945, Britain has given independence to over fifty countries, nearly all of which are members of the Commonwealth, a voluntary association of forty-nine states accounting for about a quarter of the world's population. Member states share a common language and close professional, academic, and commercial links.

Business

Manufacturing   Britain is a leading manufacturer of mechanical equipment, metal goods, motor vehicles and components, electrical and electronic goods, chemicals, and office equipment. Productivity in long-established industries such as steel manufacture and vehicle building has been increasing as a result of modernization. The use of advanced technology, especially microelectronics, is steadily increasing in many industries. The average manufacturing firm is fairly small, with three-quarters of the establishments employing under twenty people. These account for 11 percent of the manufacturing work force; in contrast some 46.8 percent of the work force is employed by only 1.6 percent of the establishments.

Steel and Mineral Processing   Britain is the world's tenth largest steel producer (by volume); it has one of Europe's largest nonferrous metal industries; and it is a major producer of specialized alloys used by the aerospace, electronic, petrochemical, and other industries. Other mineral products include glass (especially float glass, which was developed in Britain), bricks, cement, and ceramics. Britain is the world's main manufacturer of fine bone china, much of which is exported, and the world's largest exporter of china clay.

Engineering   Mechanical engineering is an important source of export earnings. Major products include machine tools, agricultural tractors and machinery, construction and mining equipment, and process plant for large-scale industries such as iron and steel manufacture, oil refining, and nuclear power generation. Britain is the largest exporter of agricultural tractors. It is also an important manufacturer and exporter of motor and railway vehicles and related components and equipment. The British aerospace industry is one of the largest in the Western world; its products include civil and military aircraft, helicopters, aero-engines, guided weapons, and satellites. Rolls-Royce is one of the world's three leading aero-engine manufacturers, and British Aerospace has been the prime contractor for all the telecommunications satellite projects of the European Space Agency. Because of worldwide overcapacity in general shipbuilding, the British industry is moving into more specialized areas such as ferries and offshore support vessels, production having been modernized through computer-aided design and manufacture.

COUNTRY PROFILES

Electronic data-processing equipment has been a growth industry; output nearly doubled between 1983 and 1985. Britain has originated many advances in microelectronics, which have had a major impact on the manufacture of office machinery, data-processing equipment, telecommunications, and consumer electronic equipment. British companies are strongly involved in the development of electronic revenue control equipment such as British Rail's computerized ticket-issuing machines. There is an advanced production capacity in optical fibers used in modern telecommunication systems.

Chemicals   The chemical industry is the third largest in Europe and the fifth largest in the Western world. About 12 percent of the world's research in pharmaceuticals takes place in Britain. Many of the basic discoveries in plastics, including polyethylene, have been British.

Textiles and Footwear   Although the textiles and clothing industries have been affected by low-cost imports, the use of automated production techniques is helping the UK become more competitive. The clothing industry, one of the largest in Europe, meets about two-thirds of the domestic demand. The wool industry is one of the world's largest, and Britain is a leading producer of woven carpets. Footwear factories supply more than 40 percent of the British market, and one-third of leather production is exported.

Other Manufactures   Other major manufacturing industries include food and drink, timber and furniture, printing and publishing, paper and board, and rubber. Security printing of bank notes and postage stamps, minted coins, jewelery, and gold and silverware are exports enjoying a good reputation.

Construction   The construction industry accounts for 6 percent of the GDP; 89 percent of work is done by private firms. Efficiency and productivity within the industry are benefiting from new techniques such as computerized stock ordering and computer-aided design. Government building regulations prescribe minimum standards of construction.

Other Services   Financial and business services, health and education, and leisure services have been major growth sectors. Computing services have grown at an annual rate of between 15 and 20 percent since the mid-1970s, with revenue standing at £2,000 million in 1985.

The distributive and allied trades (wholesaling, retailing, hotels and catering, and the repair of consumer goods and vehicles) account for some 13 percent of national income. There are some 231,000 retail businesses with 343,000 outlets, although the large multiple retailers are responsible for 58 percent of revenue. Trends include an increasing number of large self-service stores and the growing use of electronic checkouts and stock control systems. In cooperation with the main retail banks, a single nationwide system of electronic funds transfer at the point of sale is being planned for the use of consumers.

Tourism continues to be a major and growing source of employment. In 1985, a record 14.5 million overseas visitors came to Britain, 55 percent from Western Europe and 26 percent from North America.

Labor The total labor force in 1986 was over 27 million. Eleven million were members of trade unions. The Trade Union Congress (TUC), the major trade union federation, accounted for 9.85 million workers organized in 91 independent unions. The remaining 1.15 million unionized workers belonged to 260 smaller associations. Of people working for employers in 1985, 65.3 percent were in services, 25.8 percent in manufacturing, 4.5 percent in construction, and 4.4 percent in the primary sector (agriculture, forestry, fishing, energy, and water supply). Self-employment (accounting for nearly 10 percent of the work force) is at a high level, having risen from 1.9 million people 1979 to 2.6 million in 1985.

Unemployment has been a problem, and in August 1986, some 3.2 million people (11.7 percent of the working population) were without work. Unemployment levels vary regionally; Northern Ireland has suffered unemployment levels of more than 20 percent since 1983, and the rate in May 1986 had risen to 21.9 percent; in contrast, southeastern England's unemployment rate has hovered between 9.3 percent and 10.3 percent during the same period and was at 9.9 percent in May 1986. Scotland (15.0 percent), Wales (16.5 percent), and the northern (18.0 percent) and northwestern regions of England (15.7 percent) all have rates higher than the average and are regions where the decline of traditional industries such as shipbuilding, coal mining, steel manufacture, and heavy engineering has been most severely felt. Special employment training measures, including the two-year-long Youth Training Scheme, increasingly remove large numbers from the unemployment rolls.

During 1984 and 1985, Britain lost a substantial number of working days through strike action. The longest-running dispute took place in the mining industry when the National Union of Mineworkers took strike action for more than a year to oppose scheduled mine closures.

The Government and Industry   The main aim of the government's industrial policy is to encourage enterprise, initiative, and innovation in a competitive market economy. Support is provided for investment in major projects and new technologies, for new investment in regions where traditional industries have contracted, for research and development, for business and technical advisory services, and for exports. The importance of standards and good design is stressed, and small businesses are encouraged by reducing administrative burdens and through other policies.

A major feature of government policy is the stimulation of competition so that commerce can flourish. The extent of state ownership of industry is being reduced by a privatization program designed to expose the industries to market forces. Companies that have been privatized include British Aerospace, British Gas, British Telecom, and Jaguar. The privatization of British Airways and National Bus Company were under way in 1987.

Infrastructure

Financial Services   Financial services account for about 5 to 6 percent of the British economy's total output. The City of London has the world's largest insurance market; its banks are responsible for about a quarter of international bank lending and it is the principal international trading center for commodities.

The Bank of England, Britain's central bank, assists in the implementation of aspects of the government's economic policies and is concerned with management of the domestic currency and supervision of the banking system. It acts as banker to the government, to commercial bankers in Britain, and to overseas banks and international monetary institutions. There are four major retail banks based in London and three in Scotland. In addition, some 460 overseas banks and financial institutions are represented in Britain. Other financial institutions are building societies—which take deposits (on which they pay interest) and make loans for house purchase—pension and life insurance funds, investment and unit trusts, and the Post Office National Girobank.

The London Stock Exchange is the third largest in the world, its revenue being roughly equal to that of all the other EEC exchanges combined. In addition, the City of London includes the various commodity markets, the gold market, the Baltic Exchange for shipping and aviation, and Lloyd's for insurance.

Transportation and Communications   Most passenger and freight transport goes by road; private cars and taxis account for about 82 percent of passenger mileage, buses and coaches

C
O
U
N
T
R
Y

P
R
O
F
I
L
E
S

for 8 percent and rail for 7 percent. The road network totals some 231,200 mi (372,000 km), of which 1,770 mi (2,850 km) are motorways. Heavy through traffic has been removed from many towns and cities by the construction of bypasses and motorways.

Intercity travel has been improved by British Rail's diesel high speed trains, which travel on existing tracks at speeds of up to 125 mph (200 km/h). Several electrification schemes are in progress; the most important is a project to electrify the eastcoast main line between London and Edinburgh. Lightweight railbuses and new faster diesel and electric units are gradually replacing older rolling stock. Britain and France have agreed to the construction of twin, single-track rail tunnels (about 30 mi, or 49 km, long) under the English Channel in a £2,600 million project (the largest civil engineering project in Europe) to be undertaken by the private sector.

Air services are operated by British Airways and other airlines. British Airways carried 18.4 million passengers in 1985, while the others carried nearly 8 million people on scheduled flights and 14.2 million on chartered flights. British civil airports handled some 71.8 million passengers in 1985 and 850,000 tn of freight. The proportion of overseas trade carried by air mounted to 18.7 percent of the value of exports and 16.5 percent of imports. The government is planning to privatize British Airways as part of its policy to promote competition in international and internal air services; it also intends to privatize the British Airport Authority and the local authority airports.

British Telecom, now operating in the private sector, serves some 17 million residential and 4 million business telephone customers. Over 80 percent of British homes have a telephone, and international trunk dialing is available to nearly 170 countries. Optical fiber cable accounts for about 40 percent of British Telecom's network.

Health The National Health Service (NHS) provides largely free treatment for everyone normally resident in Britain. About 86 percent of the cost of the service is met from taxation, and the rest from small social security contributions and charges levied on some items. Examinations by family doctors, dentists, and ophthalmic practitioners are free, as are treatment and accommodation in hospital, and appliances such as hearing aids, walking frames, wheelchairs, and artificial limbs. People can choose and change their family doctors, dentists, ophthalmic practitioners, and pharmacists.

Education All children and young people between the ages of five and sixteen must receive full-time education. Many three-

COUNTRY PROFILES

and four-year-old children (43 percent in England, for example) receive nursery education, and about a fifth of sixteen- to nineteen-year-olds voluntarily stay on at school beyond the minimum leaving age—some until eighteen or nineteen, the age of entry into higher education. About 9.7 million pupils attend Britain's 36,500 schools, 94 percent receiving free education from public funds; the rest attend private, fee-paying schools.

Pupils at the age of sixteen and over will soon take a new examination—the General Certificate of Secondary Education—in England, Wales, and Northern Ireland; the first courses started in 1986. The new exam replaces two other examinations, and its preparatory course syllabuses and assessment procedures comply with nationally agreed guidelines. The advanced level (A-level) of the General Certificate of Education, usually taken at age eighteen, is the standard for entrance to university and other higher education courses, as well as to many forms of professional training. The Certificate of Pre-Vocational Education is intended for those leaving school who wish to prepare for work or vocational courses.

The Media   More daily newspapers, national and regional, are sold per person in Britain than in most other developed countries. National papers have a total circulation of 14.6 million on weekdays and 17.6 million on Sundays. There are about 130 daily and Sunday newspapers, 1,300 weekly papers, and about 7,000 periodical publications.

The press is not subject to state control or censorship and is free to comment on matters of public interest, subject to the ordinary laws of the land including those of libel and contempt of court. Newspapers are almost always financially independent of any political party; their political line usually derives from proprietorial, editorial, or other nonparty influences.

Much of the press is owned by large publishing groups, some of which have interests ranging over the whole field of publishing and the mass media in Britain's independent television and radio. There are, however, some safeguards against undue concentration of ownership in the means of mass communications.

Television and radio are the responsibility of the BBC and the Independent Broadcasting Authority, both of which must provide a public service disseminating information, education, and entertainment. Both are expected to show balance and impartiality in their general presentation of programs, particularly on issues of public policy or controversy. Although the government answers to Parliament on questions of broadcasting policy, and may issue directions on a number of technical and other subjects, the BBC and IBA are independent in their operations.

COUNTRY PROFILES

The BBC operates two national television channels and four national and thirty-two local radio stations (with more planned). It also transmits throughout the world radio broadcasts in English and nearly forty other languages. The domestic services are financed mainly from the sale of annual television licenses, and the external services by a government grant, although they have complete editorial independence.

The IBA is responsible for two television channels and over forty local radio stations. Unlike the BBC, the IBA does not produce programs, but supervises their operation by commercial program companies who draw their income from advertising, which is subject to a strict code of standards and practices. Advertisers do not sponsor programs.

By 1990, it is hoped that direct broadcasting by satellite will be available throughout Britain. Under this system television pictures will be transmitted directly from space into people's homes. The IBA has selected a commercial program contractor to operate three of the five channels allocated to Britain by international agreement.

Life-Style

Housing Housing conditions have greatly improved in the past three decades. About 97 percent of households in Great Britain have exclusive use of a bath or shower and sole use of an inside toilet. Clearance of the older slums has largely been achieved and greater emphasis is placed on improving existing dwellings. Grants from public funds help to meet the cost of improvements made to older homes.

Over 60 percent of all homes are owner-occupied, 27 percent are rented from public housing authorities, and most of the remainder are rented from private landlords or nonprofit-making housing authorities. The number of owner-occupied dwellings was over 12 million in 1985, compared with 4 million in 1951. Loans for home purchase are available from a number of sources, and tax concessions on interest payments are granted to borrowers.

The Arts Public support for the arts takes the form of government grants to independent agencies, of which the Arts Council of Great Britain is the most important. It gives financial help to opera, dance, and drama companies, orchestras, the visual arts, small touring theaters, experimental groups, and many other organizations. A growing source of funds is sponsorship and patronage by industry and commerce. The British Council promotes knowledge of British culture and English language overseas by initiating or supporting tours by British companies and artists.

London is one of the world's major centers for theater, opera, and dance, and there are many important companies outside

COUNTRY PROFILES

the capital. The National Theater stages classical and modern plays in its three auditoriums on the south bank of the River Thames, while the Royal Shakespeare Company (RSC) produces plays by Shakespeare and his contemporaries, as well as modern work, in its two auditoriums in the City's Barbican Centre; the RSC also performs at its theater in Stratford-upon-Avon, the birthplace of Shakespeare. Outside London, most cities and many large towns have at least one theater.

The Royal Opera, Covent Garden, and the English National Opera are the main London opera companies; Scotland, Wales, and Northern Ireland have their own companies. Some 240 professional arts festivals take place each year, including the Edinburgh International Festival. Over 1,000 museums and art galleries are open to the public, including the major national museums (mostly located in London), which contain a world-famous collection of objects of artistic, archaeological, scientific, historical, and general interest.

Profile 11   West Germany

This report has been prepared from information provided by:

"Facts About Germany, The Federal Republic of Germany." Lexikon Institut Bertelsmann, 1986.

"Welcome to the Federal Republic of Germany." Prestel Verlag München, 1985.

Department of State, Bureau of Public Affairs, *Background Notes — The Federal Republic of Germany* (Washington, D.C.: U.S. Government Printing Office, May 1987).

Geography   The Federal Republic of Germany (FRG) is located in north-central Europe, bordered by the North and Baltic Seas, Denmark, France, Belgium, the German Democratic Republic (GDR, or East Germany), the Netherlands, Czechoslovakia, Austria, Switzerland, and Luxembourg. The terrain varies from the plains of the northern lowlands through the central uplands and Alpine foothills to the Bavarian Alps. The Alps extend along the southern boundary from Lake Konstanz (Bodensee)—a lake on the Swiss border—to the Austrian border near Salzburg. The highest peak is the Zugspitze (9,720 ft–2,916 m). To the west is the Rhine River, the most important commercial waterway in

C O U N T R Y   P R O F I L E S

Exhibit **C11.1** Map of West Germany

Europe. In the southwestern corner of the country is the Black Forest, so named because of the deep green of its firs and because their thick cover keeps the forest floor in twilight.

The climate varies but is mainly temperate. The average winter temperature in the north is 35°F (1.6°C) and in the south 27°F (−2.7°C). Summer temperatures average 61°F to 66°F (16°C to 18°C) in the north and 68°F (20°C) or slightly higher in the south. Sometimes the country experiences the Foehn—a warm, tropical wind similar to the French Mistral or the Canadian Chinook—which breaks the cloud cover and melts the snow in the spring.

Demography

The population density is 247 persons per sq km, one of the highest in Europe with only the Netherlands and Belgium surpassing it. The population is distributed unevenly; major conurbation areas are the Rhein–Ruhr (Essen, Dortmund, Köln [Cologne], Düsseldorf) region, the Rhein–Main areas, the Swabian industrial belt around Stuttgart, and the concentrations around the cities of Bremen, Hamburg, Hanover, Nürnberg (Nuremberg), and München (Munich). The population density is greatest in the Ruhr district, where 9 percent of the federal German population lives in only 2 percent of its sovereign area. In the central part of this German industrial heartland, an extreme population density of 5,500 per sq km is reached. Every third inhabitant of the FRG lives in a large town or city—about 20 million were living in 65 towns with a population of more than 100,000 in 1984.

German is the mother tongue of more than 100 million people; in addition to being spoken in the two German states it is the official language in Austria and Liechtenstein and one of the official languages in Switzerland. In international political and economic usage, German plays a lesser role than English, French, Russian, and Spanish. Its importance is greater in the cultural field; every tenth book in the world is published in

Exhibit **C11.2** Geographic Data

> *Area:* 95,606 sq mi (248,577 sq km), including West Berlin; about the size of Wyoming
>
> *Terrain:* Low plain in the north; high plains, hills, and basins in the center; mountainous Alpine region in the south
>
> *Climate:* Temperate; cooler and rainier than much of the U.S.

COUNTRY PROFILES

Exhibit **C11.3** Demographic Data

Nationality: Noun and adjective—German

Population 61 million (including West Berlin),
(July 1986 est.): declining gradually because of low birth-
rates

Population Density: 638 persons per sq mi (247 per sq km)

Cities: Capital—Bonn (pop. 292,000); other cities—West
Berlin (1.8 million), Hamburg (1.6 million), Munich
(1.3 million)

Ethnic Groups: Primarily German; Dutch minority

Religions: Protestant 44%, Roman Catholic 45%

Language: German

Education: Years compulsory 10; attendance 100%; total
literacy 99%

German; among the languages most frequently translated into others it is third, after English and French, and it is the language into which the most translations are made.

A large number of foreign workers and their dependents (altogether about 4.5 million people) are residents of West Germany. Half of them have lived there for ten years or more. Most Germans and foreigners try to get along; however, relationships are not free of friction, especially in some cities where the foreigners comprise more than 20 percent of the population. The largest group—1.5 million, mainly Moslem Turks—have the greatest difficulties in adjusting to the alien life-style and culture of their host country. This sometimes generates mistrust and hostility on both sides.

Religion Freedom of faith, conscience, and freedom of creed, whether religious or ideological (*weltanschaulick*), are inviolable. The undisturbed practice of religion is guaranteed. About 90 percent of the population belong to Christian churches—half Catholic, half Protestant—with a small minority in other Christian denominations. Protestants are in the majority in the north, Catholics in the south. The *Länder* (states) of Rheinland–Pfalz (Rhineland–Palatinate), Saarland, and Bayern (Bavaria) are mainly Catholic; the two major denominations are about

COUNTRY PROFILES

equally strong in Baden–Württemberg and Nordrhein–West-falen (North-Rhine–Westphalia); elsewhere Protestants predominate. There is no state church in the FRG.

Education   The entire school system, including private schools, is under state supervision; the states are responsible for school matters, thus systems vary across the country. A federal–state commission works toward coordinated education planning and research promotion. School attendance is compulsory from the ages of six to eighteen, during which time full-time attendance is required for nine years and part-time attendance at vocational school thereafter. Attendance at all public schools is free. Study materials, in particular school books, are partly free of charge. The Basic Law demands that religious instruction be a regular subject. Girls and boys attend mixed classes except in older classes where sports are taken separately. Ninety percent of the youngsters who end their general schooling at the primary or intermediate level go into vocational training, most of them in the "dual system." This comprises practical, on-the-job learning with theoretical instruction in vocational schools. Private enterprise and the state are thus jointly responsible for vocational training. There are about 430 recognized occupations for which formal training is required. The practical on-the-job training—usually called apprenticeship—takes from two to three and a half years, depending on the occupation; in most cases the process requires three years. The apprentice is paid "training money," which increases annually.

Economy

The FRG's trade with other EEC states far exceeds that with other countries. In 1985, about 50.8 percent of the FRG's imports came from EEC states, while the FRG sold them 49.8 percent of its exports. The Federal Republic's two biggest trading partners are France and the Netherlands. On the suppliers list of German importers, the Netherlands takes first place, France second. France was the biggest buyer of German exports, followed by the United States.

Foreign Exchange   The basic unit of currency in the Federal Republic of Germany, including Berlin (West) is the deutsche mark (DM1 = 100 pfennigs), introduced in a 1948 currency reform that replaced the reichsmark.

Government

Political System   The government is parliamentary and based on a democratic constitution (Basic Law) emphasizing the protection of individual liberty and divided power in a federal structure. The republic consists of ten states (*Länder*). The chancellor (prime minister) heads the executive branch of the

C
O
U
N
T
R
Y

P
R
O
F
I
L
E
S

Exhibit **C11.4** Economic Data

> *GNP (1986 est.):* US$898.9 billion
>
> *Annual Growth Rate (1986):* 2.6%
>
> *Per Capita Income:* US$10,600
>
> *Underlying Inflation Rate:* Less than 1%
>
> *Natural Resources:* Iron, hard coal, lignite, potash, and gas
>
> *Agriculture:* (1.7% of GNP) corn, wheat, potatoes, sugar
>   beets, barley, hops, and viniculture.
>
> *Industry:* (48% of GNP) iron and steel, coal, chemicals,
>   electrical products, ships, and vehicles

federal government. The Cabinet, consisting of the chancellor and the federal ministers, is usually referred to as the government. The duties of the president (chief of state) are largely ceremonial. Real power is exercised by the chancellor. Although elected by and responsible to the Bundestag (lower and principal chamber of the Parliament), the chancellor cannot be removed from office during a four-year term unless the Bundestag has agreed on a successor. The Bundestag, also elected for a four-year term, consists of 496 deputies, plus 22 repre-

Exhibit **C11.5** Trade Statistics

> *Trade (1985):* Exports—US$298 billion in chemicals, motor
>   vehicles, iron and steel products, and electrical
>   and other manufactured products; imports—
>   US$247.2 billion in food, petroleum products,
>   manufactured goods, electrical products,
>   automobiles, and apparel
>
> *Major Markets:* EEC 49.8%; other European countries 17.6%;
>   USA 10.3%; developing countries 7.7%
>
> *Major Suppliers:* EEC 50.8%; other European countries
>   14.5%; USA 7%; developing countries 9.6%
>
> *Exchange Rate (May 1987):* About 1.76 deutsche marks
>   (DM) = US$1

COUNTRY PROFILES

sentatives from Berlin, who have no vote in plenary sessions except on procedural matters. The FRG has an independent judiciary consisting of a Federal Constitutional Court, a Federal High Court of Justice, and federal courts with jurisdiction in administrative, financial, labor, and social matters. The highest court is the Federal Constitutional Court, consisting of twenty-four members serving in two panels of twelve each. The principal functions of the Court are to ensure uniform interpretation of constitutional provisions and to protect the fundamental rights of the individual citizen as defined in the Basic Law.

Groups in Power   The eleventh Deutscher Bundestag was elected on 25 January 1987. The Social Democrats (SPD), Christian Democrats (CDU), and Christian Social Union (CSU, from Bavaria) suffered slight losses, the Free Democrats (FDP) and Greens (Die Grünen) gained. CDU, CSU, and FDP had stated before the election that they intended to continue governing together in coalition. Together they achieved quite a respectable majority in the Bundestag.

Monetary and Fiscal Policies   Prices have risen moderately in recent years, economic growth has increased, and the number of people in work is rising; nevertheless persistent high unemployment has been a problem. In this situation, the federal government has put its greatest effort into reinvigorating market forces and stimulating investment. Both are seen as important prerequisites to reducing unemployment. The same aim is pursued by retraining and further-training programs to keep workers fit for the constantly changing demands on them. The federal government's policy on small- and medium-size businesses is designed to help them improve their efficiency and contributes to the protection and creation of jobs.

Trade Policies   The Federal Republic of Germany favors free world trade and rejects all forms of protectionism. Because it exports around 30 percent of its GNP it depends on open markets. It is vital to the economy of the FRG that the European internal market be expanded and old markets outside the EEC be retained while new ones are developed.

Objectives   The foreign policy of the Federal Republic of Germany is an active and global peace policy. The FRG's security rests on the Atlantic Alliance; on the one hand, indispensable to this unity is the friendship and close cooperation with the United States, and on the other, the political, economic, and cultural future of the Federal Republic lies in a united Europe. Thus, a primary objective is further development of the EEC

C
O
U
N
T
R
Y

P
R
O
F
I
L
E
S

to a European union. The driving force in this process of uni-fication has been and remains the friendship between Germany and France; cooperation with Great Britain has also become increasingly important.

In addition, relations with the Soviet Union are of central importance to the FRG. If Soviet policy opens up new opportunities for more understanding and cooperation, the federal government will seize them. This applies especially to progress in the field of disarmament and arms control. The aim of the FRG is and will remain to guarantee security for all concerned with a balanced and low level of military strength.

The Federal Republic of Germany regards its relationship with the countries of the Third World as an ongoing, comprehensive dialogue between partners with equal rights; it supports the developing countries' struggle for independence and self-determination. The governmental development policy aims primarily to help regions with weak structures and performance. Development aid is seen as a task for society as a whole, and private initiative is encouraged.

Attitudes Toward Foreigners The CDU–CSU–FDP federal government has adopted new policies toward foreigners. These are based on three fundamentals:

- promotion of integration of foreign workers who have been in the country for a long time, whereby integration does not mean loss of their identity but coexistence with Germans with as little friction as possible
- no more recruitment of foreigners and restriction of entry of foreigners' dependents
- financial aid for those who wish to return home.

Foreign direct investment in the FRG is constantly growing and in 1983 stood at some DM81,000. Nine-tenths of this came from Europe and the United States.

Business

Industry is concentrated in the *Länder* of Nordrhein–Westfalen, Bayern, Baden–Württemberg, Niedersachsen (Lower Saxony), Hessen, and the Saarland. It underwent a rapid upswing after the war. Today industry and the crafts together account for almost half the GNP. A major factor in this development was the 1948 change over from a controlled economy to a social market economy. One of the pillars of the market economy system is entrepreneurial self-responsibility; the state restricts its intervention to furthering social balance and creating favorable economic conditions. The federal government takes the view that competition between enterprises is the best way to assure the technological and structural competitiveness of German industry in world markets.

Almost all large enterprises in the FRG have the legal form of *Aktiengesellschaft* (limited company, stock corporation). In 1984, there were 2,118 such companies with a combined share capital of DM103,000 million. West Germany was among the first countries to institutionalize democracy or worker participation at the board-of-directors level. This system is now well established and accepted both by workers and management.

Ironmaking   Until the mid-1970s, ironmaking was one of the FRG's major industries. After that it experienced a sales crisis due to oversupply on the world market. Especially hard hit by this was the heavy industry of the Ruhr and Saarland. By providing public funds the state has promoted modernization of the steel industry.

Chemicals   The most important basic materials and production goods segment in the FRG is now the chemical industry. Of its total labor force of 586,000, almost half are employed by three large enterprises that are among the eight largest in the country as a whole. In 1984, the combined revenue of the FRG's chemical industry was DM170,400 million.

Machine and Vehicle Construction   Of particular importance are capital goods industries, including machines, road vehicles, aircraft, ships, provision of electrical engineering, and the production of office machinery and data-processing equipment. In 1984, 3.5 million passenger cars, 237,000 trucks, 119,000 motorcycles, and 3 million bicycles were produced. After the United States and Japan, the Federal Republic of Germany is the third largest automobile producer. More than a million people work in machine manufacturing, which in 1984 made a revenue of DM142,000 million, representing about 10 percent of all industrial revenue. The aerospace industry employs 54,000 people. In 1984, this segment produced revenue of DM8,700 million.

Electrical Engineering, Office Equipment, and Data Processing   With its 1984 revenue of more than DM155,000 million, its 11 percent share of total industrial output, and a work force of more than a million, the electrical engineering industry ranks fifth in overall importance, after food production, road vehicle production, chemicals, and machine construction. It is one of the segments with above-average growth and employs a wide range of new technologies.

C
O
U
N
T
R
Y

P
R
O
F
I
L
E
S

Consumer Goods, Food, Beverage, and Tobacco Total revenue of consumer goods industries in 1984 was DM181,000 million. The major segments in this sector are textiles and garment manufacture, together employing more than 558,000 people. The food, tobacco, and beverage industries had a 1984 revenue of DM173,000 million. The largest share of this was in the food industry, which includes dairies and breweries. See Exhibit C11.6.

Wages West Germans' incomes come from a wide range of sources. The major source by far is dependent employment, that is, wages and salaries. In addition, there are shareholders' dividends, property and assets, and state transfer payments such as child allowances, unemployment benefits, and pensions of various kinds. See Exhibit C11.7.

Infrastructure

Banks The FRG's central bank is the Deutsche Bundesbank in Frankfurt am Main; its main administration in each of the federal states is called *Landeszentrabank*. Bundesbank bodies are the Central Bank Council and the executive boards of the *Landeszentrabank*; these operate independent of directives from the Bonn government to determine monetary policy. The executive board implements the Central Bank Council decisions. Apart from the sole right to issue bank notes, the job of the Deutsche Bundesbank is to support the general economic policy of the federal government, to ensure the stability of the deutsche mark, and to regulate the money supply in circulation. It has various means of doing this; it can inject money into the economy by purchasing securities, or withdraw money by selling them. The Bundesbank can also influence the amount of money in circulation by setting minimum reserves that com-

Exhibit **C11.6** Major Companies, 1984

Firm	Sector	Revenue (DM millions)	Employees
1. Veba AG	Energy, petroleum	48,611	76,795
2. Siemens AG	Electrical engineering	45,819	319,000
3. Volkswagenwerk AG	Motor vehicles	45,671	283,353
4. Daimler-Benz AG	Motor vehicles	43,505	199,872
5. Bayer AG	Chemicals	43,032	174,755
6. BASF AG	Chemicals	42,596	115,816
7. Hoechst AG	Chemicals	41,457	177,940
8. Thyssen AG	Iron and steel	32,430	132,954

COUNTRY PROFILES

| Exhibit **C11.7** | Average Employee Monthly Gross Earnings in Industry (in DM), 1984 | |

Branch	Male wage earners	Male salary earners
Industry overall	2,870	4,340
Energy production	3,209	4,165
Mining	3,107	4,757
Iron and steel	2,830	4,246
Petroleum process	3,671	5,397
Chemicals	3,102	4,481
Machine construction	2,856	4,295
Road vehicle construction	3,143	4,803
Electrical engineering	2,695	4,447
Textiles	2,444	3,769
	Female wage earners	Female salary earners
Industry overall	2,076	2,886

mercial banks must leave with the Bundesbank in relation to their short-term liabilities. In addition, discounting is used as a major form of lending; by raising or lowering the discount rate at which it buys bills, the Bundesbank can influence the demand for credit.

Public, cooperative, and private credit institutions operate in the FRG. At the end of 1984, there were 247 lending banks, 12 giro clearing banks, 591 savings banks, 9 cooperative central banks, 3,707 larger credit cooperatives, 37 mortgage institutions and public mortgage banks, 16 banks with special functions, and 82 installment credit institutions. Giro banks are the central credit institutions of the public savings banks in the various *Bundeslander*; as the house banks of the federal states, they concentrate their activities on regional financing tasks. Most savings banks are operated by local governments or groupings of local authorities; in their legal form, they are autonomous public enterprises. *Zentralkasen* are the regional central institutions of rural and commercial credit cooperatives. Mortgage banks are private real-estate credit institutions that give mortgages and local authority loans and raise their funds for these by issuing mortgage bonds and local authority bonds. The German capital market is characterized by a high absorption of fixed-interest securities. The circulation of bonds of real estate and local authority credit institutions of the FRG at the end of 1984 totaled DM850,000 million. Of this, DM327,000 million were local government bonds. Their proceeds are used not only to finance loans to local governments but also on a considerable scale for credits to the federation and its special funds, federal railways and the federal post office, as well as the *Länder*.

Transportation   Transportation in the FRG is one of the major concerns of social and economic policies. Transportation is also a major economic factor in terms of employment. About 940,000 workers are employed by 81,000 enterprises.

The German Federal Railways   The largest transportation enterprise in Germany is the state-owned federal railway, the Deutsche Bundesbahn (DB). This employs about 285,000 people, with a rail network comprising about 17,398 mi (28,000 km), some 11,300 of which are electrified. These routes handle 85 percent of the railway services. The railways are indispensable for bulk and heavy transports and especially long-distance passenger travel; however, competition from the motorcar poses a serious threat to the railways. Despite all efforts, the federal railway is in the red, with a 1984 deficit of DM3,100 million; although the railways that year received federal government support grants of DM13,400 million. To improve the economic performance of the railways, a number of measures have recently been taken. These include rationalization, modernization of track and rolling stock, reduction of personnel, and closure of uneconomic lines.

Roads   Roads have taken the lead in the competition with rail transport. This is mainly because the efficient network of federal, state, and communal roads enables door-to-door goods transportation without reloading. Short - and long-distance road goods transportation accounts for some 80 percent of the total and almost 50 percent of the transport output in ton-kilometers. The road network had grown to about 304,470 mi (490,000 km) by 1985, when there were 5,093 mi (8,196 km) of motorways (autobahns). The length of the network is second only to that of the United States.

Shipping   Because it is export- and import-oriented, the FRG needs a strong merchant fleet to represent German shipping interests in international maritime trade. The merchant fleet of the Federal Republic of Germany has about 1.5 percent of the world merchant tonnage and holds seventeenth place among the shipping nations. The ports of Hamburg, Bremen, Bremerhaven, and Lübeck are the main seaports. These are connected to inland centers by an efficient waterway network; the length

C O U N T R Y   P R O F I L E S .

of the rivers, canals, and lakes regularly used by inland ships is some 4,400 km.

Aviation Lufthansa is considered one of the most successful international airlines. In 1984, it carried 15.3 million passengers and 525,000 tn of freight. The airports are operated by private companies and air traffic control is operated by a government agency. They meet international safety requirements to a high degree. Their safety standards are kept up to date and their capacities are continually adapted to demand.

Medical Facilities There are about 161,000 doctors and 34,000 dentists in the FRG, or one doctor to every 380 inhabitants, and one dentist to every 1,800. This makes the FRG medically one of the best-equipped countries in the world. However, access to doctors and dentists is not equally good everywhere. In rural areas and on the urban peripheries, there is often a lack of doctors.

Schools At the age of six, children enter primary school (*Grundschule*). In general, this lasts four years and in West Berlin, six years. All children attend primary school together. Thereafter, they choose between several possibilities; most children subsequently attend a short-course secondary school (*Hauptschule*), then at the age of fifteen go into vocational training. Intermediate school (*Realschule*), as a rule, takes six years; *Realschule* leads to a graduating certificate at an intermediate level between *Hauptschule* and senior high school (*Gymnasium*). The intermediate certificate qualifies children for attendance at a technical school (*Fachschule*), specialized schools offering vocational training at upper-secondary level. The nine-year *Gymnasium* is the traditional senior high school in Germany. Graduation from the *Gymnasium*, and receiving the so-called "maturity certificate," is the entitlement for study at the university.

Some 1,300,000 students are enrolled at the FRG's universities; seventy thousand are foreigners. Traditionally, students are free to shape their own courses of study. No study fees are charged at the universities, and if the student cannot pay living expenses, the state helps.

Mass Media The Basic Law guarantees everyone the right freely to express and disseminate opinion by speech, writing, and pictures. In 1984, there were 25 million radio and 22.4 million television receivers registered in the Federal Republic of Germany. That means 95 percent of all households had radio and 87 percent had television. More than 21 million newspapers are sold every day. Four out of five West Germans read a newspaper daily. About 5 percent of the population are reached by no medium at all. The great majority keep themselves regularly informed from two or even three media. The press in Germany is privately owned. The dailies market is shared by 382 publishers. They circulate about 1,270 editions, which vary in local content. About 9,500 periodicals are published in the FRG; they cover entertainment, specialized fields, work, housing, customer service, and also include membership journals of small associations and large organizations, with circulations ranging from 250 to 7.4 million (the ADAC motoring club magazine is the largest). Economic development in the press market has led to the formation of large publishing houses and groups that influence editorial, economic, and technical trends. In the daily press sector, the biggest conglomerate is the Axel Springer AG; its share of about a fifth of the newspaper market is largely due to the high circulation of the newspaper *Bild*.

The broadcasting media are not state-controlled, but broadcasting order and freedom are regulated by law. There are nine regional combined radio–TV corporations plus two radio-only corporations set up under federal law, and a second national television network. The regional corporations are linked together in a Standing Conference of German Public Law Broadcasting Corporations. Each broadcasts several radio programs, and together they operate a nationally-seen television program officially called "German Television" but generally referred to as "Channel One." In addition, they produce regional "third" TV programs. The broadcasting media all have basically the same system of self-government. It is exercised through three main organs. First is the Broadcasting Council, which is, in effect, the parliament of the corporation and consists of representatives of all important political, ideological, and social groups; the council deals with fundamental issues concerning the corporation and elects the director-general. Second is the Administrative Council, which watches over the day-to-day management of the corporation. And third is the director-general, who is the responsible chief executive, including control of program content.

This self-administration system guarantees the broadcasting corporations' independence from the state. It does not, however, exclude all political influence. The corporations are required by law to give equal chances to express opinions to all. The broadcasting corporations obtain most of their funds in the form of listener-viewer subscription fees. A smaller share of the stations' revenues comes from commercial advertising.

COUNTRY PROFILES

Life-Style

The German nation grew out of a number of tribes. There were Franks, Saxons, Bavarians, and Swabians before there were "Germans." The old tribes have long since lost their original character; but each in its own way continued the tribal tradition.

These German tribes are distinguished from one another by their dialects. Except for those who have learned the standard German language at school, people as a rule can be identified as Hussians, Hamburgians, Thuringians, and so forth by the dialect of a particular region, even though they may be trying to speak the purer "High German" (*Hochdeutsch*).

Germany has never had a predominant center in which the nation's entire public life is concentrated. The lack of such a center has influenced cultural life, making Germany a country with many centers (for example, the central library of the Federal Republic of Germany in Frankfurt and the book trade is concentrated here; Hamburg has the largest concentration of press publishing; most theaters are in München; the central state archives are in Koblenz; there are scientific academies in Düsseldorf, Göttingen, Heidelberg, Mainz, and München; the major museums are in Berlin; and the largest literary archives are in the small Württemberg town of Marbach am Neckar). The establishment and maintenance of most cultural facilities in the Federal Republic of Germany is the responsibility of local government, but legislation in cultural matters is the prerogative of the states.

Public subsidies are generous in the worlds of music and the theater. The FRG counts 72 orchestras and 185 theaters that receive subsidies from state or local governments; to this must be added the excellent orchestras of the various radio corporations, as well as the numerous private musical societies cultivating special kinds of music and the many private theaters and cabarets with a purely entertainment function.

In Germany, festivals are as numerous as the days of the year; there is always something going on, such as a popular festival, a religious feast, a folk dance, a historical or costume parade, or simply an occasion for public merrymaking and amusement such as the famous "Oktoberfest"—the world's biggest beer festival, held in München (Munich).

Growing incomes and rapid economic advancement have meant an increased demand for quality housing; almost all new dwellings have a bath and central heating, and are connected to public electricity and water supplies. The rising standard of living is also reflected by the increasing size of dwellings. In addition, nine out of ten households have television and radio receivers, as well as telephones. Appliances that ease housework are particularly favored by German families; refrigerators,

C
O
U
N
T
R
Y

P
R
O
F
I
L
E
S

vacuum cleaners, electric washing machines, and sewing machines are taken for granted in almost all homes.

In their outward style of living and appearance, all social groups have become similar. Four-fifths of the population live completely or predominantly from their capacity to work, whereas only a small minority are able to live on the profits from their assets. About half of the employee households own their apartments or houses. The automobile has become part of most worker households and has increased mobility to an unprecedented degree; but at the same time, it has led to an expenditure on the infrastructure (road construction, environmental protection) so great as to give rise to doubts about whether individual transportation should continue to enjoy priority. Almost every employee has a small-, sometimes even medium-size sum of savings "for a rainy day." This generally high standard of living often cannot be achieved or sustained without both spouses working; it is also possible, in part, because smaller families with one or two children have become the norm in the FRG.

Profile **12** Yugoslavia

This report has been prepared from information provided by:

Department of State, Bureau of Public Affairs, *Background Notes—Yugoslavia* (Washington, D.C.: U.S. Government Printing Office, October 1985).

"Facts About Yugoslavia," The Federal Secretariat for Information, Belgrade, 1985.

"Tourism, Where, How and Why Invest in Yugoslavia," Belgrade, 1987.

Geography

Area   The Socialist Federal Republic of Yugoslavia consists of six socialist republics: Bosnia–Herzegovina, Croatia, Macedonia, Montenegro, Serbia, and Slovenia. There are also two socialist autonomous provinces—Kosovo and Vojvodina—which form part of the Socialist Republic of Serbia. Yugoslavia covers an area of 99,000 sq mi (255,804 sq km) in the southeast part of Europe, mostly in the Balkans. Its land frontiers are 1,845 mi (2,969 km) long.

Exhibit **C12.1** Map of Yugoslavia

Yugoslavia

——————	International boundary
—·—·—	Republic boundary
— — —	Autonomous area boundary
★	National capital
⊚	Republic or autonomous area capital
+—+—+	Railroad
——————	Road

0 25 50 75 100 Kilometers
0 25 50 75 100 Miles

Climate   There are three basic types of climate in Yugoslavia. The narrow coastal belt has a Mediterranean climate with hot dry summers and mild rainy winters; in the mountainous regions the summers are short and cool and the winters long with abundant snowfall; the Pannonian, or continental, climate prevails in the northern plains with hot summers and cold winters.

Topography   About 70 percent of Yugoslavia's territory is more than 650 ft (200 m) above sea level. The mountainous region lies mainly south of the Sava and Danube Rivers and extends from the extreme northwest to the extreme southeast of the country. The Alps cover the northwestern part. Lowlands extend

C
O
U
N
T
R
Y

P
R
O
F
I
L
E
S

across the north of the country, along the Danube and its trib-
utaries—the Drava, Sava, and Tisa. The Adriatic coastal region
is a geographical entity composed of islands, a narrow coastal
belt, and the hinterland, which is separated from the rest of
the country by the steep Dinaric Mountains. The length of the
coast as the crow flies is 380 mi (610 km), but the actual
coastline, which is highly indented is 1,300 mi (2,092 km).
The Adriatic Sea separates the Appenine and Balkan peninsulas.
The average winter water temperature in the southern part is
around 9°C, and in the north 6°C. The summer water temperature averages around 25°C. The Adriatic Sea is clear and trans-
parent, allowing visibility to depths of 70 to 100 ft (22 to 33 m)
(in the south). There are about 300 lakes, but only 6 of them
are larger than 4 sq mi (10 sq km). There are 1,850 rivers with
courses longer than 6.2 mi (10 km), with a total length of over
73,322 mi (118,000 km). They drain into three seas: the Adriatic
(20 percent), Aegean (10 percent), and Black Sea (70 percent).
About 34 percent of Yugoslav territory is covered by woodland—four-fifths is deciduous and one-fifth coniferous. Farmland (58 percent of the total area) comprises 10.5 million ha
(hectares) of orchards, meadows, and grazing land.

Demography

The multinational composition of the population is a distinctive feature of the Socialist Federal Republic of Yugoslavia.
In 1981, the figures were 4,428,005 Croats, 1,339,729 Macedonians, 579,023 Montenegrins, 1,999,957 Moslems, 8,140,452
Serbs, and 1,753,554 Slovenes, while 1,219,045 declared
themselves as Yugoslavs. The figures for the national minorities were: Albanians 1,730,364, Hungarians 426,666, Turks
101,191, Slovaks 80,334, Romanies 168,099, Bulgarians 36,185,
Rumanians 54,954, Ruthenians 23,285, Czechs 19,625, Italians
15,132, and Ukrainians 12,813. Persons belonging to individual Yugoslav nationalities live in their own national republics
as well as in other parts of Yugoslavia. The national minorities
are also represented in several republics.

Languages The Montenegrins, Croats, Moslems, and Serbs
speak the same language, which is variously called Serbo-
Croatian or Croato-Serbian. The Macedonians and Slovenes each
have their own languages. All three are treated as equal, official
languages of Yugoslavia, as are the two alphabets in use: Latin
and Cyrillic. The languages of the nationalities (national minorities) are also treated as equal in the regions in which they live
and are used in education, law, administration, and so forth.

COUNTRY PROFILES

Religion   Religion in Yugoslavia is divided among:

* The Eastern Orthodox Church, 41 percent
* The Roman Catholic Church, 32 percent
* The Islamic faith, 12 percent
* Other, 3 percent
* None, 12 percent

Population   According to a census taken in 1981, Yugoslavia had 22,424,711 inhabitants (in 1985 it was estimated to be 23,137,000). The average density of population was 87.7 persons per sq km (the Socialist Republic of Serbia being the most densely populated at 105.4, per sq km and Montenegro the least with 42.3 per sq km). Industrialization has led to large-scale migration from country to town.

Economy

The Yugoslav economy is founded on a socialist system in which the associated workers themselves, using socially owned means of production, manage the production process and business affairs, thus deciding themselves on the conditions and results of their work. Economic and social development and market relations are guided through social planning on a basis of self-management. Yugoslavia belongs to the group of countries that has recorded the highest rate of economic growth in the postwar period.

Despite changing policy directions, Yugoslavia's medium- and long-term economic goals have remained constant—high growth and rapid industrialization. Industrial policy has focused on developing technology in a wide range of domestic industries. The rapid industrial expansion has been conditioned on a major increase in imports of raw materials, semifinished products, key components, and industrial equipment.

Faced with the familiar problems of a developing country—rapid inflation, significant unemployment (particularly in the south), and severe balance-of-payments and debt pressures, the Yugoslav government has worked intensively to stabilize the foreign debt situation by strengthening its balance-of-payments position. Balance-of-payments surpluses were achieved in 1983 and 1984, with the assistance of debt rescheduling agreements with foreign creditors, and further refinancing arrangements for the period 1985 to 1990 were negotiated. A number of economic stabilization and adjustment measures have already been enacted, including implementation of measures for setting of prices of domestically produced goods; amendments to the foreign investment law; and measures to improve the profitability of enterprises.

Exhibit **C12.2** Economic Data

> *GNP (1984):* US$46.3 billion
>
> *Annual Growth Rate (1983–1984):* 1.7%
>
> *Per Capita GNP (1984):* US$2,017
>
> *Average Inflation Rate (1984):* 57%
>
> *Natural Resources:* Coal, copper, bauxite, timber, iron, antimony, chromium, lead, zinc, asbestos, and mercury
>
> *Agriculture:* Corn, wheat, tobacco, sugar beets, and livestock
>
> *Land:* 69% arable, 33% of which is plow land
>
> *Industry:* Wood, processed food, nonferrous metals, machinery, textiles, leather goods, and construction

Trade Yugoslavia strives for a rough balance in its trade relations with Western nations, with the Socialist bloc, and with developing countries. In 1984, Yugoslav trade with the Soviet Union and other members of the Council for Mutual Economic Assistance amounted to about 39 percent of total trade; trade with Western industrialized countries of the Organization for Economic Cooperation and Development accounted for about

Exhibit **C12.3** Trade Statistics

> *Trade (1984):* Exports—US$10.2 billion in agricultural products (including processed meats), wooden furniture, leather goods and shoes, tobacco, textiles, ships, mineral ores, metal products; imports—US$12 billion in machinery and metal products, chemicals, iron, petroleum, coking coal, steel, and agricultural products.
>
> *Major Markets:* USSR, Italy, FRG, Czechoslovakia, USA
>
> *Major Sources:* USSR, FRG, Italy, Iraq
>
> *Official Exchange Rate (July 1985):* 285 dinars (Din) = US$1

COUNTRY PROFILES

41 percent, and trade with the Third World for about 20 percent. The United States was in sixth place among Yugoslavia's major trading partners, with a 4.7 percent share of total trade. Total volume of trade between the two countries has held steady since 1982, at around US $1 billion. In 1984, U.S. exports to Yugoslavia amounted to US $620 million and imports from Yugoslavia to US $431 million.

Due to a shortage of foreign exchange, future export opportunities for Western companies will be concentrated in certain industry sectors designated by the Yugoslav government for further development; such prospects include energy, transportation, agriculture, food processing, and, in addition, any products for which demand is high, such as metalworking equipment, electronic components, computers and peripherals, analytical and scientific instruments, and telecommunications equipment. A good market will also exist for machinery and supplies intended for export-oriented Yugoslav manufacturers.

Government

Each republic or province has a government (with considerable autonomy) modeled on the federal structure. The federal government has executive, legislative, and judicial branches. The presidency of the Socialist Federal Republic of Yugoslavia is the supreme executive and policy-making body of the government. It consists of one representative from each of the six republics and two autonomous provinces, and, ex officio, the president of the party. The president's one-year term rotates each May 15 among the members in prescribed order. The other members of the presidency are elected for five-year terms by the republican and provincial assemblies in joint sessions; the last election of the presidency took place in 1984.

The Assembly consists of two houses, the Federal Chamber and the Chamber of Republics and Provinces. The Federal Chamber has 30 delegates from each republic and 20 from each autonomous province (220 total) elected from local assemblies that are themselves elected in factories, institutions, townships, and other "interest communities." The Assembly's executive and administrative arm is the Federal Executive Council, which is essentially equivalent to a cabinet. Its members are roughly selected on the principle of equal representation of the republics and provinces. Its presiding officer (called the president, and similar to a prime minister) is proposed by the presidency and elected by the assembly. Milka Planinc was elected president in May 1982.

Certain basic human rights are recognized and protected in Yugoslavia. Most Yugoslavs may travel abroad freely, and emigration is permitted. Churches are open, and seminaries are allowed to function and even expand. Private property rights

Exhibit **C12.4** Government Data

> *Type:* Federal republic
>
> *Independence:* 1 December 1918
>
> *Constitution:* February 1974
>
> *Branches:* Executive—president of the Presidency (chief of state) rotated annually from among the collective body; premier (head of government and president of the Federal Executive Council, 4-year term); legislative—bicameral Federal Assembly (308 delegates); Federal Chamber, Chamber of Republics and Provinces, Federal Executive Council (Cabinet, Assembly's executive arm); judicial—Constitutional Court, Federal Supreme Court
>
> *Political Party:* League of Communists of Yugoslavia
>
> *Suffrage:* Universal over 18
>
> *Administrative Subdivisions:* 6 Republics, 2 autonomous provinces
>
> *Defense* (1983 est.): 5.2% of GNP
>
> *Flag:* Blue, white, and red horizontal stripes with a centered five-pointed red star edged in gold

are respected—84 percent of all farmland is owned privately—and in manufacturing, firms with some private participation have begun to operate. Economic and social rights are strongly protected to the point that it is difficult to fire a worker, even if there is a good reason to. Only one political party is permitted; the press is restricted and subject to party direction (though not to the rigid controls common in Warsaw Pact countries); individuals can be jailed for criticism of the government, the party, or the late President Tito. Basic to the Yugoslav system is the concept of self-management, which affords operational control to workers' councils in factories and other organizations and institutions. The aim is to produce a genuine federalism through decentralized decision making.

The League of Communists (LCY) is the only political party permitted to function. The executive and policy management of the party is conducted by a twenty three-member presidency that includes three representatives from each republic, two

COUNTRY PROFILES

from each province, and one from the armed forces. This body establishes and implements party policy guidelines set by senior party leaders. The party does not function as a Soviet-style monolith but permits open expression of differences on some major policy issues.

Yugoslavia has succeeded in establishing friendly relations with most other countries, regardless of their sociopolitical systems. To reinforce its independence, Yugoslavia has sought to maintain diplomatic and economic ties with the West, particularly Western Europe. Relations with the Soviet Union fluctuate between periods of wary rapprochement and uneasy tension.

A cofounder of the Nonaligned Movement, Yugoslavia has made nonalignment the cornerstone of its foreign policy and a platform from which to project Yugoslav influence and leadership in the Third World and international forums. The Yugoslavs strive to create an alternative to superpower blocs, to build the Nonaligned Movement into an effective political force internationally, and to uphold the movement's traditional opposition to foreign domination, both from "imperialism" and "hegemonism"—the code word for Soviet imperialism.

Membership in International Organizations   Yugoslavia is a member of the UN and its specialized and related agencies, including the International Monetary Fund (IMF), the World Bank, the International Atomic Energy Agency (IAEA), and the General Agreement on Tariffs and Trade (GATT). It also belongs to the Council for Mutual Economic Assistance (CMEA, observer status), the Organization for Economic Cooperation and Development (OECD), and the Nonaligned Movement.

Business

The machine-tool industry has registered the most vigorous growth since the war, increasing eighteen times over the last thirty years. The production of steel, copper, fertilizers, and synthetic materials and fibers has also increased rapidly, as has electric power generation (twenty-five times). The production of consumer goods and household appliances topped the list of industrial producers in the last few years. Yugoslavia possesses various mineral and power resources that can provide a basis for more rapid and stable development and for a reduction in the balance of payments deficit. This refers primarily to such basic metals as iron, aluminium, copper, lead, zinc, and nickel, as well as hydroelectric power potential and coal. There are extremely favorable conditions for the production of sufficient quantities of staple agricultural products and foods, both for domestic consumption and export.

C
O
U
N
T
R
Y

P
R
O
F
I
L
E
S

Agriculture   Important changes in crop patterns and the wide-spread introduction of modern farming methods and machinery have made it possible to obtain much higher staple crop yields. Average wheat, maize, and sugar beet yields per ha have more than doubled. According to the livestock count carried out at the beginning of 1984, there were 5,341,000 head of cattle, 9,337,000 hogs, 7,458,000 sheep, and 74,008,000 poultry, owned primarily by private farmers. Livestock breeds have been improved, and a modern meat-packing, processing, and canning industry has been developed, with meat and milk production having risen several times over.

Forestry   In 1983, Yugoslavia had 9,369,000 ha of woodland and forest (more than one third of the total area of the country), of which 6,441,000 were socially owned and 2,928,000 were in private possession.

Tourism   The tourist industry in Yugoslavia has developed into a strong branch of the economy that is having an impact on the overall economic developments in the country. Thanks to more than 50 million foreign and almost 60 million domestic tourist nights registered in 1986, Yugoslavia ranks among the more developed tourist-receiving countries. One of the opportunities for quicker development of the tourist industry lies also in the long-term forms of economic cooperation between Yugoslav tourist industries and their foreign counterparts.

Employment   The total 1984 work force of 9.7 million was distributed among: nonagricultural, 6.4 million; agricultural, 2.3 million; unemployed, 1.0 million.

Changes in the economic structure in favor of industry and other nonagricultural activities have resulted in an appreciable increase in overall labor productivity in the socially owned sector. To a great extent, this is due to the sizable imports of the most up-to-date equipment. Between 1953 and 1980, the volume of industrial production per worker rose 3.4 times.

Economic activity is carried out in organizations of associated labor and other forms of labor organized on a self-managing basis using socially owned means of production. A work organization is founded for the purpose of pursuing economic activities that are carried out by basic organizations of associated labor, and linked by virtue of the production process. An enterprise may be founded by existing organizations of associated labor, by self-managing interest communities, local communities, sociopolitical communities, and by other juridical persons. All enterprises enjoy equal status regardless of who founded them. The enterprise is completely independent in determining and pursuing its business and development policy. It plans and organizes production, trade, and services in accordance with its financial capacity and interests. It decides independently on the volume it will produce and on its line of products on the basis of its estimate of the market situation and the flow of orders from the home market and export contracts. The enterprise is also independent in setting prices.

Trade   Yugoslavia is currently engaged in trade and other forms of economic cooperation with 140 countries, and with 82 of these countries trade agreements have been concluded. Yugoslavia is not a member of the existing European economic groups (the Common Market and COMECON) but cooperates with both, having been granted special status. The open policy pursued by Yugoslavia and its higher level of economic development have strengthened its links with foreign trade and the world market. The development of economic cooperation with other countries has been extended to include many new forms, such as the transfer of expertise and technology, industrial and financial cooperation, and so on.

Yugoslavia was one of the first socialist countries to pass regulations on the investment of foreign capital in the domestic economy. The share of foreign capital in a joint venture is no longer limited. This also applies to the reimbursement and transfer of the money invested, which now depends solely on the effect and success of the investment. The foreign investor has the right to influence business policy by participating on terms of equality in the body concerned with the success of the joint venture. Working standards may be specified in the joint-venture contract. Special tax benefits have been established for joint investments. Foreign investors are protected from changes in current economic policy insofar as they affect advantages they enjoyed when signing the contract. The procedure for obtaining approval of a joint venture has been shortened and greatly simplified.

Infrastructure

Transportation   There has been a considerable expansion in the infrastructure and capacity of the transport system, resulting in an approximately sevenfold increase in the volume of freight and passenger transport. Since the end of World War II, 31,086 mi (50,000 km) of modern roads have been built, and 1,656 mi (2,665 km) of railway tracks have been laid with 37 percent of the entire network also having been electrified. The total tonnage of the merchant fleet has more than quadrupled, while its carrying capacity is nearly twelve times greater.

C O U N T R Y   P R O F I L E S

Medical Facilities   Medical care is provided in about 15,000 outpatient units and clinics. In 1983, Yugoslavia had 138,786 hospital beds, or 5.6 beds per 1,000 inhabitants, and 36,872 physicians, 8,013 dentists, 5,047 pharmacists, and 116,014 medical personnel with auxiliary and secondary-level qualifications. More than half the doctors (57 percent) were specialists. There was one doctor to every 618 inhabitants, one dentist to 2,845 inhabitants and one pharmacist to 4,518 inhabitants. The medical services are organized on a territorial principle. Each commune has at least one health center offering all forms of basic health care, including emergency medical aid. The health service covers the entire population. In 1983, health service costs amounted to 4.7 percent of the national income. Minimum rights (compulsory and primary health care) are determined by the republican and provincial laws on health care.

Schools   The basic elements of the educational system are established in the republics and provinces and coordinated in the federation; the details are worked out and developed on a self-management basis at the local level and in schools, which are independent and self-managing institutions. The whole educational system is geared to the needs of associated labor and is subject to the direct influence of working people. Elementary or primary schooling lasting eight years is compulsory for all children from seven to fifteen years of age and is received in primary schools; this schooling is free and all pupils are covered by free health insurance. The first two years of the new system of guided secondary education offer a joint program of a general educational and polytechnical character, while optional and elective subjects train pupils in various simple skills. During the next two years, pupils acquire level III and level IV skills or qualifications, and the foundations for higher education. Those who have received a secondary education in this way may find employment and, while working, acquire qualifications as highly skilled workers or technicians or enroll at a university. In the 1983–1984 academic year, there were 19 universities with 235 faculties (or departments), 115 colleges, and three advanced schools (postsecondary level). In accordance with constitutional principles, inhabitants belonging to the nationalities of Yugoslavia are guaranteed tuition in their own language at educational institutions from preschool to university level.

Media   In 1983, a total of 3,078 newspapers (with a total circulation of 1,461,945,000 copies), and 1,537 magazines (with a total circulation of 39,784,000 copies) were published in

Yugoslavia. The daily newspapers had an average daily circulation of 2,392,000 copies. Each of the republics and provinces has a daily newspaper in the language of the nation or nationality living there.

In 1983, Yugoslavia had 200 radio stations (republican, provincial, and local), which broadcast 385,000 hours of programs; there were 4,689,000 radio license holders—an average of one radio set to every 1.3 households. In recent years, commercial radio stations have begun broadcasting mainly music, commercials, and short news bulletins. There are television centers broadcasting programs in color in Belgrade, Zagreb, Ljubljana, Sarajevo, Skopje, Titograd, Novi Sad, Pristina, and Koper. In 1983, these television centers broadcast a total of 19,464 hours of programming. Besides domestic programs, there is a high percentage of foreign programs, especially films, TV dramas, and serials, as well as cultural and educational programs. In 1983, there were 4,001,000 TV-license holders—an average of one set to every 1.5 households. The radio and television networks are independent, self-managing organizations, financing their activities mostly from license fees and commercials. The radio and television stations are associated in a single organization, Yugoslav Radio-Television (JRT), founded in 1952. JRT is a member of the European Radio Broadcasting Union and collaborates with Eurovision. It has observer status in the international organization OIRT.

Life-Style

The peoples of Yugoslavia have a long cultural tradition. As independent medieval states they achieved a high level of material and cultural development; representing a junction of routes from the Near East, Mediterranean, Asia, and Africa, many different political interests and cultural influences have met and clashed here. Assimilating the cultures of ancient Greece and Rome, Byzantium, Europe, and the Orient, the Yugoslav peoples have created a cultural synthesis, while at the same time developing their own distinctive national cultures and artistic works. The creative achievements of the Yugoslav peoples, influenced by ancient European and oriental cultures, have given Yugoslavia a wealth and variety of artistic expression that is rarely found in such a comparatively small geographical area.

After liberation in 1945, there was free development in education, science, and culture, and the educational system and institutions became more democratic. The introduction of self-management meant that educational, scientific, artistic, and cultural life in general was freed of administrative interference by the state in regard to cultural and artistic creativity.

Index for Country Profiles